WHAT'S NEW IN GARDENING

What's New in Gardening

P. P. PIRONE Plant Pathologist

The New York Botanical Garden

DRAWINGS BY REISIE LONETTE

Hanover House

GARDEN CITY, NEW YORK, 1956

To Loretta

Preface

"What's New in Gardening" was written over a five-month period, that is five months of writing at night, on weekends, and holidays, a relatively short period. But this represents only a small part of the time devoted to its preparation. Actually I have been gathering material for the book for the past five years.

Although only my name appears as the author, many persons and publications had a hand in its preparation. I am indebted to all of them.

Above everyone, I owe most to my wife Loretta, who not only carried on her own duties faithfully and patiently, but assumed many of mine around our home so that I could work with the least amount of distraction and meet the publisher's deadline.

Next, I am indebted to my good friend, Mrs. Herminie B. Kitchen, Associate Editor of *Soil Science,* for her editorial help. Mrs. Kitchen helped me with the first book I wrote, *Maintenance of Shade and Ornamental Trees,* and I agreed to take on the present assignment only after she assured me that she would help me with it.

Among the other persons who have read certain chapters or have helped in other ways are Mr. E. J. Alexander, associate curator, Dr. David D. Keck, head curator, and Mr. E. N. Mitchell, staff photographer, of The New York Botanical Garden; Alfred Graf, general manager of Julius Roehrs Company, Rutherford, New Jersey; Louis C. Schubert, of Somerset Rose Nursery, New Brunswick, New Jersey; and my secretary, Mary Louise Sutton, for secretarial and stenographic help.

I would also acknowledge the many publications such as *American Nurseryman, Trees Magazine, Popular Gardening,* and publications of state colleges of agriculture and the United States Department of Agriculture. I would single out one especially among the garden magazines, *Flower Grower,* the *Home Garden Magazine*. I have reused such material from the "Modern Gardener" column of this magazine, a column I write each month.

Finally I am indebted to all amateur and professional gardeners and to the scientists and manufacturers who made possible the plants, chemicals, the machines, and the practices described in this book.

P. P. PIRONE

New York, N. Y.

Contents

9

Introduction

When it comes to gardening, 30 million Americans can't be wrong! According to a recent survey, that number of our people garden for pleasure. Such a large number certainly indicates that gardening has become an important part of American life.

Gardening life in America now centers about small suburban homes, each with its own plot of ground for the owner to tinker with as he pleases. Gardening today is drawing housewives out of the kitchen and many of their husbands away from the golf course and the fishing boat. The housewives appear to be more interested in ornamental plants; the husbands are attracted more toward lawn management and vegetable growing.

What is it in gardening that keeps drawing more and more enthusiasts every year? One reason is that it is rewarding in many ways. The gardener can see or harvest the fruits of his labor and he can be quite relaxed while he is achieving his objective. Gardening, too, is a relatively cheap hobby. True, the initial expense for equipment and materials may be high, but when these costs are spread over the many years of good service, they are a lot lower than those for most other hobbies.

But there are other reasons for the popularity of gardening. Gardening is not static. It is a constantly changing hobby, and this accounts, perhaps, for the continued interest. It is more than a rebirth every spring, wonderful and mysterious as this is. There are always new kinds of trees and flowers, new tools, new chemicals to do a better job with less effort on the part of the gardener.

Love for gardening and appreciation of the beauty and benefits derived from it are not restricted to any particular race, color, or class. A housewife living in a cold-water flat on New York's East Side can derive as much pleasure from a few geraniums or a pot of marigolds growing on her window ledge as can a millionaire with a many-acre estate in northern Westchester County!

Nor is the acquiring of a "green thumb" restricted to any particular class or group. My faithful assistant at The New York Botanical Garden, John Walther, with no formal garden training, grows plants every bit as well as the most highly trained graduate of Kew Gardens. I have seen him nurture sickly, starved plants into robust prize winners!

Some feel that a green thumb is inherited. I do not agree with this. I will admit that you cannot make a gardener out of a person who wants only to play golf or to fish. But anyone can develop a green thumb if he or she has an urge to grow something and an honest desire to learn.

Two characteristics of a dyed-in-the-wool gardener are his short memory and his optimism. By January he has forgotten his failures of the previous year and is already planning to grow perfect plants the coming spring.

Another characteristic of any person who likes the soil is that he is a good person at heart. I have never known or heard of a true gardener who was mean. Somehow love of the soil and meanness never go together.

All of my adult life, or the last thirty years, has been spent working with plants and with people who grow plants. But I cannot honestly say that I inherited a liking for gardening. Actually, as a boy, I disliked it thoroughly because my father made me cart pail after pail of water nearly every evening to his tomato and pepper plants at the time when all my friends were playing hide-and-seek or cowboys and Indians.

My first intimate appreciation for plants was fostered by the late Professor H. H. Whetzel of Cornell University, first professor of plant pathology in America. When I first matriculated at Cornell, I, like most young men entering college, was undecided as to a career. My mother hoped that I would study medicine. My sometimes stern but thoughtful father felt that agriculture was the field for me.

It was not until I took the elementary course in plant pathology and had a "conference" with Professor Whetzel that I chose agriculture, more specifically plant doctoring, as a career. This was indeed a happy choice, for I not only selected what has proved to be a happy and exciting career for me, but both my mother and father were pleased with my decision.

As a result of this selection, the course of my life was changed. I was awarded a fellowship to work on insect and disease problems of vegetable growers in Nassau County, New York, as part of my doctorate requirements. It was while on this assignment that I met, wooed, and wed Loretta Kelly.

Almost thirty years later to the day, our eldest son, Tom, enrolled in the same course in plant pathology at Cornell that helped to decide my future. I am happy to record here that sophomore Tom received the highest term grade in plant pathology in a class comprised largely of upper classmen and some graduate students!

Besides having worked intimately with fruit and vegetable growers and professional arborists and nurserymen for twenty years, I have spent the past nine years at The New York Botannical Garden answering all kinds of garden questions. As a result, I became interested about six years ago in everything new in gardening and have attempted to keep abreast of the times. In addition, I had a hand in the development and early testing of some of the new chemicals such as maleic hydrazide and RAPIDGRO and of some of the new gardening practices such as foliage feeding and air-layering with plastics. Therefore when Harold Kuebler of Hanover House approached me to do WHAT'S NEW IN GARDENING, I was quite ripe for the assignment.

One of the most difficult decisions I had to make was to select a starting date for new plants, new chemicals, and new gadgets. In other words, how new is new or how old must something be in gardening before it is no longer new?

In the beginning, I arbitrarily selected two years prior to the preparation of this book as the starting date for new things. But I soon discovered that I could not adhere strictly to this rule because many fine plants, efficient chemicals, or excellent tools would have to be left out. I have therefore included some of the older things I believe will be with us for a long time because of their outstanding qualities.

A prominent garden editor friend of mine remarked that it would be foolish to write a book of this sort because it would be out of date the day it was printed. He argued that new developments, varieties, and chemicals would come along with every passing day.

I agree with these conclusions, but if every author of professional books took that attitude we soon would be deprived of stores of accumulated knowledge. Nevertheless, to ensure my readers the greatest benefit over the longest possible period, I have not only described the newest information on plants and gardening, but I have also included many of the fundamentals—fundamentals that can be used by gardeners for years to come.

Some professional plant growers and manufacturers of garden equipment and chemicals may feel I have been amiss in failing to mention their introductions or their products in this book. This does not imply that I look with disfavor on their plants or products but rather that they were left out because of lack of space.

This book is roughly divided into two parts: one deals with the plants themselves and the other with practices involved in successful culture of plants. I sincerely feel that I have prepared a different sort of book, a really new kind of garden book. I am hopeful that it will be of value and interest to all gardeners.

WHAT'S NEW IN GARDENING

Chapter 1

PLANTS WITH CONSTITUTIONAL RIGHTS

When Henry Bosenberg, a landscape nurseryman of New Brunswick, New Jersey, observed in 1925 that one of his rose bushes behaved unlike its sisters, he little dreamed that within a few years this particular plant would become famous in gardening history. For this rose, THE NEW DAWN, was destined to be the first plant patented in the United States. Since it was awarded U. S. Plant Patent No. 1 in August 1929, more than fourteen hundred patents have been issued to all kinds of trees, shrubs, fruits, and flowers. This may seem like a goodly number of new plant varieties in only a quarter of a century but, compared with the nearly 1 million utility patents granted in the same period, it is quite insignificant.

The story of the discovery of THE NEW DAWN is one I believe every gardener will find interesting. It was told to me by Louis Schubert, co-owner of the Somerset Rose Nursery at New Brunswick, the firm which owns Patent No. 1 and which introduced THE NEW DAWN to the gardening world.

In the spring of 1925 Henry Bosenberg purchased from a local nursery, among other roses, a bundle of ten No. 1 Grade, field-grown, climbing roses labeled DR. VAN FLEET. This particular variety had been introduced by the famous rose hybridizer Dr. W. W. Van Fleet, who was attempting to develop a race of roses that was vigorous, hardy, and disease-resistant, would flower all summer, and could withstand the extremes of heat and cold found in the United States. Quite an order!

But let's let Louis Schubert tell the story in his own words:

"Most of the DR. VAN FLEET climbing roses purchased by Mr. Bosenberg were used in various places during the spring. One rose was left over, and was 'heeled in' temporarily.

"Weakened by abuse and overgrown with weeds, it struggled to survive. Improvement of the area added to its woes. Topsoil was

19

dumped on it, trucks and tractors pounded it, but its will to survive was greater than its troubles. The ground was graded and sowed to grass.

"In July a tiny shoot poked its head about a foot above the surface and produced a single pink flower. For some reason it was not cut off but instead was protected with stakes. The tiny shoot produced another flower, and several weeks after the first bloom, another flower opened, and another and another right into November.

"Something had happened. My theory is that the plant's chromosomes were rearranged in the same way they are when colchicine or X rays are used on seeds or plants. Somewhat similar changes had occurred in roses through the so-called process of 'sporting,' but in most cases either the reblooming characteristic or the climbing habit was lost in the process. Never before had there been a hardy, recurrent-blooming, climbing rose.

"With some misgivings, we budded several hundred seedlings from this rose during the summer of 1926. The resulting plants bloomed and rebloomed as maidens in 1927. Our doubts as to their fixed habits were resolved when again in 1928 all maidens bloomed and rebloomed. Through some freak of nature, Dr. Van Fleet's dream had been realized. Here we had a hardy, vigorous rose that could be grown as a climber or as a spreading bush with glossy, disease-resistant foliage. Its flowers were of good quality, fairly double, very fragrant, and produced on good stems for cutting.

"Because Henry Bosenberg was not in the rose-growing business, he did not want to go to the trouble of introducing a new variety. So we, as the Somerset Rose Nursery, made arrangements to introduce it. Mr. J. D. Eisele, president of Henry A. Dreer Company in Philadelphia, one of the largest retail seed and plant companies of the time, helped us.

"Meanwhile, the Townsend-Purnell Plant Patent Act was passed by Congress and was signed by President Herbert Hoover on May 23, 1930. We immediately applied for a patent. We were not the first applicants, but perhaps because we named the rose THE NEW DAWN, which was symbolic of a new era, both in everblooming climbers and also in plant patents, we were fortunate in being granted the first plant patent. The resulting publicity created a demand we were unable to supply for several years, and even today THE NEW DAWN is still one of the more popular varieties of climbing roses."

Here, then, is the story of the world's first patented plant. I personally believe THE NEW DAWN was so distinctly different from any of its predecessors that the patent officials felt they were on firm ground in making the historical award.

Protecting Plants with Patents

Before the plant patent law was passed, hybridizers, plant breeders, and amateur gardeners had no protection for their discoveries, though inventors in other fields were amply protected by patents for their brain children. One of the reasons for passing the act was to provide new incentives to horticulturists, in line with the Constitution's provision "To promote the Progress of Science and useful Arts, by securing for limited Times to Authors and Inventors the exclusive Right to their respective Writings and Discoveries."

As the plant patent law is now interpreted, any kind of plant, except certain types of tubers, may be patented, provided it has been produced asexually, that is, other than by seeds. This means that patentable plants must be reproduced by budding, by grafting, or from cuttings. Plants arising from sports or mutants and as hybrids are therefore all patentable. But no plant found in the wild can be patented even though it has never before been described.

Some seedsmen look forward to the day when certain seeds also may be covered by patents. In this category would come those formed by artificial pollination, such as the so-called F_1 hybrid seeds discussed in some detail later in Chapter Seven.

Any person who feels he has discovered or developed a new variety of plant may apply for a patent. His first step usually is to hire a plant patent attorney to file the application with the Patent Office in Washington. Complete specifications of the plant must be outlined. They must tell where the plant originated and include a complete description in addition to a water-color drawing of the flower or plant "artistically and competently" executed. The cost for securing a patent varies from a hundred and fifty to three hundred dollars.

Many of the new plants developed and patented in recent years have been direct results of planned research sponsored by large horticultural concerns. In this country firms like Bobbink and Atkins, of Rutherford, New Jersey; Jackson and Perkins, of Newark, New York; Armstrong's Nurseries, of Ontario, California; Brownell's of Little Compton, Rhode Island; Conard-Pyle Company, West Grove, Pennsylvania; and Germain Seed Company, Los Angeles, have introduced many of our finest present-day roses. Other firms and individuals, not only in this country but also in Europe, have, of course, aided in the development of new plants.

The job of developing a new plant is not a simple one and it costs several thousands of dollars to produce a new rose, for instance. It means first making a large number of crosses; that is, transferring the pollen or male element from one desirable variety to the stigma or female part of another variety. Seeds that develop from each of these crosses are then planted and the resulting plants grown to flowering.

When one individual is found to have properties superior to those of its parents, it is subjected to further study to be sure that the desirable properties are fixed and reproducible. It is only then that the professional plant breeder feels the new variety is worthy of a patent. It is the Patent Office that has the final say as to whether or not the new plant is sufficiently different from older kinds to merit a patent. Incidentally, about half of the plant patents thus far issued have gone to roses.

The person who develops and patents a new plant or the company to which he assigns his patent is entitled to a royalty on each plant sold. Royalties and licensing for plant patents are the same as for mechanical patents. The holder of the patent may license anyone to reproduce his plants asexually. And the person or firm that grows the plant for resale must report the number of plants so grown and pay the holder of the patent a royalty agreed upon.

Thus are the constitutional rights of plants assured. And this is as it should be, for plants worthy of patents represent long hours of patient research by trained men like Eugene Boerner of the Jackson and Perkins Company, Martin Jacobus of Bobbink and Atkins, and Herbert Swimm and Dr. Walter Lammerts, both of whom were formerly with Armstrong Nurseries of Ontario, California, who not only know what qualities to look for in the breeding of new varieties of plants, but also how to make the most of any new or unusual characters they discover.

Like the introduction of new varieties of plants, most of the other developments in gardening, whether they be new materials and methods for stimulating growth of desirable plants and for combating their enemies or new devices to conserve the gardener's time and energy, are results of continuing research by firms and individuals who would make gardening more and more rewarding for you and me.

Chapter 2

ANNUALS, PERENNIALS, AND BULBS

ANNUALS

Most of us gardeners like annuals because they are so easy to grow and are available in every color, in every size, and for every purpose. Moreover, they grow from tiny seeds into lovely flowers within a single season, sometimes within a few months. They provide lots of color during periods when color is usually lacking in the more permanent kinds of plants.

How to Start Annuals

In the northern United States and Canada the seeds of many of the slow-starting annuals like snapdragons, petunias, salvias, verbenas, and annual dahlias should be started indoors in February. Faster-growing ones like balsam, marigold, and zinnias are better started in March.

A soil that is loose in texture, drains well, and yet holds moisture readily is best. A good mixture for growing seedlings indoors is 2 parts by volume of good garden loam and 1 part of coarse sand.

Seeds should be sown at the depth indicated on the seed packet and held at a temperature of about 70 degrees. After the seedlings appear they should be kept at a cooler temperature and in a south window so they will get as much light as possible. Seedlings grown in dim light and at high temperatures tend to become pale green, tall, and spindly.

In the warmer parts of our country the seeds of annuals are usually sown out-of-doors.

The trouble most frequently encountered in growing seedlings is the disease known as damping-off, in which soil-inhabiting fungi rot the seeds before they germinate (pre-emergence damping-off) or kill the young seedlings after they push through the soil (post-emergence damping-off). Finer seeds or seedlings of snapdragons, petunias, rhododendrons are particularly susceptible to this disease.

Any one of a half dozen methods will prevent damping-off. The soil can be baked in the oven, or it can be treated with formaldehyde, chloropicrin, or oxyquinoline benzoate before the seeds are planted. Or the seeds can be coated with special seed-treating chemicals like ARASAN, SEMESAN, or SPERGON. Finally, you can avoid damping-off without resorting to either heat or chemicals if you use sifted sphagnum moss for seed growing. For some unexplained reason damping-off and seed decay do not occur in sphagnum moss. The same cannot be said for peat moss. Sphagnum may be bought in sifted form ready for use, or ordinary baled sphagnum may be rubbed through a sieve.

The standard procedure is to fill flats or pots with unsterilized soil to 1½ inches of the top. Then add 1 inch of shredded sphagnum, and water until the moss is thoroughly wet. Seedlings will be stronger if a solution of a soluble fertilizer is added in the initial wetting. Then broadcast the seeds over the surface of the sphagnum and press them in gently. Small seeds need not be covered. Place a pane of glass over the flat or pot. If no glass is available, it is best to cover even the fine seeds with a thin layer of sifted sphagnum moss. Put the flats away from direct sunlight until the seeds have germinated, then admit air and sunlight as the seedlings develop.

Some gardeners prefer to fill the seed-starting container completely with sphagnum. While this makes the flats easier to handle, a nutrient solution must be used on the young seedlings to keep them growing vigorously.

Seedlings can be readily lifted out of the sphagnum two weeks or so after germination and transplanted to the usual soil mixture. Roots come out almost intact.

After the seedlings have attained a fair size and the weather is favorable, the annuals can be moved outdoors in the flats, boxes, or cans in which they were grown, to harden them off, that is, condition them for the outdoors. They can finally be moved from their growing containers to the permanent location in the garden within a week or so after the conditioning period.

Most annuals thrive in sunny locations and in reasonably fertile, well-drained soil. Tall-growing kinds like the giant zinnias, tall snapdragons, big marigolds, cosmos, and spider plants can be used for background plantings. Medium-tall plants like asters, cornflowers, calendulas, scabiosas, and the marigolds and zinnias of medium height should be used in the central sections of flower borders. Low-growing plants like dwarf zinnias, French marigolds, sweet alyssum, ageratum, portulaca, verbena, and dwarf petunias can be used to edge flower beds, cover a bank, or brighten up a rock garden.

New or Unusual Annuals

In 1955 there were only two annuals to win an All-America Award. One is the celosia TOREADOR. This celosia is not the first of its kind to do so, however. FLAME OF FIRE cockscomb won in 1935 and ROYAL VELVET in 1939.

TOREADOR is a distinct improvement over any existing variety of the rather stiff cockscomb, *Celosia cristata,* if only because of its color. Its clear, vivid red is much more appealing than the dull, purple-tinged blooms of the older varieties. The flower heads are larger on sturdy stems, and the light green leaves provide a bright contrast to the striking flower heads. (Illustration following page 64)

Another unusual celosia is GILBERT'S GOLD DUST, whose ruffled combs are at first silvery, then change to a rich yellow, and finally a deep gold or chartreuse with a silver sheen.

The other annual to win a 1955 All-America Award is the petunia PRIMA DONNA, an F_1 hybrid with large and delicately frilled rose-pink flowers. It grows uniformly to about 12 inches high and fully as wide and is good for bedding, in the garden, in pots, and for window or porch boxes. (Illustration following page 64)

The beautiful petunia FIRE DANCE received the All-America Award for 1956.

Other new or unusual petunias are: PALEFACE, a white, slightly ruffled kind for borders and beds that grows 16 to 20 inches high; JEWEL, a brilliant cerise that makes a spectacular ground cover; and MARTHA WASHINGTON, ruffled lavender blue that is low-growing. BLUE MOON, a deep violet blue that is remarkably true to color, is one of the more notable doubles introduced recently. Other really spectacular doubles are ALLEGRO, SONATA, BURPEE'S ORCHID, NOCTURNE, and RHAPSODY.

CROWN JEWELS petunias have five clear and brilliant colors, including a golden yellow. These are F_2 hybrids grown as separate colors, then mixed in the seed shed for just the right variety.

Marigolds are also extremely popular annuals. Among the new African or tall-growing kinds is KON-TIKI, which flowers early and has large yellow incurved blooms. MAN-IN-THE-MOON is creamy white and looks especially nice as a cut flower under artificial lights. (Illustration on page 64)

The dwarf or French marigolds have more striking color mixtures. ROYAL SCOTT has gold- and mahogany-striped flower petals; SUN-BRITE produces very early golden yellow, carnation-like blooms; PARISIAN HYBRIDS has blotched or striped double flowers 2½ inches across; and ORANGE FLAME has a gold crest and mahogany guard petals. LULU forms tiny canary-yellow flowers almost hidden in its finely cut foliage.

Zinnias are also popular and easy to grow. BLAZE, an All-America winner in 1954, has brilliant mandarin-red flowers, which change to a fiery orange scarlet, and GLAMOUR GIRLS has large informal and fluffy flowers in different colors.

Among the salvias are both dwarf and tall varieties that bloom early and late. Best known of the low-growing reds are ST. JOHN'S FIRE and BLAZE OF FIRE, which grow to about 10 inches. FIREBALL is just as red but is even more dwarfed. BRIGHTNESS, AMERICA, and BONFIRE are three tall-growing kinds.

Gardeners who feel the fire-engine reds of most salvias are too gaudy may want to try ROSE FLAME, a coral pink, considered by many to be the best of the pinks.

One of the finest annual phlox is the STAR MIXED strain from Holland. It has well-blended colors on plants of uniform height and with large numbers of perfect star-shaped flowers.

The new F_1 hybrid snapdragon, HIT PARADE, has 6- to 8-inch flower spikes on 18- to 24-inch stems.

PERENNIALS

Perennials, when properly managed, are the backbone of the flower garden. But no perennial, no matter how easily grown, will thrive for long if it is neglected during long periods of drought, permitted to become choked with weeds, or allowed to go to seed.

Perennials last from a few to many years, depending on where they are planted, the kind used, and, as I have just suggested, the care they receive.

Avoid poorly drained areas, because perennials will die out within a year or two in such spots.

The perennial border should be located where it can be most enjoyed by the family. It must have full sun for at least half a day, and the soil must be well prepared at the start.

Nor should perennials be planted haphazardly. The over-all habit of each kind must be kept in mind. Some, like peonies and day lilies, develop large clumps of foliage that are attractive all through the season. So give these plants plenty of space, and set some low-growing colorful plant in the foreground to utilize their green lush foliage as a background.

New or Unusual Perennials

The first perennial ever to receive an All-America Award was MC KANA'S GIANT COLUMBINE. The flowers of this 1955 award winner are in clear, bright colors, of extra-large size, and with long spurs borne on long, wiry stems. The bushy plants grow to about 3 feet, and the flower colors include blue, deep yellow, primrose, pink, red, purple, maroon, and showy combinations of these. (Illustration following page 64)

Two new hardy asters are RADAR, with ruby-crimson blooms in September on 2-foot-high plants, and N. A. RED STAR, a 3½-foot-tall plant with deep carmine-rose flowers appearing in September and October. Aster EVENTIDE has very dark blue, semi-double blooms.

Among the new dwarf hardy asters are CANTERBURY CARPET, with masses of blue flowers on 10-inch stems, and PERSIAN ROSE, with rose-pink flowers on 15-inch stems.

Chrysanthemums New and Old

Each year dozens of new kinds of chrysanthemums are introduced. Unless one has followed developments in the "mum" world, it is difficult to appreciate that within recent years an endless variety of shapes, colors, and color combinations have turned up. Some are so outstanding that they will stay with us for a long time. Others do not differ sufficiently from, or are no improvement over, older, established kinds, and hence soon will be forgotten.

Chrysanthemums thrive in a well-drained garden loam that is slightly acid and is well supplied with organic matter. They do best in full sun, although they will do fairly well in a semi-shaded area, provided they get full sunlight for at least six hours a day.

They are heavy feeders. Besides mixing in 4 pounds of a 5-10-5 fertilizer into each 100 square feet of bed area before planting, I have found that they can take additional plant food through the leaves during the growing season. Spraying the foliage four or five times with RAPIDGRO, 1 pound in 44 gallons of water, gives larger, huskier plants and bigger flowers. The RAPIDGRO can be mixed in most of the commonly used insecticide-fungicide mixtures instead of plain water and thus will kill two birds with one stone. That is, one can give the mums an extra boost of plant nutrients and control pests and diseases in the same operation.

Recently six more of the so-called "Bird Series" chrysanthemums were introduced to gardeners. They are RUFFED GROUSE, light strawberry red; KINGFISHER, another red; THRASHER, burnt orange to brown; CUCKOO, a clear lemon yellow; DESERT QUAIL, a soft lavender pink; and ORCHARD ORIOLE, orange bronze. At this writing there are twenty-seven hardy, early- or medium-blooming, large-flowering mums in the Bird Series.

Gardeners in the more northerly parts of the country will welcome three early varieties. They are CHIPPA RED, similar to the well-known Chippewa, with turkey-red to maroon blooms in early September; NEW MARJORIE MILLS, with ruby-red blooms by September 10; and SPELLBINDER, which produces lemon-chrome blooms in late September.

Northern gardeners will also welcome the so-called "Granite Series," recently released by the New Hampshire Experiment Station. These are extremely hardy and require a minimum of maintenance. They are GRANITE BRONZE, GRANITE BUTTERCUP, GRANITE GEM, GRANITE GLOW, GRANITE HARVEST, GRANITE ENCHANTMENT, GRANITE PAGEANT, GRANITE PROMISE, GRANITE RANGER, and GRANITE RADIANCE.

The so-called cushion mums, which are dwarf, dense plants of mound-shaped habit of growth, rarely exceeding a foot in height, have become increasingly popular with many back yard gardeners. When these mums are in flower, the blossoms are so numerous they virtually hide the leaves. Two new ones in this group are MAIDEN'S DREAM, a delicate peach shade, and POT OF GOLD, with bronze flowers.

More recently cushion mums with the same growth habit but with much larger flowers, 2 to 3 inches across, have been developed. These produce no more flowers than the ordinary cushion mums, but because the individual flowers are larger, the over-all result is far more impressive. The following kinds were introduced after twenty years of breeding work:

STAR FROST, with two-toned, very large flowers. The center petals are deep rose pink and the outer ones light frosty pink. The blooms take bad weather and early frosts remarkably well.

GOLD STAR, double, rich yellow with center petals remaining incurved for a long time.

LILAC STAR, pinkish lilac, stiff petals. The very double blooms eventually open wide to reveal deep gold centers.

MAROON STAR, maroon-red flowers with even, rounded form.

MOONLIGHT STAR, 3-inch blooms with yellow center petals and very light yellow outer petals. Very early-flowering and compact plants, 3 feet across and 15 inches high.

Among the late-flowering giant- or exhibition-type chrysanthemums are the huge white ATLANTA, and the rosy-purple with lighter overcast MARY PALMOUR.

In the so-called "Queen Series" of anemone-type chrysanthemums the ray petals surround prominent yellow centers. Two interesting ones introduced a few years ago are QUEEN ELIZABETH, orchid pink, and QUEEN VICTORIA, wine red. More recently QUEEN MARY, which combines a rich yellow center with softer yellow petals, and QUEEN ANNE, with dazzling white petals around a bright yellow center, have come into the picture.

Another group of anemone-flowered mums is known as the "Princess Series." They were originated by Louis Reichert of Bell Harbor, New York, and have crested or pincushion centers. Among the Princess Series are: PRINCESS ANNE, a golden yellow; PRINCESS DOROTHY, silvery lavender pink; PRINCESS MARIE, Indian red; PRINCESS VIOLETTA, rich rosy purple; and PRINCESS POCAHONTAS, deep mahogany bronze.

Two outstanding yellow chrysanthemums are SUNBURST, with deep yellow, cactus-like blooms more than 4 inches across, and VALIANT, a compact, bushy plant with light yellow incurving blooms.

MURIEL RICE is a large-flowered, light buttercup yellow. One of the pinkest mums is the salmon-pink ADORABLE, which begins to bloom in mid-September in the latitude of New York City.

REAL GOLD has pointed petals and a rich color; PURPLE WATERS is a deep purple with quilled petals.

PATRICIA LEHMAN, with geranium-pink blooms and a peach center, starts to bloom in early September.

YELLOW SPOON has warm golden quilled petals.

In the spider mum classification is LIMELIGHT, a lime yellow chartreuse overcast, which was developed after five years of inbreeding from the "green" chrysanthemum NIGHTINGALE. Three new white spider mums are YOUTH, MILADY, and LA BELLE.

CAPISTRANO is an early-flowering purple, and GOLDEN THREAD is a fine-petaled yellow spider.

Chrysanthemum hobbyists and exhibitors will want to try MRS. HERBERT C. LEGG, a very large soft pink with incurved petals.

The famous botanist and horticulturist Dr. E. J. Kraus recently developed several new small-flowered, double chrysanthemums. These are: THERESA STONE, a light yellow, and MARGARET KELLAR, a spiky-petaled rose. Two new large-flowered yellow doubles also developed by Dr. Kraus are BUTTERSCOTCH and GARLAND POWELL. CORALIE SCHMIDT, a salmon pink; ROSETONE, a rosy lavender; and MOJAVE DESERT, an orange yellow, complete his recent introductions.

The Faithful Iris

Iris is another old reliable perennial that gives years of satisfaction with relatively little care.

A recent unique introduction is CARMELA, a heavily crinkled, lace-edged variety. THORWALD has yellow and orange blossoms in mid-season, and SUB-DEB has rose blooms set off by rosy-tangerine beards. CLEMENTINA has blooms resembling clematis, with all its petals lying flat or on one plane.

PLUMED DELIGHT has soft yellow-cream flowers (Illustration following page 64); DRESS PARADE has white ones veined and stippled with blue; and PINK SENSATION has deep, pure pink flowers.

Because iris is such a dependable plant, many new gardeners should try more varieties of them. The following list presents, by color, three dozen of the most popular old and fairly new kinds:

White: NEW SNOW, SNOW FLURRY, LADY BOSCAWEN.
Cream and pale yellow: TRULY YOURS, PINNACLE, AMANDINE.
Bright yellow and orange yellow: OLA KALA, ROCKET, CLOTH OF GOLD.
Light blue: GREAT LAKES, HELEN MC GREGOR, CAHOKIA.
Medium blue and violet: BLUE RHYTHM, CHIVALRY, BLUE VALLEY.
Dark blue and purple: SABLE, PIERRE MENARD, SABLE NIGHT.
Bicolor: WABASH, AMIGO, EXTRAVAGANZA.
Red and maroon, including brown red: SOLID MAHOGANY, RANGER, SUNSET BLAZE.
Pink: MARY RANDALL, PINK CAMEO, HAPPY BIRTHDAY.
Plicata, light ground, edged or sanded deeper color: BLUE SHIMMER, MINNIE COLQUITT, FIRECRACKER.
Blends: ARGUS PHEASANT, BRYCE CANYON, MULBERRY ROSE.
Onco hybrids: LADY MOHR, ELMOHR, BLUMOHR.

According to F. W. Cassebeer, noted iris authority, the following are among the best of the Siberian irises: SNOWCREST, white; MOUNTAIN LAKE, bright blue; TROPIC NIGHT, deep blue; CAESAR'S BROTHER, dark purple; TYCOON, mulberry purple; ERIC THE RED, purple red; and HELEN ASTOR, rosy mauve.

Four bearded irises, introduced during the last two years, that come closest to a true red color are DEFIANCE, DRESS REHEARSAL, PRIVATEER, and YLEM.

Something new and different from the ordinary bearded iris is the so-called horned iris, in which the beards project up and out like horns instead of lying flat on the lower flower petals. UNICORN, introduced in 1954, was the first of the horned irises. Its standards, or upright petals, are mulberry-colored and its falls, or lower, flat petals, are pure white edged with mulberry. PLUMED DELIGHT and MULBERRY SNOW were introduced in 1955. The former has soft yellow-cream standards and creamy white falls bordered with pale yellow. The latter has wine-colored standards and pansy-violet falls.

West coast gardeners who go in for iris are more fortunate than their eastern friends, for they are able to use iris varieties that flower twice every year. In the Pacific Northwest these kinds flower in early May and again in October, whereas in the warmer parts of California they bloom even earlier and continue for a longer period. The rhizomes of the twice-flowering irises mature in a few months. Those of ordinary irises require a full year. The following are some of the smaller-growing (2 feet or less), twice-flowering iris available from western growers: AUTUMN QUEEN, white; OLIVE WHITE, yellow; SURPRISE, blue; AUTUMN ELF, purple; and OCTOBER BLAZE, red.

The Favorite Peony

Hardy, easy, and economical to grow, the peony will long remain one of our favorite perennials. The plants need lots of sun, good drainage, and a deep, rich, loamy soil. Because of the deep-rooting character of the peony and because the planting is rather permanent, the soil should be thoroughly prepared.

The first two herbaceous, yellow-flowered peonies known to exist in the United States were introduced in the spring of 1954. These are CLAIRE DE LUNE and ORIENTAL GOLD.

CLAIRE DE LUNE originated from a cross of the pale yellow single species *Mlokosewitschi* with a *lactiflora* variety. Dr. E. B. White of Daytona Beach, Florida, made more than four thousand crosses before this exceptionally beautiful flower developed. Its guard petals are pale creamy yellow surrounding a large center of orange stamens.

ORIENTAL GOLD is a slightly fragrant, clear yellow double. Another double yellow herbaceous peony, recently introduced from Japan, is YOKI HI. It has deeper yellow petals than CLAIRE DE LUNE but no stamens.

Other new peonies are ANN COUSINS, a pure white double; LA LOR-RAINE, a flesh-colored double; DOLORODELL, light pink; ENSIGN MORIARITY, dark pink; KANSAS, red; and SEA SHELL, a pink single.

One of the most beautiful peonies, THERESA, introduced more than fifty years ago by the famous French originator of many fine peonies, Auguste Dessert, is still extremely popular. Despite many introductions in recent years, it is still considered the queen of the light pinks. It has long petals of translucent, old-rose pink, paling toward the base and illuminated by a golden yellow glow in the depths. It has leaves of truly splendid form, texture, and color, a decided advantage for exhibition purposes.

New Dahlias

Modern dahlias offer a vast range of forms and colors. Although mostly grown from tuberous root sections, they can also be grown from seeds and cuttings. Because it is a favorite among men gardeners, the dahlia has become known as the "man's flower."

Some outstanding new kinds are: MRS. ALTON B. PARKER, golden-yellow flowers flushed with vermilion; CERAMIC BEAUTY, large rose red, with ox-blood centers; CHEROKEE BEAUTY, large rich pink; FIRST LADY, primrose yellow; MARGARET DUROSS, yellow, flushed scarlet to orange; MARVELOUS, lavender; MR. PRESIDENT, pink and yellow; SEQUOIA, primrose yellow; YELLOW MASTERPIECE, soft, clear yellow; and YOSEMITE, apricot with metallic luster. BETTY BLOSSOM, another new dahlia developed by Herman Rindfleisch of Mamaroneck, New York, opens a cream yellow and develops a rose blush on yellow petals.

Three new dwarf dahlia strains now available from most seedsmen are UNWIN'S DWARF HYBRIDS, COLTNESS HYBRIDS, and MIGNON MIXED. In the latitude of New York City seeds sown outdoors in late May will produce blooming plants by July. These low-growing kinds will continue to bloom until frost.

Modern Day Lilies

With the hundreds of excellent day lilies already available, one might wonder why new ones each year? As a matter of fact, most ornamental plants go through the same process. Plant breeders are constantly being called on to meet a demand for larger, smaller, or more numerous flowers, earlier or later blooms, new colors, and more fragrance. Hence the ever increasing numbers of new kinds. One of the most famous of the day lily hybridizers was our own Dr. A. B. Stout of The New York Botanical Garden.

Because day lilies are long-lived perennials, especially where there is plenty of space for them to spread, they have become increasingly popular in recent years. Varieties are now available which will provide a succession of blooms from May to October. They are most effective when planted in a curving border against broad-leaved evergreens.

A few of the newest day lilies are PRECIOUS TREASURE, buff peach; JACK FROST, pale yellow; CANARI, cream yellow; OLIVER TWIST, yellow; HIGH NOON, orange; HER MAJESTY, pink; PICTURE, light rose; PETROUCHKA, dark eye zone on buff petals and cream midrib; PIRATE'S TREASURE, red and purple; HAWTHORNE ROSE, dusky rose petals, edged and ribbed in cream; and RED RESPLENDENCE and KRIS KRINGLE, both reds.

REVOLUTE, a green-yellow day lily, won the Stout Medal in 1953, the highest award of the Hemerocallis Society of America.

Hardy Phlox

Hardy phlox is highly desirable because it flowers so abundantly during the hot summer months when, except for day lilies, colors from most perennials are indeed scarce.

Phlox requires a rich soil, good air and soil drainage, and more sun than shade. As the clumps age, the lowermost leaves have a tendency to turn brown, a condition often attributed to spider mite infestation or infection by fungi. While studying this problem at Cornell many years ago, I found that the blighting of the lower leaves can occur in the absence of pests and fungus parasites. In fact, the blighting is actually an inherited characteristic of all hardy phlox of the *paniculata* type, whereas it never occurs in the *suffruticosa* varieties like MISS LINGARD, HERCULES, EMPRESS, and MISS VER-BROOM. The latter, however, are notably subject to the powdery mildew disease. I described my work with this trouble in the June 1938 issue of *Nursery Disease Notes* when I was at the New Jersey Agricultural Experiment Station. So far, no one has disputed my theory of the cause of the trouble. Incidentally, this trouble is incurable no matter what sprays are used. There are, of course, fungus diseases that will cause the leaves to turn brown, as will mites. But these troubles are preventable with sprays.

Phlox flowers should be removed when they have passed their best.

Otherwise seeds will form, and the resulting seedlings will soon crowd out the parent plant and will produce those horrid magenta-colored flowers so frequently seen in neglected phlox plantings.

Among the newly introduced phlox varieties are WINDSOR, a bright salmon carmine; BALMORAL, amaranth rose; SANDRINGHAM, persian rose; and B. SYMONS-JEUNE, soft pink rose with dark red eye. PURPLE HEART is a rich violet blue that will probably become extremely popular.

More New Perennials

Some other new outstanding perennials are:

Campanula WEDGWOOD, which produces dozens of brilliant violet-blue flowers on rigid stems.

Dicentra BOUNTIFUL, a hardy, perpetual-flowering "bleeding heart." It blooms almost all summer and produces 30 to 40 stalks of dainty, fuchsia-red flowers during its flowering peak in May and again in fall.

A truly double shasta daisy, HORACE REED, blooms from June until late summer. Shasta daisy COBHAM GOLD is the first break from white. It has lovely flowers, fully 4 inches across, with high-crested centers of fine pale yellow enhanced by a double row of creamy white guard petals. It blooms freely until frost.

Three English varieties of veronica that are completely hardy and ideal for borders are BACCAROLE, a deep rose pink; MINUET, a dusty pink; and PAVANE, a clear pink. They bloom lavishly during July and August.

PFITZER'S DWARF canna is a new dwarf form in soft, pleasing colors varying from Chinese coral, primrose yellow, and shell pink. It flowers prolifically all summer long.

Lovers of old-fashioned pinks will want to try JOHN BALL, with large, fully double white and crimson flowers on 12-inch stems. The flowers are pure white at the center, and each petal has a narrow crimson edge and a crimson zone surrounding the white center.

BULBS

In the spring garden hardy bulbs probably produce more color than all other groups of flowers combined. This, plus the fact that they are easy to grow, makes them extremely popular. Of the spring-flowering bulbs, perhaps daffodils and tulips are planted in greatest numbers.

Daffodils. Because they last for many, many years, daffodils are probably the best bulb investments.

Several that bloom early are ADA FINCH, a white giant trumpet, and FEBRUARY GOLD, a robust yellow trumpet. ADVENTURE is a huge yellow trumpet, and MOUNT HOOD an excellent white.

In the medium-trumpet and short-cup group are some with brilliant red or orange centers. Among these are KANSAS, SELMA, DICK WELL-BAND, and FIREBIRD. LA ARGENTINA has a white trumpet with a white cup marked with radiating bands of gold.

PINK FANCY and MRS. R. O. BACKHOUSE are two good pink daffodils.

The so-called pheasant's-eye daffodils have brilliant white petals and small red-rimmed yellow cups. New or unusual kinds in this group are MINUET, ACTEA, and LADY KESTEVAN.

CRAGFORD, a cream white with deep orange center, is one of the newer, fragrant poetaz or cluster-flower sorts.

Tulips, too, are extremely popular spring flowers because of their flashy colors. Many wonderful kinds have been developed by crossing Darwins with the *fosteriana* hybrids. These have the long, strong stems of the Darwins and the glowing orange-red color of the other parent. The first of this group to become generally available was APELDOORN, with large, oval, orange-scarlet and yellow-edged black base. Other very desirable ones in this group are GENERAL EISEN-HOWER, a superb scarlet; OXFORD, a vivid orange scarlet with a very large yellow base; DOVER, a yellow-ringed oriental scarlet with a purple-black base; and LONDON, a very early variety, scarlet with a yellow-margined blue base.

Darwins crossed with the species *T. Greigii* have yielded such lovely kinds as ORIENTAL SPLENDOUR and MARGARET HERBST. These have large red, or yellow and red, blooms on yard-long stems with the form and mottled leaves of *T. Greigii*.

FANTASMA is an early-flowering *T. Eichleri* hybrid with stunning red flowers.

The so-called peacock tulips are a cross between *T. Greigii* and *T. Kaufmanniana,* which flower very early and for a considerable period. Many of them—red, white, pink, and yellow—have the beautifully spotted leaves of *T. Greigii* and the true lily form of *T. Kaufmanniana.* They are low-growing and hence ideally suited for rock gardens.

Among the newer or outstanding parrot tulips are GARDEN PARTY, which is like sculptured white TRIUMPH with a glowing deep pink edge, and TEXAS GOLD, a very large yellow with green strokes in its outer petals. Another very popular parrot is FANTASY, with emerald-green markings on deep-rose petals.

SWEET HARMONY, an ivory-white-margined lemon yellow, and DEBORAH, a soft pink, are two new Darwins.

Two new cottage tulips are ARTIST, a green-striped dull lilac rose, and ROSY WINGS, a salmon pink which gradually turns a sparkling pink.

For beginners in tulip culture, I present a baker's dozen of the more popular ones. MRS. J. T. SHEEPERS, PRINCESS ELIZABETH, MOUNT TACOMA, RED EMPEROR, CLARA BUTT, THE BISHOP, ARISTO-CRAT, BLUE PARROT, ECLIPSE, NIPHETOS, PRIDE OF ZWANENBURG, SMILING QUEEN, and CAPTAIN FRYATT.

Gladioli. Another very popular, though later-flowering plant is the gladiolus. As with many of the other popular flowers, new kinds by the dozens appear each year. Hence it is difficult to select those that will be with us for a long time until we see how well they are received and how great will be their demand by gladiolus growers, both amateur and professional.

Some of the outstanding new gladioli are: SNOWDRIFT and WHITE RAIN, both whites; HEART OF FLAME, white with a prominent red throat; LORELEI, lively ruffled cream; STALWART, a huge deep cream; CHAMOIS, buff suffused with pink; ROSE SPIRE, light rose with ivory throat; CABELLERO, reddish orange; EXCALIBUR, ruffled fiery red; WILLOW ROSE, medium rose; SAN ANTONIO, red with rose throat; JAUNTY, cream-throated rose pink; BLUE RADIANCE, light blue with deeper blue throat; LILAC TIME, ruffled lavender; GOLDEN BOY, yellow; CONRAD, deep yellow; and ERIN, with green petals, the first large green-flowered gladiolus ever introduced!

The 1956 All-America gladiolus selections are APPLEBLOSSOM, with white-edged pink flowers, and ROYAL STEWART, with rich red ones.

Some of the best of the miniature and small-flowering kinds include: ALECIA, pure white; CADETTE, ruffled scarlet; DAINTINESS, creamy white and heavily ruffled; GOLDETTE, yellow and ruffled; FROLIC, yellow with a huge red throat blotch; LITTLE GOLD, orange with floret edges slightly crinkled; LOVELY MARY, salmon; FLASHLIGHT, a salmon and scarlet bicolor; TOYTOWN, orange-tinted scarlet with a yellow throat; CHERUB, dainty pink; ZIG ZIG, red; FIFTH AVENUE, deep red;

TONY BOY, rose; JUDY, lavender with cream throat; LITTLE JOE, chocolate petals distinctly edged by white; and PETER PAN, ruffled salmon colored petals.

For beginners here are a dozen older glads in a variety of colors that are inexpensive, vigorous, and of fine quality: SPICK AND SPAN, ruffled deep pink; PACTOLUS, buff; BURMA, rose; MID AMERICA, red; POLYNESIA, salmon; RED CHARM, red; EVANGELINE, pink; ELIZABETH THE QUEEN, lavender; FLORENCE NIGHTINGALE, white; and RAVEL, blue.

Lilies. Among the showiest of all flowers grown from bulbs are the hardy lilies. Unfortunately because of the widespread publicity some years ago on the high susceptibility of lilies to diseases, many gardeners even now have the impression that the queen of flowers is difficult to grow. This is certainly not so.

Disease-free and disease-tolerant kinds are now available which can be grown with as little trouble as many other kinds of plants that are far less attractive. For example, a number of kinds either escape the destructive virus disease known as mosaic or are able to tolerate it even if they become infected. In this group are *L. Brownii, Henryi, Martagon,* and varieties; *Martagon-Hansonii* hybrids; *pardalinum* and varieties; *Wilmottiae;* and certain Backhouse and Preston hybrids.

New and more efficient insecticides and fungicides also help to combat the insect pests and fungus diseases of these plants. Moreover, many of the new hybrids do better because they are garden-grown. Hence they are better adapted to garden conditions than are wild species.

We now have a goodly number of easy to grow Aurelian hybrids (SUNBURST, HEART'S DESIRE, and GOLDEN CLARION strains) in pink, yellow, and golden yellow, developed by crossing *L. Henryi* with best trumpet lilies. (Illustration following page 64) Outstanding in the field of hardy lily introductions is the famous lily hybridizer Jan de Graaff of Gresham, Oregon. PROSPERITY, with pure lemon-yellow blooms facing outward, is one of his most recent introductions, as are a number of trumpet lilies in shades of rich pink, gold, and white.

Jillian Wallace is one of the newest auratum hybrids developed by Roy M. Wallace in Australia. Flower petals are carmine red with white margins, spotted with intense deep crimson. Individual flowers are 8 inches across, and one plant will bear as many as 7 flowers on a 5- to 6-foot stem.

There also are the early-summer-flowering Green Mountain hybrids stemming from *L. Sargentiae,* with widely opened flowers in varying shades of ivory and green white.

The Potomac hybrids are fine crosses between *L. auratum* and *L. speciosum,* developed by Dr. S. L. Emsweller of the United States Department of Agriculture.

HARMONY, TANGELO, VALENCIA, and SERENADE are all Mid-Century hybrids and come in striking shades of orange, yellow, and salmon.

The golden regal lilies have blooms ranging from clear yellow to deep gold, with exteriors flushed with rosy pink. These were developed by LeVern Freimann of Bellingham, Washington. He crossed a creamy yellow strain, possibly containing some *L. Wardii* blood, originally obtained from Luther Burbank, with some *gloriosum* seedlings.

These are but a few of the extremely beautiful and increasingly popular lilies to appear in recent years. More will no doubt follow.

I would like to conclude my discussion on bulbs by calling bulb enthusiasts' attention to the *American Gardener's Book of Bulbs,* by The New York Botanical Garden's horticulturist, T. H. Everett. I think it is one of the finest books of its kind.

HOW TO KEEP CUT FLOWERS

Because most if not all the flowers described in this chapter can be used as cut flowers in the home, I feel it would be wise to include here a few words on how to get the most out of cut flowers. After combing the literature carefully on this subject, I found that I could not improve on the suggestions made by a former colleague of mine, the late Dr. Kenneth Post, professor of floriculture at Cornell.

Here are Dr. Post's nine suggestions for increasing the longevity of cut flowers:

1. Wash the container before using it for cut flowers to remove bacteria. A dirty container enables the bacteria to multiply so rapidly that they clog the water-conducting tubes in the stems and cause the flowers to wilt.

2. Cut the lower stems, either on a slant or straight across, with a sharp knife or sharp shears. A fresh cut absorbs water freely.

3. Remove all leaves that will be below water, because submerged leaves decay and hasten fading of the flowers.

4. Always place stems in water at 110 degrees, or about bath temperature, and let the water cool naturally. Warm water moves easier and faster in the stem than does cold water. The warm water

probably clears the stem of air bubbles. The base of the stem must be covered, though deep water is not necessary.

5. After the stems are placed in warm water, wrap a piece of paper around the upper stems and flowers. The paper prevents rapid air movement over the flowers and reduces water loss. The flowers should become completely turgid, or perked up, within two hours, after which the covering is removed and they can be rearranged if necessary.

6. In the water use a commercial flower food containing sugar, acidifiers to prevent bacterial growth, and a mild fungicide to kill fungi. These will make the flowers keep longer, if, after they are added, the water is quite acid, around pH 4.5. They do not work in some city water that is high in carbonates, but will work if the water is acidified to around pH 4.5.*

7. Keep flowers cold when not in use. Flowers keep longer at 30 to 35 degrees than at higher temperatures. The life of flowers can be doubled if they are placed in a cold room or refrigerator at night, or when not in use. Most orchids should not be placed in temperatures below 50 degrees.

8. Never place flowers over a radiator or in a draught. Warm air removes water from flowers faster than they can absorb it. Heat also makes them mature sooner. Air blowing over flowers causes water loss faster than it is absorbed.

9. Boil the lower stems of poinsettias, poppies, and dahlias. The milky, viscous substance that oozes from the stem of poinsettias, poppies, and dahlias plugs the water-conducting tubes. Place the base of the stem in boiling water for thirty seconds and then in 110-degree water as for other flowers, and they will keep. The treatment is necessary each time the stem is cut.

* Several materials that prolong the life of cut flowers are ALLADIN, BLOOM-LIFE, FLORALIFE, SURVIVAL 77, and Borden's CUT FLOWER FOOD.

Chapter 3

ROSES, OTHER SHRUBS, AND HEDGES

POPULAR ROSES

The rose is America's favorite flower. As such, it makes a fitting start for the chapter on new or unusual shrubs.

PEACE is unquestionably the most popular rose in America. How long it will hold this place is difficult to forecast, but it probably will do so for many years. More than two thousand rose growers in the United States rated it highest in quality in 1954, giving it 9.6 points out of a possible 10.

The favorite color of roses is red. Americans are also partial to variations of red such as pink and salmon and to orange, yellow, and gold. Up to 1955, of the forty-three All-America winners, fifteen have been red, thirteen pink of varying shades, ten yellow, 2 orange, one two-toned, one buff and one multicolored. In other words, about two thirds of the award winners have been among the reds.

How to Grow Good Roses

For best results in growing roses, follow six important steps:

1. Buy only top-quality plants, preferably No. 1, two-year old, field-grown and field-budded. Plant them as soon as they arrive; or if you can't, "heel them in," that is, dig a shallow trench for the roots and cover them with soil until you are ready to plant the bushes.

2. For best results, plant them in a sunny, well-drained spot away from trees or their roots. Dig the planting hole 12 to 18 inches across and at least 2 feet deep. Set budded plants with the bud union 2 inches below the soil surface, and fill the hole with a good loamy soil mixture.

3. Keep up the fertility of the rose bed by applying 4 pounds of 5-10-5 to each 100 square feet every spring after the new growth is 4 to 6 inches long. Working in 5 bushels of well-rotted manure for

each 100 square feet every spring will also help. As with chrysanthemums, I have found that 3 or 4 leaf sprays of RAPIDGRO plant food make better roses and more vigorous bushes. Dr. L. C. Chadwick, horticulturist at Ohio State University, reported, too, that this plant food applied as a foliage spray produced finer roses in the test gardens of his university during 1953 and 1954.

4. Mulch with buckwheat hulls, corn cobs, or peat moss during the summer months to conserve moisture and to keep weeds down.

5. Control diseases like black spot and mildew and pests like aphids, thrips, Japanese beetles, and red spiders with a good combination spray containing the following materials for each 5 gallons of water: 2 ounces of 25 per cent wettable malathion powder, 1 ounce of ferbam, ⅕ ounce MILDEX, and a few drops of the wetting agent SANTOMERSE S. Another effective combination contains ARAMITE, zineb, and MILDEX as the active ingredients. Remember that roses heavily infested with mites and black spot winterkill more readily than uninfested plants.

Gardeners who do not want to bother mixing their own combination spray can buy one of several ready-mixed kinds such as BOBBINK AND ATKINS ROSE SPRAY, JACKSON AND PERKINS ROSE SPRAY, DU PONT'S ROSE INSECTICIDE AND FUNGICIDE, SCIENCE ROSE AND FLORAL DUST, or SWIFT'S END-O-PEST ROSE DUST. And there are literally dozens of other good brands on the market.

6. Prune properly. Hybrid teas and other bush types should be pruned in early spring when the buds begin to swell. Remove all wood killed or injured during the winter, all showing fungus lesions, and all weak, twiggy growth. Prune ramblers and similar climbers after blooming by removing old unwanted canes at the base.

Classes of Roses

Except for dyed-in-the wool rosarians, most gardeners are confused by the various classes of roses grown in this country. Hence a few words on this subject are in order.

The largest class is the HYBRID TEA (HT.), large-flowered types usually borne one flower to a stem. These are the kinds usually sold in florists' shops. Many of them are not reliably hardy in the northern parts of the United States and therefore should have some sort of winter protection.

FLORIBUNDAS (FL.) are generally easier to grow, hardier, and more vigorous than the hybrid teas. They bloom more or less continually, but their flowers are smaller and are borne in clusters.

The new GRANDIFLORA class (GR.) combines the chief characteristics of the hybrid tea and the floribundas. The plants are relatively tall, very free-flowering, and produce blooms similar to the hybrid teas in size and form. The flowers are borne in clusters, but the individual stems are long enough for cutting.

RAMBLERS (R.) are vigorous, hardy, tall growers which form small flowers in clusters once a year.

CLIMBING HYBRID TEAS (CHT.) have typical hybrid tea blooms and and are grown only in the warmer regions.

LARGE-FLOWERED CLIMBERS (LC.) make moderate growth, are generally hardy, and may bloom more than once a season.

EVERBLOOMING CLIMBERS (EVBL. C.) have large flowers, bloom in spring and fall, and sometimes during summer.

Here is the list of the American Rose Society's 1955 top-rated roses by classes:

HYBRID TEAS

Red: CRIMSON GLORY, CHARLOTTE ARMSTRONG, ETIOLE DE HOLLANDE.

Pink: DAINTY BESS (single), PICTURE, RADIANCE.

Yellow: ECLIPSE, GOLDEN ANNIVERSARY, GOLDEN DAWN.

White: PEDRALBES, MCGREDY'S IVORY, WHITE WINGS.

Blends: PEACE, TIP TOES, MME. HENRI GUILLOT.

FLORIBUNDAS

Red: RED PINOCCHIO, DONALD PRIOR, FRENSHAM.

Pink: THE FAIRY, FASHION, ROSENELFE.

Yellow: GOLDILOCKS, KING BOREAS, DENNY BOY.

White: SUMMER SNOW, DAGMAR SPATH, IRENE OF DENMARK.

GRANDIFLORAS

Pink: QUEEN ELIZABETH. Only official member. Some catalogues will also include the following:

Red: CARROUSEL.

Yellow: BUCCANEER.

Pink: DEAN COLLINS.

CLIMBERS

Red: PAUL'S SCARLET (LC.), CLIMBING CRIMSON GLORY (CHT.), CHEVY CHASE (Climbing Rambler).

Pink: THE NEW DAWN (LC.), CLIMBING PINKIE (CFL.), DR. W. VAN FLEET (LC.).

Yellow: CLIMBING GOLDILOCKS (CFL.), HIGH NOON (CHT.), DOUBLOONS (LC.).

White: CITY OF YORK (LC.), WHITE DAWN (LC.), SILVER
  MOON (LC.).
Blend: CLIMBING MRS. SAM MCGREDY.

This list includes the best of the roses, some of which have been
available for many years and thus have withstood the test of time.
But every year new roses are introduced, and in time a goodly number of the new introductions are sure to be included in the most
popular list.

Hybrids. Perhaps the finest of the brand-new hybrid teas, TIFFANY,
named after the world-famous jewelry store, produces long-stemmed,
graceful, warm pink flowers that hold their color regardless of
weather conditions. The plant is vigorous, highly productive, and its
flowers are fragrant, a quality most hybridizers overlook when developing modern roses. (Illustration following page 64)

The best of the new yellow hybrid teas is GOLDEN MASTERPIECE.
It has long, slender, graceful buds that open to majestic, high-
centered, deep yellow blooms nearly 8 inches across.

Among other yellow hybrid teas are SUN KING, the first all-yellow
offspring of PEACE, whose long-pointed buds open to a vivid lemon
yellow with approximately 40 petals; LEMON CHIFFON, a rich lemon
yellow that holds its color well in the sun; and BURNABY, yellow with
a delicate fragrance.

Another offspring of PEACE, GRANDMERE JENNY has more pink
in its petals than has its parent.

Several other fine hybrid teas were introduced in 1955: RONDO, a
fiery orange with flowers 4 inches across; BIG DADDY, a deep velvety
red, still another offspring of PEACE; COURTSHIP, with yellow petals
overlaid with cerise pink; DAMON RUNYON, a glowing vermilion; KATE
SMITH, a rich apricot with abundant foliage and good vigor; LA JOLLA
(as in Spanish *La Hoya*), with soft yellow and pale apricot flowers
overlaid with varying amounts of crispy pink; PRESIDENT EISEN-
HOWER, a fragrant, brilliant red, which its originators call the modern
"American Beauty" rose; YELLOW RUFFLES, a sport of ORANGE RUF-
FLES, which is said to be resistant to black spot disease; RED SPLEN-
DOR, a brilliant red that is large and fragrant; and HANDSOM RED,
which is probably the most brilliant fully double red rose.

LOVE SONG, introduced in the fall of 1955, is another offspring of
PEACE. It is a brilliant bicolor, salmon pink with yellow on the
reverse side, very double and very large. BINGO, introduced in the
fall of 1955 by the Ilgenfritz Nurseries of Monroe, Michigan, is a

fiery red hybrid tea developed by the famous French hybridizer Marcel Robichon.

The nearest to a true blue rose ever offered in this country is TWILIGHT. Actually its color is a lavender lilac with a light silvery sheen on the reverse side. It is a full, double hybrid tea with a beautiful pointed bud tinted a soft pink lavender. TWILIGHT is not to be confused with VEILCHENBLAU, a rambler available for nearly fifty years and widely publicized and sold as the "blue rose." The color of its flowers more nearly approaches a magenta.

Floribundas. Among the newest floribundas and the only rose to receive the coveted All-America Award for 1956 is CIRCUS. Its bright yellow and orange buds open to display changing and additional tones, including buff, pink, and bright red. CIRCUS was developed by Armstrong Nurseries of Ontario, California, and is the first multicolor rose to win an All-America Award. (Illustration following page 64)

Yellow floribundas are not very plentiful. Hence a welcome addition to this group is GOLDEN FLEECE, introduced by Jackson and Perkins in the fall of 1955. It is tawny gold in bud and opens to a lighter gold and finally finishes a bright canary yellow.

Among the new floribundas is an All-America winner in 1955, JIMINY CRICKET, named after Walt Disney's famous character. It has tangerine-colored buds that open to a coral orange and finally to pink coral similar to FASHION.

Other exciting floribundas are ALPINE GLOW, bright vermilion; E. I. FARRINGTON, a brilliant, velvety red double; RED CAP, a fiery red, excellent for mass bedding and hedges; RED WONDER, oxblood red; BABY BLAZE, cherry red with a lighter center, which is also excellent as a hedge plant or as a low shrub in foundation plantings; and LULLABY, a fine white. SPARTAN, released by Jackson and Perkins in the fall of 1955, is a sparkling, warm, orange red that softens to a reddish coral at the finish. The plant is constantly in flower from early spring to severe frosts, and the flowers are produced both in large clusters and individually on long stems.

Grandiflora. The first rose to be placed in the new GRANDIFLORA class is QUEEN ELIZABETH, an All-America selection for 1955. It is a tall, free-flowering plant with flowers that are a blend of soft carmine rose and dawn pink, which become richer as the blooms age. QUEEN ELIZABETH is a vigorous grower with glossy leaves. (Illustration following page 64)

In addition to the three other grandiflora types mentioned in the American Rose Society's list, the following have also been mentioned as outstanding new candidates for this class: ROUNDELAY, with pointed buds and high-centered, vivid red blooms; SUGAR PLUM, a clear pink; and MONTEZUMA, a beautiful scarlet orange.

Climbers. Ever since the discovery and the patenting of THE NEW DAWN ROSE, hybridizers have been busy in their search for other everblooming hardy climbers. As a result, a number of fine everblooming climbers have been developed, and the future holds promise for even finer ones.

Outstanding in this group are the BROWNELL EVERBLOOMING PILLARS, which come in pink, light pink, light yellow, yellow, and red colors. These will grow as tall as the ordinary hardy climbers and bloom as freely as hybrid tea roses.

Among other new ones in this category are:

MORNING DAWN with clear, soft pink flowers that are just as large, double, and perfect in shape as any hybrid tea rose. Besides being an everbloomer, it has the old-fashioned fragrance and grows on long stems that are ideal for cutting.

RUBY GLOW is a red with dependable hardiness; RED FLARE, another red, grows to 7 or 8 feet; RITZ makes clusters of small, lively red flowers through the summer and fall; and GLADIATOR has brilliant, rose-red, 5-inch blooms on 8- to 10-foot high plants.

Other fine everblooming climbers available for the last four or five years are DREAM GIRL, which flowers profusely in early June and continues with a succession of spicy blooms throughout the summer; INSPIRATION, similar to DREAM GIRL but a stronger grower in some areas and with more and longer canes; and TEMPTATION, with vivid red blooms that look their best after the plants become thoroughly established.

Low-Growing Varieties. Other recently introduced roses are CHARLIE MC CARTHY, a low-growing variety that grows about 18 inches tall and has creamy white buds and a continuous show of pure white flowers on a bushy, compact plant with very shiny leaves; and an everblooming shrub rose, AUTUMN BOQUET, with carmine-red blooms.

Miniature or dwarf roses seldom grow more than a foot high. Though small and dainty, they are relatively hardy. They are best planted in sheltered spots in rock gardens or as a border to the rose garden, but never among the larger roses. They do well in a greenhouse, but though they are sometimes sold as house plants, they do not thrive in the average home. Their worst pest is spider mite, which can be controlled with occasional applications of ARAMITE or malathion spray.

SWEET FAIRY, with deep pink buds and 1-inch, very double, apple-blossom-pink flowers; PIXIE, a fully double white; RED IMP, a bright, unfading crimson; BABY GOLD STAR, a yellow; and MIDGET, a red, are among the more popular miniatures.

PINK CAMEO is the first everblooming miniature pink climber. It has long-lasting deep pink buds and flowers.

In a book of this sort it is obviously impossible to go into minute detail on roses because of their many different kinds. Those who want to delve into the pedigrees of modern roses will find that the book *Modern Roses,* the latest edition of which is *Modern Roses IV,* contains descriptions of all the roses in commerce or of historical or botanical importance. It is published by the J. Horace MacFarland Company of Harrisburg, Pennsylvania, in co-operation with the American Rose Society.

OTHER WOODY SHRUBS

Rhododendrons. Among the broad-leaved evergreen shrubs, few can rival the rhododendrons. Besides their very showy flowers, they produce beautiful evergreen leaves.

Most rhododendrons prefer an acid soil, one which ranges between pH 4.5 and 6.0, well drained and containing a goodly amount of organic matter.

Don't plant rhododendrons in deep shade if you want them to flower freely. But you can plant them under deep-rooting trees like oaks and pines, if the trees' branches are high and allow some light to pass through and if you water the shrubs during extended dry spells. The ideal spot to plant rhododendrons on larger properties is beyond the spread of the trees' branches along the edge of a clearing, where the shrubs can get sunlight for four or more hours on sunny days.

Rhododendrons are attacked by a number of pests, including lace bugs, mealy bugs, midges, and spider mites, and by several fungi that cause leaf spots and blights. These can be controlled by spraying with a mixture of malathion and either ferbam or captan.

There are a number of excellent rhododendrons that will do well where the climate is not too cold, that is, where the temperature does not fall below the zero mark. Best known in this group are the

Dexter hybrids, developed by the late Charles O. Dexter on Cape Cod, and the Gable hybrids, developed by Joseph C. Gable of Stewartstown, Pennsylvania.

The Dexter hybrids belong mostly to the *Fortunei* series, which have large, trumpet-shaped flowers 4 or more inches in diameter, in colors ranging from white to pink and rose.

Some of the Gable hybrids, which also have very beautiful flowers, are hardier than the Dexters; others are less so. Any nurseryman who specializes in rhododendrons can supply some of these newer kinds.

The Guyencourt rhododendrons are a new race of low-growing kinds developed by Guy S. Nearing of New Jersey. They grow to a height of several feet in climates similar to that of New York City and in favored locations much farther north.

Among the named garden varieties are: DELAWARE, pink-tipped flowers with yellow throats; LENAPE, pale yellow; BRANDYWINE, rose pink; HOCKESSIN, pinkish yellow; MONTCHANIN, clear white; and CHESAPEAKE, yellowish pink.

Azaleas. Although azaleas are classified botanically as rhododendrons, gardeners and nurserymen usually call the evergreen sorts rhododendrons and the deciduous sorts azaleas. Actually the distinction is not quite that sharp because there are deciduous rhododendrons and evergreen azaleas.

Among the most famous azaleas developed in this country in recent years are the Glen Dale hybrids. The first experimental crosses were made a little more than twenty-five years ago by hybridists in the Division of Plant Exploration and Introductions of the United States Department of Agriculture under the direction of B. Y. Morrison.

The color range of the four hundred and fifty named varieties runs the gamut from a snowy white, unmarked and clear with no blotch of green or yellow, through the tangerine tones to the deep rose end of the spectrum. The color range, however, is only part of their unusual qualities. Many are striped, sanded, flaked, and margined with color, producing a double-tone effect which intensifies the ground color.

The Glen Dale azaleas are not reliably hardy north of New York and hence must be given some protection when grown in the northeastern states.

Following are twelve outstanding varieties grouped according to their blooming periods:

Early bloomers: CYGNET, white touched with very pale yellow; SAMITE, pure white with an occasional hose-in-hose flower; DAY-SPRING, pale pink with white centers; and BALLET GIRL, a combination of light with deep red that gives an over-all orange effect.

Midseason bloomers: CARNIVAL, salmon; GAIETY, rose pink blotched with red; MARTHA HITCHCOCK, white margined with rosy purple patches at the edge of frilled petals; and HELEN FOX, with the outside of the petals red and the insides light pink blotched with darker pink.

Late bloomers: SAGITTARIUS, pink with salmon undertone and tiny, boxwood-like leaves; SNOWSCAPE, greenish white; CRUSADER, pink with a showy blotch of rose; and EROS, orange pink.

Viburnums. The viburnums are among the most versatile groups of shrubs because the many members have unusual flowers, fruits, or growth habits, all of which are highly desirable. Among the better kinds are the FRAGRANT VIBURNUM *(V. fragrans)*, which opens its clustered pink buds from November to April; *V. Carlesii,* with fragrant early-spring flowers; the DOUBLE FILE VIBURNUM *(V. plicatum* var. *tomentosum),* with flowers that grow in very striking layers along the branches; and perhaps the most desirable of all, *Viburnum Carcocephalum,* the FRAGRANT SNOWBALL, considered to be the finest spring-flowering shrub offered to American gardeners in the last fifty years. It originated in England from a cross between *V. Carlesii* and *V. macrocephalum.* A profusely flowering shrub with exceedingly fragrant, large clusters of blossoms, some 6 inches across, it is indeed appropriately named. Its dense foliage closely resembles that of *V. Carlesii* except that it colors brilliantly in autumn.

An older viburnum considered one of the best all-round shrubs is the SIEBOLD VIBURNUM *(V. Sieboldi).* Its white, flat flower clusters, resembling those of the wild carrot, or QUEEN ANNE'S LACE, are borne in profusion in late May. These are replaced by berries that are red at first but turn black late in the season. Besides the lovely flowers and the striking fruit, the plant has thick, rugose leaves about 6 inches long and 2 inches wide that are also highly ornamental.

Yews are considered by many as the best narrow-leaved evergreens. Although practically unknown a quarter of a century ago, they now constitute the "backbone" of many ornamental plantings.

Yews come in all sizes and shapes—from tall columnar forms to dwarf spreading types. The upright and spreading Japanese yews, first to be used, are rapidly being replaced by more attractive slow-growing kinds.

Two fine slow-growing yews which frame the entrance to my home were given to me by William Flemer of Princeton Nurseries. I cannot recall how large they were when I planted them, but after eight years of healthy, compact growth they are only 18 inches tall and about 30 inches wide!

Yews are desirable for a number of reasons. They grow in full sun or shade, although perhaps not quite as well in the latter situation. They have the darkest green leaves of all evergreens and the female, or pistillate, plants produce fleshy red berries that are quite attractive and that frequently remain on the plants for several months.

Like hollies and a few other kinds of trees, a male, or staminate, plant must be within 100 feet or so of the pistillate plant to provide pollen for fruit formation.

The leaves are said to be poisonous to animals if consumed in large quantities, and the hard seeds in the fleshy berries are said to be poisonous to humans. I frequently suck the sweet juice from the ripe berries without, of course, chewing or swallowing the seeds.

There are two serious pests of yews: mealy bug and black vine weevil. The former attacks aboveground stems and can be controlled with malathion sprays. The latter does most of its damage below ground, where the roots are chewed or girdled by the larval stage. Treating the soil with chlordane will give reasonably good control of the larval stage, and spraying the lower branches and leaves with dieldrin will control the adult, or weevil, which feeds on the leaves.

Camellias are usually considered tender shrubs, and hence their growth outdoors is confined primarily to the southern part of our country. They are apparently more cold-resistant than most gardeners realize, however, for some are being grown outdoors rather far north. For example, Dr. P. W. Zimmerman of 2,4-D and plant hormone fame has been growing selections of *Camellia japonica* var. *elegans* in his garden at Yonkers, New York, since 1928. The only severe injury to his plants occurred in the winter of 1933-34, when the temperature dropped to 20 degrees below zero. Some leaves, flower buds, and stem tips were damaged at that time, but the plants survived.

In more recent years his camellia selections have come through the winter as well as many other plants that are usually considered fairly winterhardy. The plants in his yard withstood 2 degrees below zero on February 3, 1955, without showing injury to leaves or flower buds. These plants have been well established and are now approximately 4 feet tall.

Some of the named varieties of camellias being tested by Dr. Zimmerman are "Z," ELEGANS, KUMASKA (LADY MARION), MME. LE BOIS, SARA FROST, and COMTE DE GOMER. Among the winter-resistant kinds he recently named are MRS. WILLIAM T. WOOD, red-flowered, and MRS. WILLIAM G. GEROW, a small-flowered dark red.

Some selections of the SASANQUA camellias *(C. Sasanqua)* also tolerate considerable cold. They are now being grown along most of the Atlantic coast and inland as far north as the Great Lakes. Their gorgeous colors range from velvet white to rose, pink, deep pink, cherry red, and deep red.

Apparently camellias can withstand low temperatures far better once they become thoroughly established. Dr. Zimmerman feels that, with a little more selection and care in planting, hardy camellias will soon be a reality.

Lilacs have long been favorites of gardeners who like early spring-flowering shrubs. The new yellow PRIMROSE is said to be the only yellow lilac now in existence. Its flowers are a soft cream yellow on young plants but are a deeper yellow as the plants age and become better established. PRIMROSE is a sport of MARIE LEGRAYE, a single white which has been available for a long time and which is popular with florists who force lilac blossoms under glass.

Showiest of the white lilacs presently available is MONUMENT. MONT BLANC is late-blooming, white, and single.

Three late-blooming lilacs recently released by the New Hampshire Plant Growers' Association are NELLIE BEAN, purple; MRS. ANNA AMHOFF, white; and MISS KIM, light purple. The first two are open-pollinated seedlings of a Canadian introduction, MISS PRESTON'S ROYALTY. MISS KIM is a seedling of the Korean species *Syringa Palibiniana*. It makes low, compact growth and has mildew-resistant dark green leaves that turn to a burgundy-wine color in autum.

When all other lilacs have faded, usually by early June, the tree lilac *Syringa amurensis japonica* comes into its own. This produces big, fluffy, flat-topped panicles of small white florets. Tree lilacs are usually trained to grow like trees, that is, on a single stem, and often reach a height of 25 or more feet. Their shiny green foliage is much more attractive than that of the more common bushy French hybrids.

Besides the new lilacs, there are other recently introduced shrubs that are exceptionally outstanding.

Other New Shrubs

Pyracantha SENSATION is an improvement over older kinds in that it produces berries on very young growth. Thus young plants, when established, are covered in early fall with coral-scarlet berries that later turn to brilliant red. This variety is also less thorny than the older varieties and is said to be very hardy.

One of the newest forsythias, LINWOOD GOLD, originated in Ireland, produces great numbers of deep yellow flowers that are more striking than those on older forsythias.

DR. MERRIL is a relatively new hardy magnolia that transplants easily and grows rapidly. Its white star-shaped flowers appear in early spring. Its foliage is particularly good, and hence even when not in flower the plant makes a fine lawn specimen.

A delightful, deep-blue autumn-flowering shrub, Caryopteris HEAVENLY BLUE, does well in light sandy soils and in full sun.

A little-known shrub from North Africa *Cytisus Battandieri,* was recently introduced to American gardeners. Golden-yellow lupine-like flowers in tight clusters are produced in late May and June.

PINK CASCADE tamarix produces pink flowers in panicles or loose pyramids from July to September. Its narrow blue-green foliage is quite distinctive. It does best in seashore plantings.

The new daphne hybrid MANTENSIANA looks like an important addition to gardens in the northwestern parts of the country. Its parents are daphne SOMERSET and *D. rugosa.* It is a slow, compact grower, the eventual size being 15 inches high and about 30 inches wide. The orchid-purple flowers are very fragrant and appear as thimble-like clusters at the ends of the branches.

Abeliophyllum distichum, more popularly known as white forsythia, is a strong, compact shrub with white flowers appearing in February and March in the latitude of central Ohio.

The hybrid lantana GOLDRUSH is the first trailing lantana in a clear yellow. Like all lantanas, it is cold-sensitive. In the cooler parts of our country it is usually grown indoors in a hanging basket. In the milder regions it can be used as a ground cover.

A new dwarf mock orange, FROSTY MORN, which eventually grows to about 40 inches tall, has pure white double blooms in late June and July.

Lonicera tatarica ARNOLD RED, recently introduced by the Arnold Arboretum, has the darkest red flowers of any of the tatarian honeysuckles. It is a vigorous grower and is hardy throughout most of the northern United States.

Some Older "All-Stars"

Although all these new shrubs are fine and are certainly worth growing, let us not overlook some of the older American shrubs that have stood the test of time and will continue to be tops in any shrub planting. Included in this category are six evergreen shrubs, some with the most beautiful flowers in the plant kingdom. If planted in the proper place, they will do well for years and years.

Here are the six all-stars: Carolina rhododendron, mountain-laurel, Japanese andromeda, American andromeda, drooping leucothoe, and boxleaf holly.

All six have a number of things in common. They all do best in loamy acid soils and dislike alkaline soils. They like lots of organic matter in a soil that is well drained. Because their leaves stay on through the winter, they are, with the possible exception of the box-leaf holly, extremely susceptible to wind burn, sunscald, and winter drying. Hence they should not be planted in wind-swept areas or where they are constantly exposed to strong sunlight.

Carolina rhododendron has the smallest leaves of all the rhodo-dendrons native to the eastern United States. Most members of this species have clear pink trusses of beautiful flowers in late April and early May, although the color may range anywhere from pure white to a deep rosy pink in some individuals.

Mountain-laurel, considered by many America's most beautiful shrub, is a long-lived evergreen when planted with due regard to its susceptibility to wind burn and sunscald. Two very common fungus diseases frequently associated with it, leaf spot and blight, can now be easily controlled with occasional sprayings of ferbam or captan during the growing season.

Both the Japanese and American andromedas have bell-like florets and are sturdy growers. The flower clusters on the Japanese species droop gracefully, whereas those on the American species are erect. The former does better over a wider range of temperature and soil conditions than does the latter.

Drooping leucothoe has arching branches which in early spring are heavy with white flower clusters hanging beneath rows of dark, leathery, pointed leaves. This plant tolerates shade better than any of the others in this group.

Boxleaf holly *(Ilex crenata convexa)* has the least showy flowers of the six, but it is perhaps the toughest plant of them all. It grows almost anywhere, in the full sun, in shade, and even in the relatively poor soil of our larger cities. Its small, shiny, boxwood-like leaves are attractive at every season of the year. Some fine forms of the Japanese holly, *I. crenata,* are HELLERI, KINGSVILLE, and KINGSVILLE GREEN CUSHION.

Other deciduous shrubs have long given satisfaction to gardeners and should not be completely overlooked in favor of the newer kinds. These include autumn eleagnus *(E. umbellata);* black alder *(Ilex verticillata);* buddleia FORTUNE, lilac with orange eye; CLANDON BLUE-BEARD *(Caryopteris clandonensis);* creeping cotoneaster *(Cotoneaster adpressa);* Hypericum SUNGOLD, golden-yellow flowers in summer and fall; redvein enkianthus *(Enkianthus campanulatus);* Scotch broom *(Cytisus scoparius);* silky broom *(Genista pilosa);* thicket shadbush *(Amelanchier canadensis),* white flowers and beautiful, edible fruits; weigela BRISTOL FAIRY, garnet crimson; white-flowering quince *(Chaenomeles lagenaria* var. *nivalis);* winged euonymous *(Euonymous alata);* and winter honeysuckle *(Lonicera fragrantissima).*

The climbing hydrangea, *H. petiolaris,* has been with us for many years but only recently has come into its own. It forms large, beautiful clusters of white flowers and is excellent for rambling over old stone piles, growing up stone or brick walls, and even on the trunks of tall trees. Trees never seem to suffer from the close association.

Modern Hedge Plants

A few new hedge plants are worthy of mention. The new dwarf privet SUWANNEE RIVER introduced in the fall of 1954 has small, slightly curled dark green leaves that almost hide its woody stems. It was originated by Larry M. Bartlett of Forest Park, Georgia, from a cross between *Ligustrum japonicum* and *L. coriaceum.* Twelve-year-old plants average only 5 feet high. This hedge grows on a wide variety of soils, in either sun or shade, and requires little or no pruning. Although its northernmost limit is unknown, it has proved hardy in the last two years at Philadelphia and Harrisburg, Pennsylvania, on Long Island, and along the eastern seaboard south of New York. Because of its growth habit, SUWANNEE RIVER is ideally suited for landscape plantings around the modern ranch-type home and therefore is discussed further in *Chapter 10.*

Another very slow-growing dwarf privet, VICARI, has a golden foliage and is suitable for edging walks and flower beds. It is said to be hardy as far north as Ohio.

An excellent privet for use as a hedge or as a specimen plant in the southern Great Plains area and other mild-wintered, semi-arid areas of the country is *Ligustrum Quihoui.*

A dwarf form of the red-leaved barberry, CRIMSON PYGMY, is now available. It is a slow-grower, a three-year plant measuring 18 inches across and only a foot high. Like the standard red-leaved kind, CRIMSON PYGMY must also be planted in full sun to bring out the deep red color in the leaves.

Several other kinds of plants make excellent hedges if sheared occasionally. Among these are: Amur maple, *Acer ginnala;* cornelian cherry, *Cornus mas;* European larch, *Larix decidua;* shingle oak, *Quercus imbricaria,* and the Chinese lilac *Syringa chinensis.*

Because of the highly desirable habit of gradually developing a wider plant at the base than at the top, MOON'S COLUMNAR YEW makes one of the finest plants for hedges.

An unusually fine new hedge plant, LUEDY FASTIGIATE GLOSSY BUCKTHORN, *Rhamnus frangula,* developed by the Cole Nursery Company of Painesville, Ohio, will be available to gardeners by the fall of 1956. It grows narrow and upright, without trimming, and the ratio of height to width is about 3 or 4 to 1.

Chapter 4

TREES: SHADE, ORNAMENT, FLOWERS, FRUIT

Styles change in shade, flowering, and fruit trees as well as in other plants. The trend today is toward smaller trees, that is, smaller in permanent stature, for the modern, average-sized property. On extremely narrow properties and along narrow streets, the slender-growing, or fastigiate, shade trees are the ones to plant.

One of the outstanding exponents of lower-growing trees with specific forms to fit the planting situation is Edward Scanlon of Olmsted Falls, Ohio, editor and publisher of *Trees,* a magazine devoted to tree care, and formerly Shade Tree Commissioner for Cleveland. Mr. Scanlon already has built up a good supply of young trees that have upright, columnar, globe-shaped, and other desirable forms for use on smaller properties or along narrow streets.

So far as I can determine, Mr. Scanlon is the first to grow the famous GLASTONBURY THORN or the HOLY THORN OF GLASTONBURY in sufficient quantity to make it available commercially.

The legend, tradition, and verifiable history about this tree make a rich and moving story, which was well told by Dr. Donald Rogers of The New York Botanical Garden in the Garden's *Journal* a few years ago. Here is the first paragraph of Dr. Rogers' story, which should whet the appetite of readers who want to know more about this famous tree:

"When Joseph of Arimathea, worn by his pligrimage from the Holy Land, had climbed to the summit of Wearyall Hill at Glastonbury, he thrust his staff into the ground as a sign that his wanderings were at an end. The staff put out roots and leafy branches, and in the course of time blossomed, not only in the spring, when the hawthorn was flowering elsewhere in England, but also on Christmas morn. The tree that sprang from St. Joseph's staff is the Holy Thorn of Glastonbury."

A direct descendant of the GLASTONBURY THORN is growing in front of the Museum Building at The New York Botanical Garden.

Low-Growing Ornamental Trees

The following low-growing trees are suggested for small-sized properties:

AMUR CORK TREE, *Phellodendron amurense,* grows in northern parts of the country in all kinds of soils at a pH ranging from 5.5 to 7.0. It resists smoky city conditions, tolerates very dry soils, and is rather free from insect attack. Its light, deeply fissured bark is conspicuous in winter.

AMUR MAPLE, *Acer ginnala,* does best in northern United States in rich, well-drained soil at a pH of 5.0 to 6.0. It will thrive either in full sun or in partial shade. It has excellent foliage and will grow in dry spots. It is more effective when planted in groups of two or three.

BLACKHAW VIBURNUM, *Viburnum prunifolium,* grows well in the eastern United States in almost any soil with a pH range of 5.0 to 6.0. It has white flowers in spring and blue-black fruits in fall. Its handsome foliage gives off a disagreeable odor when frost strikes it. Nevertheless, it is a highly desirable tree.

Crab apples, *Malus* species, can be both ornamental and utilitarian. Some produce bright-colored fruits that make excellent jelly in addition to truly magnificent flowers in early spring. Others are grown primarily for their flowers.

Among the best known kinds that serve the dual purpose are ARNOLD CRAB and ALDENHAM CRAB. Two recent introductions that fall in the same category are REDFIELD and REDFORD. Both are hardy and produce good-sized fruits with flesh that is red throughout. Other good varieties are DOLGO and YOUNG AMERICA. The former is a Russian variety introduced into America by the South Dakota Experiment Station, while the latter is an old variety of unknown origin. Both make excellent jelly.

Among the older varieties of crab apples grown primarily for their flowers are BECHTEL'S CRAB, with fragrant, double pink blossoms; CARMINE CRAB, with large rose-madder flowers; and DOROTHEA, with bright tyrian rose flowers. Newer ornamental crab apples are *Van Eseltine,* which produces double pink blossoms and which retains its small fruits during the winter and thus provides food for birds; and the very hardy CRIMSON BRILLIANT, with semi-double, vivid crimson flowers.

The dogwoods are among the most popular of the low-growing

flowering trees. Best known and most widely planted is the FLOWER-
ING DOGWOOD, *Cornus florida*. It does best in the eastern United
States in well-drained soils with a pH ranging from 5.0 to 7.0. It
flowers either in full sun or partial shade. Its large white bracts surrounding the flower are very conspicuous in spring, and its leaves
and fruits are colorful in autumn. It is most successfully transplanted
in spring immediately after flowering. There are a number of pink
or red strains of the FLOWERING DOGWOOD. Latest to appear is the
PROSSER FLOWERING DOGWOOD, which is said to have deeper red
blooms than the older red-flowering kinds.

FLOWERING DOGWOOD is attacked by borers, but these can be
controlled by spraying with DDT three or four times at two-week
intervals starting the third week in May.

During very rainy springs and summers this lovely tree is subject
to three fungus diseases—spot anthracnose and Septoria leaf spot,
which cause circular spots on the leaves and flowers, and Botrytis
blight, which blights the flowers and leaves. These diseases can be
prevented by spraying with captan or MANZATE once a month starting
in April, when the flower buds are in the cup stage, and continuing
until flower buds for the following year are formed in late summer.
The most destructive disease affecting dogwood is crown canker,
caused by the fungus *Phytophthora cactorum*. No control measure is
known. Because this fungus may enter the tree through wounds,
injury by lawnmowers and other implements should be avoided.

A close relative of our native dogwood, the JAPANESE DOGWOOD,
Cornus Kousa, grows about 20 feet tall and blooms about three weeks
after the FLOWERING DOGWOOD. Its small yellow flowers, which last
for about a week, are surrounded by 4 conspicuous white bracts
which are pointed at the tips and not notched and rounded as are
those of the FLOWERING DOGWOOD. Because the flowers and fruit
are borne on the upper side of horizontal branches, the tree is best
planted where it can be seen from above. The CHINESE DOGWOOD,
C. Kousa chinensis, is supposed to have larger bracts than the
Japanese species.

FRINGETREE, *Chionanthus virginicus,* grows best in the East and
in Gulf coast states in moisture-retentive sandy loam soils ranging
from pH 5.5 to 6.0 and in sunny locations. It is fairly tolerant of
smoky city conditions. In late May and early June it forms numerous
white blossoms.

GOLDENRAIN TREE, *Koelreuteria paniculata,* grows almost anywhere
but is most common in the Midwest and does especially well in dry

soils at a pH of 6.5 to 8.0. It is drought-resistant and has average resistance to windstorms and ice. It forms conspicuous panicles of yellow flowers in summer.

Hawthorns, *Crataegus* species, like the crab apples, are especially attractive when in flower and in fruit. They do best in the northern and eastern states, in well-drained, fertile soils with a pH of 6.0 to 7.0. Nursery-grown trees are transplanted easily. As mentioned in *Chapter 10,* hawthorns are excellent trees to plant around the modern ranch-type homes.

Best of the older kinds are Paul's SCARLET THORN, with clusters of half-inch blossoms of deep rose color, and the WASHINGTON THORN, with white blossoms in May followed by scarlet berries and brilliant foliage in autumn.

The latest kind available commercially is the GLASTONBURY THORN, described earlier in this chapter. Its flower and fruit characters are like those of the WASHINGTON THORN.

Hawthorns, like other members of the Rose family, are susceptible to the bacterial disease fire blight, which can now be controlled with sprays containing antibiotic streptomycin. These are sold under such trade names as AGRIMYCIN, AGRISTREP, and PHYTOMYCIN, and are discussed in greater detail in *Chapter 13.* A fungus leaf spot is also common in wet summers. This disease frequently causes premature leaf drop. It can be prevented by periodic applications of a MANZATE or FERMATE spray.

HEDGE MAPLE, *Acer campestre,* is an unusual low-growing tree that thrives in the eastern United States in well-drained, deep, fertile soil with a pH of 6.0 to 7.0. Its growth resembles that of Japanese maples, and its foliage is yellow in fall.

MOUNTAIN MAPLE, *Acer spicatum,* grows well in the northern states on rocky hillsides in soil with a pH ranging from 5.0 to 6.0. It is a very hardy tree, with light green leaves that turn orange and scarlet in fall, and with fruits that are bright red in summer.

Two outstanding low-growing Asiatic maples are DAVIDS STRIPED-BARK MAPLE, *Acer Davidi,* with zebra-like black and green striped bark, and the CHERRY-BARK MAPLE, *A. griseum,* with birchlike, curly bronze-red bark, and blazing red foliage in fall.

REDBUD, *Cercis canadensis,* may be grown throughout the South and in the eastern United States as far north as Boston along the coast. It prefers a rich soil with a pH of 6.5 to 7.5 and a sunny or slightly shaded area. Its pea-shaped rose-pink flowers are very showy in early spring. It is used as a street tree in the South and as a lawn specimen in the North. A white-flowering form is also available. A highly destructive fungus disease, canker, affects the branches. Unfortunately there are no control measures. Pruning infected branches and burning them is the best way to prevent spread of the disease.

RUSSIAN OLIVE, *Eleagnus augustifolia,* is one of the hardiest of the low-growing trees, withstanding extremely low temperatures far up into Canada. It has beautiful gray-green to near-silver leaves, which are very striking when ruffled by the breeze. It will grow even in dry, barren soils. Unfortunately it does not transplant easily, and hence large specimens must be moved with a soil ball.

The JAPANESE SNOWBELL, *Styrax japonica,* is a small tree of flat-topped form with curved, horizontal branches, dense foliage, and pendulous, bell-shaped flowers appearing after the foliage, but not hidden by it.

Sorbus alnifolia is a handsome small mountain ash from Asia. Bright green leaves turn orange and red in autumn, and deep pink berries persist well into the winter months. *Sorbus Aria* is another pleasant small mountain ash. Its leaves, bright green above and white tomentose below, contrast with the large orange-red to scarlet fruit. The variety *aurea* has yellow leaves; those of *chrysophylla* are even deeper yellow.

SORREL TREE, *Oxydendron arboreum,* is an eastern tree that grows well in acid soils, pH 5.5 to 6.5, and in partial shade. Its late fall flowers are very striking, as is the scarlet color of its leaves at the same season.

The outstanding magnolia for northern areas, except for the extremely cold regions, is the STAR MAGNOLIA, *M. stellata.* It produces semi-double white flowers more than 3 inches across. The variety *rosea,* with pink buds that open to pinkish flowers, is even more striking. A newer form, *M. stellata rubra,* has dark pink or purplish-red petals. WATERLILY is a white hybrid with slightly smaller flowers but more compact growth than the species.

STAR MAGNOLIA does best in rich, porous soil, although it tolerates clay soils. It prefers a soil pH of 5.0 to 6.0 and definitely dislikes lime and fresh manure. It is most successfully moved with a soil ball in spring after growth starts.

Other low-growing trees are the TRIDENT MAPLE, *Acer buergerianum,* COLISEUM MAPLE, *A. cappadocicum;* MONTPELIER MAPLE, *A. monspessulanum;* and AMERICAN HOPHORNBEAM, *Ostyra virginiana.*

Most of the low-growing trees discussed here reach a height of 25 feet or so when they are mature, which with most kinds is in about

sixty years. A few like AMUR CORK, GOLDENRAIN, and FLOWERING
DOGWOOD may eventually grow to 40 feet.

Tall-Growing Shade and Ornamental Trees

Countless tall-growing or standard shade and ornamental trees have
long been favorites for large properties or for wide city streets. These
trees reach heights varying from 50 to 120 feet at maturity. Because
they are difficult to spray, to prune, and to maintain, they are losing
their popularity in many communities.

Beeches. There are, nevertheless, many new or interesting kinds that
are worthy of mention. Among the beeches, for example, are the
DAWYCK BEECH, *Fagus sylvatica fastigiata,* a beautiful fastigiate form;
the GREEN-LEAVED WEEPING BEECH, variety *pendula;* a red-leaved
variety *purpurea;* a golden-leaved variety *aurea;* the green fern-leaved
form, *asplenifolia;* the red fern-leaved beech, *Rohannii;* an improved
purple-leaf, *Spaethi;* and finally, the TRICOLOR BEECH, with pink,
white, and green leaves that turn coppery bronze.

Elms. The AMERICAN ELM, *Ulmus americana,* is rapidly disappearing
from the American scene because of the inroads of both Dutch elm
and phloem necrosis diseases. Besides being highly susceptible to
these diseases, it is subject to attack by a number of insects, particularly the elm leaf beetle. Hence the upkeep cost of one of America's finest shade trees are unusually high.

HANSEN MANCHURIAN ELM was introduced into America by the
late Dr. N. E. Hansen, who collected it in the rugged mountains near
the Manchurian-Siberian border, where it withstands temperatures of
60 degrees below zero. It has strong, sturdy limbs which branch out
with firm crotches that do not split easily like those of the American
and Chinese elms. The leaf is similar to the Chinese elm but is
larger and more glossy green. The MANCHURIAN ELM grows fast, as
much as 8 to 12 feet in one season, and, like most Asiatic elms, is
decidedly resistant to the Dutch elm disease.

Two close relatives of the American elm that appear to be somewhat more resistant to the Dutch elm disease than are their American
cousins are the JAPANESE KEAKI, *Zelkova serrata,* and *Buisman,* a
variety of the European smooth-leaf elm, *U. carpinifolia.* The former
is vase-shaped, with bark resembling beech and with elm-like foliage
that turns red in fall. The latter is a handsome, glossy-leaved, pyra-
midal-shaped tree that also appears to be somewhat resistant to the
phloem necrosis virus disease.

The AUGUSTINE ASCENDING ELM is an unusually fine columnar-shaped elm for use along narrow city streets and for landscaping that needs an accent tree. It is unusually resistant to wind and ice storms and is resistant to the Dutch elm disease, according to the organization sponsoring its sale and distribution.

The GOLDEN ELM, *Ulmus carpinifolia Wredei,* has a pyramidal shape and rich golden leaves that hold their color all season.

Ginkgo. In a chapter on new kinds of trees there seems little reason to mention the GINKGO, *G. biloba,* because it is actually one of the world's oldest. But it is worth mentioning because it is one of the few present-day trees that we know existed on earth millions of years ago. Impressions of its fan-shaped leaves, with veins radiating from the base to their curved top edges, are found clearly imprinted as fossils in ancient rocks.

The GINKGO is also mentioned here because it happens to be one of the few trees that are almost free of insect pests and fungus parasites. It is excellent for planting along streets of large cities because it is tolerant of polluted air. It is best to plant male trees only, because female trees bear brown, olive-like fruits with a disagreeable odor. By spraying the trees at blossom time with a dilute solution of maleic hydrazide, discussed in *Chapter 12,* gardeners can prevent the fruits from forming on female GINKGO trees already planted.

Dawn Redwood. One of the most unusual trees recently introduced into America or, more correctly, reintroduced after an absence of millions of years, is the DAWN REDWOOD, *Metasequoia glyptostroboides.* Fossils from Elko, Nevada, show that this tree existed in North America about fifteen million years ago.

In 1941 a Japanese paleobotanist described Metasequoia from fossil specimens at a time when the tree was believed to be extinct. Three years later several large specimens were discovered growing in a remote village in Central China. Shortly after their discovery Dr. E. D. Merrill of the Arnold Arboretum sent two hundred and fifty dollars to Dr. W. C. Cheng, a Chinese forester at Nanking, and asked Dr. Cheng to send an expedition to collect seeds. Literally bushels of seeds of the DAWN REDWOOD were shipped to America as a result, and hundreds of young trees are now growing all over the United States. Seedlings vary greatly in their growth rates. Some make as much as 4 feet of growth in one summer; others about half as much. A seven-year-old specimen in Northampton, Massachusetts, is already 20 feet tall. This rapid growth rate suggests that the tree might eventually serve as a good source of timber.

Locusts. The MORAINE LOCUST, one of our newest shade trees, described in *Chapter 7,* is now widely available from nurseries in the United States. It seems to be doing well in all parts of the country where it has been tried. (Illustration following page 64)

The locust SUNBURST with bright, golden-bronze foliage, is completely free of thorns and is more resistant to insect pests than the common honey locust. Its brilliant coloring is limited to 8 or 10 inches of branch tips. It is a slow, compact grower and is as hardy as the common honey locust. SUNBURST was developed by the Cole Nursery Company of Painesville, Ohio.

Horse Chestnuts. The red-flowering horse chestnut, *Aesculus carnea,* is a very very beautiful tree when in bloom. It is a cross between the common white-flowering horse chestnut and the red-flowering buckeye.

LONDON PLANE, *Platanus acerifolia,* sometimes incorrectly listed in nurserymen's catalogues as the ORIENTAL PLANE, can be grown in all but the colder parts of the country. One of the most popular trees along city streets and in parks, it is subject to several fungus diseases, including cankerstain and Dothiorella canker. Both of these diseases appear to be more prevalent in trees under which leaf fires have been set. In other words, fires seem to contribute to the severity of these diseases.

The cankerstain fungus can be spread in branch-pruning operations, during which contaminated sawdust is transferred from an infected to a healthy tree. Tree paints used to cover wounds also can become contaminated and hence can spread the fungus, unless a disinfectant is added.

Until recently plant doctors thought the disease could not be spread by way of contaminated saws if pruning was done in winter, from December 1 to February 15. But newly uncovered evidence suggests that this belief was only wishful thinking and that all pruning tools should be sterilized with 70 per cent denatured alcohol after use on each tree regardless of season.

Maples. The NORWAY MAPLE, *Acer platanoides,* is another widely planted street tree that does well in almost any kind of soil in the eastern United States and on the Pacific slope. It is an easily transplanted, fast-growing tree. Its dense foliage and especially vigorous, fibrous root system combine to make lawn-growing beneath it virtually impossible. It is subject to a goodly number of pests and diseases but is rather resistant to wind and ice.

The newest strain of NORWAY MAPLE to appear on the market is CRIMSON KING, *Acer platanoides nigra*. It holds its bright red color throughout the spring and summer and hence is a decided improvement over the red-leaved, long-planted SCHWEDLER MAPLE, which loses its red color with the advent of warm weather.

Because of its striking foliage, CRIMSON KING should be planted in a spot where it will not detract from the rest of the landscape planting. The back yard is an ideal spot for it because there the family can admire its rich color and enjoy the welcome shade of its dense foliage on warm summer afternoons. CRIMSON KING originated in the nursery of Barbier and Company in Orléans, France. The original tree is no longer alive.

A strain closely resembling CRIMSON KING, FAASSEN'S BLACK, is said to have originated in a Belgian nursery; and another, GOLDWORTH'S PURPLE, in an English nursery.

Two narrow, upright forms of the sugar maple are NEWTON SENTRY and TEMPLE'S UPRIGHT. The original tree of the former grew in a grammar school yard at Newtonville, Massachusetts. The origin of the latter is unknown, but the tree from which presently available nursery stock was grown still stands in Rochester, New York.

NEWTON SENTRY has many ascending branches, no dominant central leader, and dark green leaves with leathery texture and wavy margins like those of black maple. TEMPLE'S UPRIGHT has few ascending branches; a strong central leader which produces stubby lateral branches, especially when secondary branches are removed; and yellow-green non-leathery leaves.

Acer nigrum, a fastigiate form of black maple, is a taller-growing tree with clear yellow fall color and more compact growth than the species.

ARMSTRONG is a narrow, upright red maple with growing habit resembling LOMBARDY poplar. Not quite so narrow and with more dense foliage is another variety of red maple, BOWHALL.

EVERGREEN TREES

No tree suggests "Christmas" better than holly, with its shiny green leaves and bright red berries. Its use as a festive symbol, in fact, antedates Christianity by many years.

In recent years interest in holly has grown by leaps and bounds. Holly aboreta have been established in different sections of the country under the guidance of the Holly Society of America. One of the finest private collections in the eastern United States is at St. James, Long Island, where Mrs. F. Leighton Meserve operates a holly arboretum and nursery under the name "Holly-by-Golly." Her collection includes literally hundreds of species, varieties, and clones of American, European, and Oriental hollies. I spent a very pleasant afternoon not long ago looking over this wonderful collection.

There are species of holly for every part of America. In the Pacific Northwest and in a narrow belt along the eastern seaboard, which is exposed continually to moist sea air, the true English holly, *Ilex Aquifolium,* grows. The Brownell Farms in Portland, Oregon, started one of the first commercial groves of this holly and has been marketing it as cut holly since 1919.

Although holly is commonly thought to be dioecious, that is, with male flowers on some trees and female flowers on others, some plants do exist with so-called perfect flowers, which carry both the male and female elements. A strain of this sort available on the west coast is known as *Ilex Aquifolium fertilis.* Some catalogues list it as VAN TOL or DUTCH HOLLY. Also available are fertile hollies that are primarily female plants on which a male branch has been grafted to supply pollen for fertilizing the female flowers.

The American holly, *Ilex opaca,* is more tolerant of low temperatures than is the English holly and can be grown in colder regions of the country, but not in extremely cold areas.

More than two hundred and fifty varieties of American holly are grown in the United States at present. Many now on the market have appeared as a result of the keen interest of members of the Holly Society of America, particularly Earl Dilatush of Robbinsville, New Jersey; Wilfrid Wheeler of Falmouth, Massachusetts; Dr. Charles Connors of Highland Park, New Jersey; Clarence Wolf of Millville, New Jersey; and Judge Thomas Brown of Rumson, New Jersey.

The best holly for warmer climates is Burford holly, *Ilex cornuta Burfordii,* with oval, glossy leaves that do not resemble the usual kinds. Unlike most hollies, also, it has perfect flowers and hence produces berries without the need of a male plant.

One of the most beautiful hollies I have seen is *Ilex altaclarensis,* JAMES G. ESSON, named by T. H. Everett. It has large glossy leaves resembling the finest English holly and large clusters of bright red berries that are far more striking than any strain of American holly.

Celosia *Toreador*, All-America Award
Winner 1955, with petunia *Paleface*
in foreground.

McKana's Giant Columbine,
All-America Award Winner 1955.

Petunia *Prima Donna*,
All-America Award Winner 1955.

Marigold *Man-in-the-Moon.*

Iris *Plumed Delight.*

W. ATLEE BURPEE CO.

RAINBOW HYBRIDIZING GARD[

How new lily varieties are developed.
The orange *Lilium Henryi* (lower) was crossed
with a white trumpet lily (left) to produce
the "sunburst strain" (right).

JAN DE GRAAFF

Tiffany, one of the finest
of the newer hybrid teas.

The multicolor floribunda rose, *Circus,*
the only rose to win an All-America
Award for 1956.

Queen Elizabeth, the first rose to
be placed in the new grandiflora
class, was an All-America selection
for 1955.

This *Moraine* locust in Dayton, Ohio, is the parent tree from which all others have come. This beautiful new shade tree is the result of twenty-five years of painstaking development by John and George Siebenthaler.

Two unusually fine specimens are growing near the main conservatories at The New York Botanical Garden. The variety JAMES G. ESSON is available in the trade.

Holly comes in other shapes and sizes. There are, for example, many varieties of Japanese hollies with small leaves. The low-growing kinds are discussed earlier in this chapter.

Corliss Brothers Nurseries of Gloucester and Ipswich, Massachusetts, just released four excellent evergreen euonymous: EMERALD LEADER, EMERALD PRIDE, EMERALD CHARM, and EMERALD CUSHION. They are vigorous and hardy, and make bushy, compact erect growth.

Pinus Thunbergii Compacta-Hrenii, an attractive, compact pine especially suited for wind-swept beach areas, was recently introduced to the trade by Joseph Hren, a nurseryman of Easthampton, Long Island. As early as 1939, Mr. Hren started gathering cones from the most attractive, hurricane-resistant Japanese pines planted along Montauk Highway at the eastern end of Long Island and the presently available trees are the result of this work.

Tsuga caroliniana ARNOLD PYRAMID is a bushy, dense-growing form of Carolina hemlock with many trunks coming from the base of the plant. It will be distributed to nurserymen in 1956, who should have young plants available for gardeners by 1958.

FRUIT TREES

Even fruit trees have succumbed to the rage for lower-growing types to fit today's smaller properties. For example, the gardener can buy apple trees to fit any size property—they will grow to a certain height and no more. This is achieved by grafting the popular standard apple varieties on so-called Malling dwarf rootstocks originally developed at the East Malling, England, Research Station. If a standard variety is grafted on Malling IX stock, for instance, the tree will grow only 6 to 10 feet high. If grafted on Malling I, it will be 12 to 15 feet high.

One of the most serious pests of dwarf apples is the wooly aphis. Soon to be made available are the so-called Malling-Merton (MM) rootstocks. These are wooly-aphis-resistant rootstocks developed in a co-operative project between two English institutions—the John Innes Horticultural Institute and the East Malling Research Station. None of the MM rootstocks is so dwarfing as Malling IX mentioned above, however. MM 106 is the most dwarfing one developed thus far and it is more vigorous than Malling IX.

Besides being suitable for smaller areas, dwarf fruit trees solve another problem. Where gardeners are growing varieties like McIntosh and Delicious, which require pollen from another tree to set fruits, their dwarf size permits the planting of several kinds.

Until recently only apples and pears were available in dwarf form. Gardeners can now buy dwarf peaches, plums, and cherries. During my annual summer vacation in Genesee Valley in western New York State, I frequently drive by the extensive acreages of Kelly Brothers Nurseries at Dansville. In these plantings I have seen literally thousands of dwarf CORTLAND, DOUBLE RED DELICIOUS, NORTHERN SPY, RED MC INTOSH, and YELLOW DELICIOUS apples; dwarf BARTLETT, DUTCHESS, CLAPP'S FAVORITE, and SECKEL pears; and dwarf METEOR and NORTH STAR cherries.

Besides using dwarf fruit trees, gardeners with very limited space have recourse to several other substitutes. One is to plant a single standard tree on which three, four or five different varieties of fruits have been grafted. Apple and peach are the two kinds more commonly available with multiple species of fruits.

Although not practical, the number of different varieties that may be grafted on one tree is astounding. For example, Dr. C. E. Meyers, plant breeder at Pennsylvania State University, has an apple tree on which 52 different varieties have been grafted. In 1954, twenty-seven of these bore fruit.

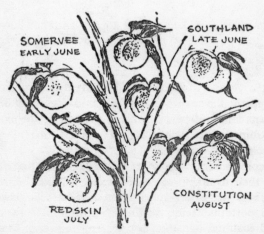

Peach and apple trees are available with several varieties on the same tree. The varieties sketched on this tree will provide fruits for several months.

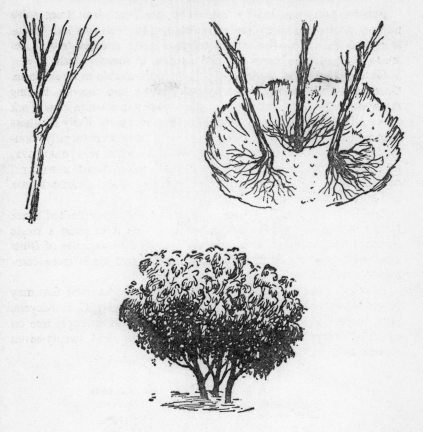

Another method recently advocated on the west coast is to plant three different kinds of peach trees, for example, in one hole, each tree being trained as if it were a single branch on one tree. Before planting, each tree is cut back to a strong lateral branch about 2 feet above the soil surface. The roots on the side opposite the lateral branch are then trimmed off. The three trees are finally set in the same large hole with their lateral branches facing outward and the root-pruned portions facing toward the center of the hole. A very important precaution to observe when growing trees in this manner is to see that the growth of each tree is kept in balance. If one is allowed to grow larger than the others, it will soon crowd them out. Summer pruning will help keep the fastest grower in line.

Finally, fruit trees may be grown in confined areas if they are trained as espaliers along fences or walls. This type of fruit culture is not the easiest because of the constant need to prune and train. Amateurs will have most fun and success if dwarf or semi-dwarf apple and pears are used. Henry Leuthardt of Port Chester, New York, is one of America's foremost growers of espaliered fruits. His catalogue tells all about the art of growing trees by this method. *The Pruning Manual,* by E. P. Christopher, also tells of the different ways to train trees.

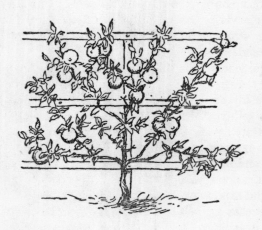

Culture of Fruit Trees

The two basic requirements of all fruit trees are a well-drained soil and full sun. When the soil is heavy and drains poorly, roots do not develop normally and they are more subject to fungus decay. Plenty of sunshine is necessary for fruit bud development and for proper ripening of the fruit.

To grow high-quality fruit it is also necessary to supply the tree with plant food. In most soils and with most fruit trees, nitrogen is usually the most limiting plant food element. It is wise for amateurs not to apply this element by itself but in a so-called complete plant food containing the other two major plant food elements, phosphoric acid and potash. The amounts to use will depend on the kind and size of the fruit tree, so be guided by these factors when following directions on the fertilizer package.

LEGAL HOLIDAYS IN THE UNITED STATES

	1973	1974
New Year's Day	Jan. 1	Jan. 1
Lincoln's Birthday	Feb. 12	Feb. 12
Washington's Birthday	Feb. 19	Feb. 18
Memorial Day	May 28	May 27
Independence Day	July 4	July 4
Labor Day	Sept. 3	Sept. 3
Columbus Day	Oct. 8	Oct. 14
Veterans Day	Oct. 22	Oct. 28
Election Day	Nov. 6	Nov. 5
Thanksgiving Day	Nov. 22	Nov. 28
Christmas Day	Dec. 25	Dec. 25

OFFICIAL HOLIDAYS IN THE UNITED KINGDOM

	1973	1974
New Year's Day in Scotland only	Jan. 1	Jan. 1
Good Friday in England & Wales	Apr. 20	Apr. 12
Easter Monday in England & Wales	Apr. 23	Apr. 15
Spring Bank Holiday in England & Wales	May 28	May 27
Spring Bank Holiday in Scotland	May 7	May 6
Summer Bank Holiday in England & Wales	Aug. 27	Aug. 26
Summer Bank Holiday in Scotland	Aug. 6	Aug. 5
Christmas Day, England, Scotland & Wales	Dec. 25	Dec. 25
Boxing Day, England, Scotland & Wales	Dec. 26	Dec. 26

LEGAL HOLIDAYS IN CANADA

	1973	1974
New Year's Day	Jan. 1	Jan. 1
Good Friday	Apr. 20	Apr. 12
Easter Monday	Apr. 23	Apr. 15
Victoria Day	May 21	May 20
Dominion Day	July 1	July 1
Labor Day	Sept. 3	Sept. 2
Thanksgiving Day	Oct. 8	Oct. 4
Christmas Day	Dec. 25	Dec. 25

The British-American Chamber of Commerce
655 Madison Avenue
New York, N. Y. 10021
Tel: 212-752-2270

Dear Chamber Member:

I trust you will find your Member's Book useful and informative and that it will assist you in learning who your fellow members are, what they do, and where to contact them.

By publishing these listings, the Chamber hopes to encourage mutually profitable business relations among members.

As an added convenience, the dates of 1973 and 1974 official and legal holidays in the United States, United Kingdom, and Canada are listed on the reverse side.

> O. C. Cochrane
> President, The British-American Chamber of Commerce

Thos. Cook & Son, Inc. have kindly provided this bookmark for the convenience of other members.

Whenever, wherever you travel, travel through Cooks.
Always protect your funds by carrying Cooks Travel Cheques, encashable worldwide since 1874.

Finally, because they are so subject to insect pests and diseases, fruit trees must be sprayed with a combination fungicide-insecticide at periodic intervals. A good mixture is presented later in this chapter.

The standard or tall-growing fruit trees propagated on ordinary seedling rootstocks should be planted so that the point of union of the scion and rootstock is about 4 inches *below* the soil surface. This will prevent the understock from forming shoots or suckers and also permit the scion eventually to form roots of its own just above the union. On the other hand, dwarf fruit trees should be planted so that the point of union is at least 4 inches *above* the soil surface. If the point of union is planted below the surface, roots will form at the base of the scion, smothering the dwarfing roots, and the tree will revert to standard type.

Home gardeners planning to grow fruits must bear in mind that some fruit trees require more than one variety to set fruit. If space is available for but one large tree, a self-fruitful kind is necessary. Among the self-fruitful apples than can be set out singly and still produce fruits are YELLOW TRANSPARENT, GRIMES GOLDEN, WEALTHY, JONATHAN BEAUTY, and ROME BEAUTY. The following cannot be set out singly and must have a pollinator to produce fruits: DELICIOUS, MC INTOSH, RHODE ISLAND GREENING, STAYMAN WINESAP, WINTER BANANA, and NORTHERN SPY.

Most peaches are self-fruitful, but J. H. HALE is not. It will bear fruit only if another variety of peach is somewhere in the vicinity. Nurserymen's catalogues will list those kinds of fruit trees that can be planted alone and those that require more than one kind for fruit production.

New or Unusual Fruits

Apple. JERSEYRED, the first apple variety introduced by the New Jersey Agricultural Experiment Station, came from crosses made by the late Professor M. A. Blake. Its parents were WHITE WINTER PEARMAIN and GALLIA BEAUTY. JERSEYRED forms large fruits with more red color than ROME BEAUTY. It retains a crisp, snappy flesh longer than ROME, and is a better eating apple and fully equal to ROME for cooking. JERSEYBRED trees are vigorous, with strong branches and twigs, and large, tough, leathery leaves. It is resistant to fire blight and is not particularly susceptible to other common apple diseases.

RUBY, a recent introduction by the Ohio Station, has deep red color, firm and fairly juicy flesh, and is recommended for cooking. Its parents are GALLIA BEAUTY and STARKING. (Illustration following page 96)

WELLINGTON, a handsome, early-maturing, red-streaked variety was recently introduced by the New York Agricultural Experiment Station at Geneva.

A dwarf apple, DELCON, introduced by the Missouri Agricultural Experiment Station has red, medium-sized fruits, shaped like DELICIOUS, but it makes a half-sized tree. It is an excellent tree for home orchard planting and is available from several nurseries in Missouri and Iowa.

JONADEL, a new apple developed at Iowa State College by crossing JONATHAN and DELICIOUS, will be introduced into the trade during the winter of 1957-58. It is less susceptible to fire blight than JONATHAN and has superior solid red fruits that retain their juice and flavor to the end of the storage season.

SPARTAN, a high-quality, late-keeping McIntosh type, and MANTET are two recent Canadian introductions that are doing well in northeastern United States apple orchards.

Peach. In the last ten years or so, fruit breeders and nurserymen in the United States and Canada have introduced more than a hundred new peaches. Only a few of the most promising kinds are listed here in their order of ripening.

Early yellow-fleshed varieties:

SPRINGTIME, one of California's earliest-ripening kinds (late May), was developed after years of research by Armstrong's Nurseries, Ontario, California. (Illustration on page 96)

SOMERVEE, developed at the Horticultural Experiment Station, Vineland Station, Ontario, Canada, ripens very early, about six weeks before ELBERTA. It is decidedly hardy and is resistant to low temperatures when in bloom.

GOLDEN EARLY BIRD, a patented variety that ripens six weeks ahead of ELBERTA, is attractive, semi-clingstone, and fairly productive.

DIXIRED, developed at the Fort Valley, Georgia Experiment Station, ripens three days after GOLDEN EARLY BIRD. It is an attractive highly colored clingstone with firm flesh and good size and flavor.

PRAIRIE DAWN, ripening three days after DIXIRED, is a very productive red-striped clingstone with firm though somewhat coarse flesh of good flavor. It is one of the hardiest of all yellow-fleshed varieties.

CORONET, ripening four days after PRAIRIE DAWN, is a highly attractive, nearly freestone peach with firm flesh and excellent flavor.

JERSEYLAND, a New Jersey introduction, ripens two days after CORONET. It is a highly colored, firm peach of good quality.

Midseason yellow-fleshed varieties:

REDHAVEN, one of the oldest varieties in this list, was introduced by the Michigan Agricultural Experiment Station in 1940 and is now being planted extensively all over the United States. Ripening four weeks ahead of ELBERTA, it is highly attractive, with firm flesh and good flavor. It must be thinned early and heavily to produce fruit of best size and quality. SUNHAVEN, recently introduced by the same station, is similar to REDHAVEN but matures ten days earlier.

SOUTHLAND, from the Fort Valley, Georgia, Station, ripens about three weeks ahead of ELBERTA. It is a highly colored, attractive freestone peach with good flesh firm enough to withstand handling.

FAIRHAVEN, another Michigan State introduction, ripens a day later than SOUTHLAND, is an attractive, productive freestone with firm flesh and good flavor.

BLAKE is another New Jersey introduction. It is fully freestone, with skin three-fourths covered with an attractive red over bright yellow, and has unusual consumer appeal. It ripens a week before ELBERTA.

SUNAPEE is a yellow freestone hardy peach developed in New Hampshire, where it ripens in late August. In contrast to most peach trees, whose fruit buds winterkill at about 15 degrees below zero, it has withstood temperatures as low as 22 degrees below and still borne a crop. MEREDITH is another hardy variety, which ripens a few days after SUNAPEE.

Late yellow-fleshed varieties:

REDSKIN ripens just before or with ELBERTA and has better color than ELBERTA. Its quality is good.

CONSTITUTION, developed in New Jersey, ripens ten days later than ELBERTA. It produces attractive fruit of good quality but of small size.

White-fleshed varieties:

White-fleshed peaches are not grown nearly so commonly as the yellow-fleshed kinds. Three recent introductions are available to provide a succession of high-quality fruit throughout the season.

EARLY WHITE GIANT, a patented variety, ripens six weeks before ELBERTA. It is a productive semi-freestone with large, highly colored fruits.

SUMMERROSE, from New Jersey, ripens two weeks ahead of ELBERTA. It is a productive freestone with large, attractive fruits.

LATERROSE ripens five days after ELBERTA and is a very productive, attractive freestone of good quality.

No discussion of peaches would be complete without some mention of peach borers. Two kinds attack peach trees. The most common one attacks the tree near the base of the trunk and is easily controlled with DDT. The other, the lesser peach borer, occurs higher up on the trunk and scaffold branches, and is not controlled with DDT.

Unlike DDT, malathion has been found to control both kinds of borers and is recommended for areas where the two pests occur. The trunk and scaffold branches should be sprayed four times at two-week intervals, starting June 15, with a mixture containing 1½ cups of 25 per cent wettable malathion powder in 5 gallons of water.

Pear. The Tennessee Agricultural Experiment Station recently introduced four new pears—DABNEY, AYRES, MOOERS, and HOSKINS—which have the fine eating qualities of European pears and the disease resistance of Oriental pears. They have good quality and are virtually immune to the fire blight disease. In Tennessee, DABNEY ripens in late July and early August. Its fruits are sweet, subacid and medium-sized. AYRES, which ripens in late August, has golden-russet, attractive fruit. (Illustration following page 96) MOOERS matures from late October onward as a golden-russeted fruit with crisp, subacid flesh. It is especially good for canning. HOSKINS, a winter pear, harvested about October 1, has golden-russet fruit of subacid flesh that is good for both dessert and canning.

Cherry. METEOR, a red tart cherry recently introduced by the Minnesota Station, is suitable for the colder regions of the country. Its parents are MONTMORENCY and a very hard, small-fruited, medium-dark red, unnamed variety obtained from the Canadian Agricultural Station at Morden, Manitoba. Fruits are large with bright red skins and yellow, medium-firm, and medium-juicy flesh. In relation to maturing dates of standard varieties of red tart cherries, METEOR ripens about midseason.

Plum. OREGON TRAIL is a hybrid produced by crossing the purple-leaved plum *Prunus cerasifera* variety *Pissardi* and the delicious yellow-fruited plum SHIRO. The fruit, with cherry-red skin and yellow-orange flesh, is excellent for eating fresh. The foliage, bright red in spring, changes to red green on the upper surface and to bright red purple on the lower surface as the season advances. This variety can be grown for both fruit and ornament.

Spraying Fruits

A simple, safe, and very effective "general purpose" spray mixture for fruit trees is prepared from the following:

Ingredient	Per cent of Mixture	Quantities required to make	
		1 gal.	25 gals.
Water		1 gal.	25 gals.
Methoxychlor (50 per cent wettable powder)	35	3 tbsp.	¾ lb.
Malathion (25 per cent wettable powder)	30	2 tbsp.	½ lb.
Captan (50 per cent wettable powder)	35	3 tbsp.	¾ lb.
Complete Mixture	100	8 tbsp.	2 lbs.

Most garden supply stores carry these separate materials under different brand names and in 1 to 4-pound packages.

Curculio, Japanese beetles, fruit maggots, and worms are controlled by the methoxychlor; aphids, pear psylla, and mites by malathion; and apple scab, peach brown rot, and certain other diseases by captan.

NUT TREES

Most kinds of nut trees require cross-pollination. Hence at least two varieties of each species that flower at the same time must be grown near each other. Nurserymen handling these trees will advise as to the proper kinds to use.

As with most trees, the most important factor governing successful culture of nut trees is climate. It is very important to plant varieties that have originated locally or under similar climatic conditions and that are of proved worth. For example, it is risky to buy a variety developed in the South and expect it to survive the extremely low temperatures of Upstate New York or Minnesota.

Following are some varieties of nut trees that are successful in many parts of the Northeast:

Black Walnut. THOMAS, ELMER MYERS, SPARROW, and STAMBAUGH.

Butternut. CRAXEZY, IRVINE, KENWORTHY, and LOVE.

Heartnut. BATES, FAUST, LANCASTER, and WALTERS.

Hickory Nut. DAVIS, FOX, MANN, and WILCOX.

Pecan. BURLINGTON, GREENBRIERS, MAJOR, and ROSEY. BARTON, a recent introduction by the U. S. Department of Agriculture for more southerly areas, is a good yielder with nuts that are thin-shelled and with kernels that keep well. A highly noteworthy paper-shell, hardy pecan, STARKING HARDY GIANT, just introduced by Stark Brothers of Louisiana, Missouri, matures its nuts in 138 to 145 days, or in about the time it takes DELICIOUS apples to mature.

Filbert. COSFORD, MEDIUM LONG, and ITALIAN RED.

Chestnut. In recent years many home gardeners have become interested in growing hybrid chestnuts that are resistant to blight, a disease which has all but wiped out the American chestnut. These chestnuts are of Asiatic origin, where blight has been present for centuries and where the trees have apparently developed resistance to it.

Given plenty of space, the Chinese chestnut grows to the size and shape of a large apple tree. It makes a good-looking shade tree if its lower branches are pruned, and its white flowers are very showy in spring. It will grow in any climate where peaches are hardy. Because Chinese chestnuts are not self-fruitful, more than one seedling is needed for cross-pollination.

The variety HOBSON, which produces medium-sized nuts of good quality, is considered a reliable bearer.

Among other hybrid chestnuts that are particularly promising are ABUNDANCE, CARR, KULING, MEILING, NANKING, and YANKEE.

Dr. G. F. Gravatt of the U. S. Department of Agriculture has crossed American and Chinese chestnuts. The hybrid resembles the American chestnut in growth, form, and leaf shape. Its resistance to disease is less than that of its Chinese parent but greater than that of its American parent. It is better suited for reforestation than is the low, spreading Chinese chestnut. First-generation trees have increased about 2½ feet in height and about ½ inch in diameter each year.

They are now fence-post size, and in twenty to twenty-five years, if they survive, will be tall enough to use as telephone poles.

A few of the nurseries which sell Chinese chestnuts are: Bulk's Nurseries, Babylon, Long Island; Carrol D. Bush, Eagle Creek, Oregon; Fairview Evergreen Nurseries, Fairview, Pennsylvania; John W. Hershey, Downingtown, Pennsylvania, and Sunny Ridge Nursery, Swarthmore, Pennsylvania.

Chapter 5

VEGETABLES AND BUSH AND VINE FRUITS

Interest in back yard and community gardens reached an all-time high in America during World War II, when more than 20 million gardens were grown. How well I remember that period! Not only did I keep my family and friends well supplied with vegetables from my 50- by 100-foot garden plot, but as executive assistant to New Jersey's Victory Garden Chairman, Frank G. Helyar, I helped, by means of publications, lectures, and demonstrations, to teach thousands of amateurs how to garden. It was on this assignment that the training I received from Cornell's vegetable crop specialists and my many years of working with vegetable growers on Long Island and in Upstate New York really came in handy.

Although the number of home gardens has decreased since World War II, interest still continues high with many home owners because no vegetable or fruit tastes better than a properly home-grown one.

Ample sunshine—at least five or six hours every clear day—is a prime requisite for a successful vegetable or small-fruit garden. Gardens should never be planted near large trees. Not only is shade detrimental, but the tree roots will compete for water and plant nutrients and so prevent proper development of vegetables and fruits.

Many vegetables and some fruits prefer a relatively sweet soil, a pH of 6.5, for best growth. Hence a soil test is in order to find out what the reaction is. If it is more acid than 6.5, enough ground limestone should be incorporated into the soil in early spring to sweeten it. County agricultural agents and state and federal garden experts will advise on how much lime to add for the crops to be grown.

A few vegetables like potatoes and some bush fruits like blueberries do better in a more acid soil. Do not lime such crops.

To assure an abundant supply of the essential elements, at least in the early growth stages, chemical fertilizers should also be incorporated into the soil at the time the garden is prepared for planting.

I have found AGRICO, which comes in various mixtures for use in specific situations, to be excellent. The package shows the amount to apply per 100 square feet of garden.

Vegetable and fruit plants watered with a nutrient solution when they are set in the garden take hold faster and frequently outyield those that are merely watered in. I have found that a cupful of nutrient solution, prepared by dissolving an ounce of RAPIDGRO plant food in 2 gallons of water, poured around each plant at transplanting time helps the plant to become established more quickly in its new location and to make new growth sooner.

New or Unusual Vegetables

Asparagus. Professor Lyman G. Schermerhorn of the New Jersey Agricultural Experiment Station, who developed such famous vegetables as the RUTGERS and QUEENS tomatoes and the WORLD BEATER pepper, recently added another to his list of fine contributions. RARITAN ASPARAGUS, the result of a twenty-five-year breeding program, is reasonably free from rust disease and produces a good crop of uniform spears, medium to dark green in color. The spear tips remain tight until the stalks reach a height of 18 to 20 inches. The variety is suitable for either processing or the fresh market.

Beans are extremely popular for vegetable gardens because they are easy to grow and yield a lot in a little space.

TENDERGREEN has been a very popular round-podded snapbean for a number of years. But improved forms like TENDERLONG, SLENDERLONG, and TOPCROSS are beginning to replace it because they produce longer pods and more of them and they are more resistant to the mosaic disease.

SEMINOLE, a bush snap bean, with very round, straight, stringless and fiberless pods was an All-America selection for 1955. It outyields TENDERGREEN by as much as a third, and its flavor is said to equal that of the highly coveted pole beans.

WADE, another All-America winner, is a high-quality bush bean that is also disease-resistant.

BLUE LAKE and POTOMAC are two straight-podded pole beans that are vast improvements over the old KENTUCKY WONDER with its gnarled and twisted pods.

Cabbage. EARLY DANISH, a new cabbage resistant to the fungus disease known as yellows, is especially adapted to the northeastern United States. Other yellows-resistant cabbages, developed at the Wisconsin

Agricultural Experiment Station, have been available for many years but are better suited to the Middle West.

Carrots. GOLD PAK is an excellent new carrot which received an All-America Award for 1956.

Celery. EMERSON PASCAL is a celery that is highly resistant to both early and late blight fungus diseases.

Sweet Corn. An outstanding sweet corn introduced in 1955, GOLDEN BEAUTY, is early maturing, sixty-eight to seventy days, and produces kernels of fine quality. Its main advantage over the older, early-maturing NORTH STAR is its resistance to bacterial wilt disease. Introduced by the Massachusetts Agricultural Experiment Station, it produces uniform ears about 8 inches long with twelve to fourteen rows of golden-yellow kernels. It was awarded a silver medal by the All-America Awards Committee for 1955.

WONDERFUL is a new hybrid sweet corn with long ears and golden kernels that mature in midseason.

FARIBO GOLDEN MIDGET CORN has ears only 4 inches long with yellow sweet kernels. These are produced in less than sixty days on plants only 30 inches tall.

Cucumber. Two new pickling cucumbers resistant to mosaic are OHIO MR 25 and WISCONSIN SMR 12. The latter is also resistant to scab disease.

MARKETER has climbed to the leadership in both home and market gardens because of its prolific, trim, medium-sized fruits of high quality.

Lettuce. SIMPSON'S CURLED and GRAND RAPIDS are still the best loose-leaved lettuce varieties.

MATCHLESS, intermediate between COS (ROMAINE) and leaf lettuce, retains its crispness and fine flavor during hot weather, when most other kinds become bitter-tasting and "bolt" to seed. It grows in a loose cluster of slender leaves and tastes very much like BIBB lettuce.

Onion. Among the dozen or so new onion hybrids to appear on the market recently, ARISTOCRAT, CHAMPION, EPOCH, and SPOTLIGHT look especially promising for eastern gardeners.

Pea. WANDO is a new pea that bids fair to become extremely popular because of its ability to tolerate hot weather. Most pea varieties must be grown during the cooler parts of the year to produce good crops.

Potato. SACO and MERRIMACK are two new varieties of high-yielding, disease-resistant potatoes.

Rhubarb. Another recent introduction by Professor Schermerhorn of the New Jersey Station is JERSEY RHUBARB, a cross between MAC-DONALD and SUTTON'S SEEDLESS. It has an upright habit of growth, unusual vigor, reasonably good color, and produces a heavy yield of long, broad, thick stalks of fine flavor. (Illustration following page 96)

Squash. An attractive F_1 hybrid of squash, SENECA PROLIFIC HYBRID, is an improvement over YANKEE HYBRID and EARLY PROLIFIC STRAIGHTNECK in that it matures earlier and has much smoother fruits.

Tomatoes are perhaps the most extensively grown home garden vegetable. As with other popular vegetables and fruits, new varieties appear every year. Some become popular, but many are soon forgotten. RUTGERS is still the most widely planted variety east of the Mississippi River, with the still older variety, MARGLOBE, in second place.

Tomatoes, like many other vegetables and fruits, are developed to meet the needs of a particular area or for their resistance to certain diseases. Some, like the RUTGERS tomato, turn out to be suitable for large parts of the country in addition to the relatively limited areas for which they were first developed.

BIG BOY, an F_1 hybrid introduced several years ago, continues to be an outstanding tomato. Large red fruits of uniform size, with relatively few seeds, form until frost, when the plants are grown in a fairly heavy, fertile soil and managed properly.

BIG EARLY, another F_1 hybrid, produces smooth, bright scarlet fruits, each averaging slightly less than half a pound.

CENTURY, an early, globe-shaped tomato, is exceptionally free from cracks. Each fruit averages about 5 ounces.

DOUBLERICH is a new variety developed by Dr. A. F. Yeager of the New Hampshire Experiment Station, famous for his many new kinds of fruits and vegetables. It has twice as much vitamin C as ordinary tomatoes.

FIREBALL is a large, early-maturing, mild-flavored tomato that withstands unfavorable growing conditions better than most sorts.

MANALUCIE, developed at the Florida Experiment Station, is resistant to a number of fungus diseases, including fusarium wilt, gray leaf spot, early blight, and leaf mold.

MORETON HYBRID is an F_1 hybrid with large, red, slightly flattened fruits. It begins to bear early and continues until late fall.

SIOUX, VALIANT, and VALNORTH are three tomatoes developed to meet the need for a quick-maturing fruit in the northern parts of the country, where the growing season is relatively short.

SUNRAY is a golden-orange tomato with all the fine qualities of the older JUBILEE and in addition with resistance to blight.

GERMAN BUSH TOMATO, a dwarf variety which rarely grows more than 15 inches tall and with leaves that curl upward, is an extremely prolific bearer. A single plant is reported to have produced seventy smooth, bright red fruits, each about 2 inches in diameter.

Small Fruits for Back Yard Gardens

Fruits that grow on bushes or vines are popular with back yard gardeners because most such fruits require relatively little space. Some, like grapes, can be grown on trellises, along fences, and on walls, where few other plants can be easily grown.

New varieties of small fruits appear on the market every year. In some states these varieties are thoroughly tested before being released. In New York State, for example, the New York State Fruit Testing Association at Geneva propagates and distributes, on a co-operative basis, promising fruits which New York Agricultural Experiment Station specialists believe to be worthy of trial.

In addition to describing some of the new or unusual varieties of bush and vine fruits, I felt that it would be well to mention briefly some of their cultural requirements.

Blackberries are best grown as hedgerows in all parts of the country except in the Great Plains, the Rocky Mountain region, and the colder parts of the northern United States. Since certain varieties do better in one region than another, the gardener should find out from his state horticulturist or from local nurserymen which are best for his area.

Two varieties for the Northeast recently developed at the New York Experiment Station are BAILEY, with large, attractive, moderately firm, subacid fruits of good quality, and HEDRICK, with large, glossy, attractive fruit that is pleasantly acid and ripens a few days before BAILEY. Another good variety for the Northeast is ELDORADO.

Scientists at the same experiment station at Geneva, New York, have succeeded in crossing a blackberry with a red raspberry to produce an upright-growing bramble hardy enough for the northeastern United States. It produces fruits similar to the popular LOGANBERRY of the Northwest. Although these plants are not commercially available at this writing, they should be within a year or two.

Blueberries grow best in a sandy, acid soil below pH 5.3, that is moist but well drained. The soil surface should be mulched rather than cultivated. Ammonium sulfate is the best fertilizer for blueberries under most conditions. They can be grown in all but the coldest regions of the United States. For the northern states BLUECROP, HERBERT, BERKELEY, EARLIBLUE, COVILLE, and JERSEY are recommended. In the South the RABBITEYE varieties do best.

Currants and Gooseberries do best in medium to heavy, well-drained, highly fertile soil in the cooler parts of the country. They should not be grown in areas where white pines are important forest trees because they carry the blister rust fungus. In white pine areas, gardeners would do well to consult with their state department of agriculture before planting currants or gooseberries. It is permissible to plant some kinds.

RED LAKE is the best currant, and POORMAN, the best gooseberry.

A tree form of the ENGLISH GOOSEBERRY, widely publicized in the last two years, is produced by grafting *Ribes Grossularia* on vigorous understock of the mountain currant, *Ribes aureum*.

Elderberry. Wild elderberries have long been popular for pies and homemade wine. A new cultivated variety, ADAMS, with fruit clusters and berries considerably larger than those of wild sorts, is available.

Grapes grow well in all parts of the country except the cold and dry regions of the Great Plains and the Rocky Mountain area. As with many other fruits, however, certain kinds can be grown in only limited areas. The European or *Vinifera* varieties, for example, are not hardy and grow well only in certain southwestern states and in California.

In the cooler parts of the country the so-called American or *Labruscan* varieties, which are much more winterhardy, are grown. Even in these areas, where the growing season is relatively short, early-maturing varieties like FREDONIA, ONTARIO, PORTLAND, SENECA, VAN BUREN, and WORDEN should be chosen. In the very cold regions BETA and JANESVILLE are best. CONCORD and NIAGARA have long been the most popular kinds for arbors in eastern back yards.

The so-called muscadine or scuppernong grapes grow well in the

South from Tennessee to Florida. The best of the dark-colored varieties are CREEK, HUNT, and THOMAS and of the light-colored, SCUPPERNONG and TOPSAIL. A male or nonfruiting vine must be planted near the female fruiting vines to assure pollination and fruit development. Recently the University of North Carolina developed self-fruitful kinds, which do not require a male plant. These are a dark-colored fruiting variety, BURGAW, and a light-colored one, WALLACE.

In my opinion, the development of seedless varieties for eastern gardens is perhaps the greatest single advance in grape culture in recent years. These varieties were developed in a co-operative grape-breeding project by Dr. A. B. Stout of The New York Botanical Garden and the New York Agricultural Experiment Station at Geneva. The first seedless grapes were obtained from a cross between the hardy early ONTARIO seeded grape and the SULTANINA or THOMPSON SEEDLESS that has long been known in southern Europe and is widely grown in California. The latest of the seedless kinds to be made available to gardeners is ROMULUS, which produces large and compact clusters of small, yellow, sweet, and seedless berries. Parents will like this kind for their children because there is no problem with seeds.

Among other new or unusual grapes developed in recent years are:

Henry Leuthardt, already mentioned in *Chapter 4,* will introduce the JOE LANE grape in the spring of 1956. Large black berries with very tiny seeds and a tender skin, and a sweet but subdued flavor of the American grape, characterize this excellent table grape named in honor of a man long associated with gardening in America who was awarded the Gold Medal of the Massachusetts Horticultural Society in 1954.

GOLDEN MUSCAT, which forms unusually large clusters of large, seeded berries of golden color and with the tang of the European muscat grapes. Although hardy, its berries do not ripen well in regions with a relatively short growing season.

SENECA is a very early white grape of excellent quality for eating out of hand.

SCHUYLER is an early-maturing blue-black grape that ripens three weeks ahead of CONCORD and has the sweet vinous flavor of many European varieties.

The first colored seedless grape to be produced by a plant breeder is BEAUTY SEEDLESS, a jet-black, early-ripening grape with a heavy bluish bloom. It is about the size of THOMPSON SEEDLESS. A tender variety, BEAUTY SEEDLESS, can be grown only in climates similar to that of the California coastal valleys.

Other relatively new grapes for milder climates are CARDINAL, an early-maturing, large red; ITALIA, an attractive, large-fruited white; and PERLETTE, a firm, crisp seedless, maturing much earlier than THOMPSON SEEDLESS.

In the cooler sections of the west coast it is better to grow the so-called American or hardy grapes, such as CATAWBA, CONCORD, DELAWARE, NIAGARA, and FREDONIA.

Before leaving the subject, we ought, perhaps, to point out that grapes are extremely subject to diseases in some parts of the country and at times control measures must be adopted. Bordeaux mixture, long recommended as a good fungicide for preventing grape diseases, has been found to reduce both vine growth and fruit yields. Where black rot disease is a problem, a fungicide like ferbam or captan is recommended. Where mildew is troublesome, gardeners should use a so-called fixed copper with extra lime added, instead of bordeaux mixture.

Raspberries should be planted in a sunny, well-drained soil. Select virus-free plants grown by reliable nurserymen. Raspberries are shallow-rooted and hence are responsive to fluctuating soil conditions. Mulching the plants over the winter will reduce heaving and winterkill.

Here are some recent introductions:

AMBER, developed at the New York Agricultural Experiment Station, has beautiful amber-colored berries that ripen about mid-July. Its unusual color and high quality make it worth while for home gardens.

BLACK HAWK is a hardy black variety developed at Iowa State College. Its fruit is excellent and freezes well.

BURGUNDY has large purple fruits of delicious flavor and a vine that is unusually robust.

CANBY is particularly suited to the Pacific Northwest. The fruits are large, bright red, and excellent for eating fresh or for freezing.

NEW HAMPSHIRE is a vigorous, winterhardy variety with firm, conical, red berries ripening in New Hampshire in midseason.

PURPLE AUTUMN is a large-fruited, purple raspberry which matures in midseason in the Middle West.

SEPTEMBER is an autumn-fruiting, or so-called everbearing, raspberry with medium-sized, very firm, bright red berries of fair quality in summer. The flavor of the late or fall crop is far better than that of the early crop.

Strawberries are popular in home gardens because they produce good crops in a small space and are relatively easy to grow. Like raspberries, however, they are shallow-rooted and hence respond readily to fluctuating soil conditions. Mulching the soil with salt hay or some other suitable material will help to make conditions more favorable for the plants.

One of the limiting factors in successful culture and a principal reason for the premature dying of strawberry plants used to be virus disease. As a result of co-operation between scientists of the United States Department of Agriculture and those at several state agricultural experiment stations, virus-free strawberries that will outyield and outlive non-virus-free plants are now available.

Gardeners can obtain virus-free plants from all the leading nurseries that handle strawberries. Among the currently available virus-free plants are such long-popular kinds as CATSKILL, FAIRFAX, PREMIER, and SPARKLE, as well as some of the more recently introduced kinds, including STELEMASTER, POCAHONTAS, DIXIELAND, and VERMILION.

Root nematodes have been the second major affliction of strawberries and another major cause for the premature death and poor yields of plantings. Now that virus-free strawberries are a reality, research workers are perfecting ways to grow nematode-free plants as well. Preliminary tests indicate that dipping dormant plants in hot water and setting them out in fumigated, nematode-free soil will eliminate these pests from planting stock.

The following are some recently introduced or unusual strawberries:

EMPIRE, with bright, glossy, medium red, large fruits; EDEN, with fruits that have firm red flesh and tart flavor and hence are excellent for slicing and freezing; and ESSEX, with small fruits of excellent quality, suitable for home gardens. All three varieties were developed at the New York Agricultural Experiment Station at Geneva.

JUMBO is a June-bearing variety especially good for freezing.

STARKRIMSON produces currant-red fruits with firm flesh that is crisp and juicy. It matures in the latter part of May in the Midwest.

STRAFFORD is a late-maturing strawberry developed at the New Hampshire Experiment Station.

STELEMASTER, developed by the United States Department of

Agriculture in co-operation with the Maryland Agricultural Experiment Station, is the first strawberry bred to resist all strains of the fungus that causes red stele disease. Virus-free plants are also available.

JERSEYBELLE, developed at the New Jersey Station, has large, bright, shiny, firm fruits that ship and freeze well.

Home gardeners who prefer to grow the everbearing kinds will like ARAPAHOE, BRILLIANT, GEM, SUPERFECTION, and RED RICH. RED RICH has, in all probability, enjoyed a greater sale to home gardeners than any other everbearing variety offered in recent years.

New Melons

Two members of the Cucurbit family, muskmelon and watermelon, are popular in home gardens where the soil and climate are favorable. Most kinds require relatively light sandy soils and a long growing season. A few have been bred to mature early for growth in areas with short growing seasons.

As with many fruits that require rather specific growing conditions, melons are developed for particular areas. Again, the gardener is best guided by the recommendations of horticulturists in his own state.

In certain parts of the Northeast soils have become infested with the fusarium fungus, making it impossible to grow the ordinary varieties of muskmelons. For such areas HARVEST QUEEN is recommended because it is resistant to the fusarium disease. It is a medium-sized, firm-fleshed, high-quality melon. Other fusarium-resistant melons available are IROQUOIS and DELICIOUS 51.

PENNSWEET, developed at the Pennsylvania Agricultural Experiment Station, is an early-maturing, very sweet, salmon- to orange-fleshed melon better suited for home gardens than for commercial culture.

MINNESOTA HONEY, a muskmelon adapted for northern areas, has solid, juicy flesh and weighs 7 to 9 pounds at maturity.

Most gardeners think of watermelons as red-fleshed, but there are kinds, with delicious cream, yellow, or golden flesh.

GOLDEN HONEY CREAM is a deep-yellow-fleshed, early-maturing watermelon of superior quality. It has a thin rind, small seeds, a high sugar content, and matures in eighty-nine days.

One with red flesh like the commonest kinds but which is of ice-box size, that is, no larger than a muskmelon, is NEW HAMPSHIRE MIDGET, which matures in sixty-five to seventy days. This small-sized watermelon is another of the many valuable contributions to gardening by Dr. A. F. Yeager. It matures in such a relatively short period that it is ideally suited for the more northerly regions, where the growing season is short.

CALIFORNIA HONEY watermelon is dark-skinned, medium-sized and with crisp red flesh. It is adapted to areas with a short growing season.

To gardeners who want more details on growing fruits, I can highly recommend *Fruits for the Home Garden,* by the late Dr. U. P. Hedrick.

Chapter 6

HOUSE PLANTS

Styles in house plants change from time to time, though not nearly so often as do styles in automobiles and women's apparel! Among the many factors that influence the change are the introduction of new house furnishings, the development of new house designs, and the use of new construction materials such as aluminum, glass brick, and large plate glass or picture windows. The human factor also plays its part. Many ultramodern-home owners have lost interest in such old-time favorites as rubber plants, sansevierias, palms, and ferns even though most of these plants are still "old reliables" in some homes.

In recent years house plants have become part and parcel of interior decoration. Home owners are selecting them as carefully as draperies and carpets.

Plant collectors must also be credited with the increased use of new kinds of plants. Men like Alfred Graf of the Julius Roehrs Company at East Rutherford, New Jersey, have traveled all over the world looking for new kinds of plants that will do well in homes, apartments, hotels, and business offices. Another such individual is Mulford B. Foster of Orlando, Florida, who has introduced into this country a goodly number of South American plants, particularly bromeliads. Besides introducing new varieties, he has developed more new varieties in this group by hybridization than anyone before him.

Although the newer house plants are better adapted to up-to-date homes, they must still receive a certain amount of care and must be provided with certain growing conditions if they are to last long indoors. Success with house plants, then, depends on choosing the kinds of plants that will thrive in the surroundings in which they are to be placed and under the care they are to receive.

Among the more important environmental factors to be considered are light intensity, temperature, and humidity. The commonest cause

87

for house plant failures are lack of sufficient light, too much or too little heat, low humidity, lack of plant food, and lastly insect pests and diseases.

TODAY'S POPULAR HOUSE PLANTS

Many of today's more satisfactory house plants are natives of the tropics, where the humidity is high, rains are frequent, and the light is bright though diffused by overhanging trees. The surprising thing about some of the more desirable kinds, however, is that they do so well in the average home, where the humidity is unusually low and temperatures vary widely.

Philodendrons

The most popular of all house plants today are the philodendrons. They can adapt themselves better to the extremely dry conditions of modern homes and stay green in the dim light of corners and hallways for longer periods than any other group of plants. Moreover, they are relatively free from pests, they require little plant food, and can withstand far more than most house plants.

Although there are more than three hundred different kinds, most of them natives of the tropical jungles of Central and South America, only a few dozen kinds are generally available.

Their leaf shapes, growing habits, and textures vary so widely that it is easy to find one kind that will fit into any modern décor or period style. Some are vinelike, others grow as rosettes, and still others are treelike. Many of the vine type are potted with a slice of bark or wood so that the aerial roots can cling as they climb. These types soon get out of hand in most homes, especially if growing conditions are favorable. Hence in recent years there has been a greater demand for the rosette types, which remain compact on the order of a bird's-nest fern. However, they require more room and are particularly favored in southern patios. Their popularity bids fair to continue on the increase.

The philodendrons make such satisfactory house plants that it seems worth while to list the principal species among the three groups now generally available, together with a brief description of each and other pertinent information.

Philodendron Andreanum, a vine type with large dark green leaves, resembling iridescent satin, marked with prominent ivory veins. It

Among the more desirable or unusual philodendrons are the following species: (top) panduraeforme; Wendlandii; *(middle)* elegans; erubescens; *(bottom)* laciniosum; hastatum; sodiroi.

requires higher humidity than most other philodendrons and therefore is not easily grown in apartments.

P. dubium, a vine type with deeply segmented dark green leaves having slightly raised light green midribs.

P. Duisbergi, a rosette type from Central America with creased leaves.

P. elegans, a vine type with large, deeply lobed, fernlike leaves that grow slowly.

P. erubescens, a climbing type whose sagittate leaves are reddish on their upper surfaces and have red stems.

P. gloriosum, a slowly climbing species with large, cordate, velvety, grayish-green leaves, ivory veins, and a distinctive red leaf margin. It is a native of Ecuador.

P. hastatum, a low-climbing type with large arrow-shaped leaves. In very dry atmospheres and as the plant ages, the new leaves become smaller and smaller. A new variety, not yet widely available, is a variegated form with leaves boldly marked with yellow streaks.

P. Imbe is similar to *P. hastatum* but has dark red spots on the petioles, or leaf stems, and reddish lower leaf surfaces.

P. lacerum, a robust-growing climber with large leaves that have indented margins.

P. McNeilianum, a tree type with large, wavy, lobed leaves, is a new hybrid. One of its parents is *P. selloum,* a variety unusually resistant to low temperatures. The hybrid has inherited some of this resistance.

P. Mandaianum, a climbing-type hybrid with mature leaves that are dark green and young leaves that are tannish salmon pink.

P. micans, a vine type with small, silky, dark green leaves that have a red sheen. It requires high humidity and does not tolerate chilly temperatures.

P. nobile, an easy-flowering rosette type with long, leathery, straplike leaves.

P. oxycardium, commonly known as *P. cordatum,* a fine type with small heart-shaped leaves. There is also a variegated form.

P. panduraeforme, a vine type with large dark green leaves shaped like a horse's head, is perhaps one of the finest house plants in form, texture, and durability. It is also sold under the common name "Panda plant" although the name HORSE'S HEAD PHILODENDRON is more appropriate. Moreover, another plant, *Kalanchoe tomentosa,* is better known as the "panda plant" because of its woolly texture and peculiar markings.

How *P. panduraeforme* gained entry into this country is an unusual story worth the telling. Native of Peru, the plant had been grown for a long time at the Royal Botanic Garden in Kew, England. During World War II an American GI is said to have "lifted" a few cuttings from the aroid greenhouse at the Garden and "sneaked" them into the United States. The few cuttings so introduced served as the nucleus of the tremendous population of HORSE'S HEAD philodendrons now on the market.

P. pittieri, a vine type with broad, heart-shaped leaves, more tolerant to dry apartment conditions than most philodendrons.

P. sanguineum, a vine type with arrow-shaped leaves, blood red on their lower surfaces.

P. selloum, a tree type with deeply lobed, fernlike leaves, which eventually grow to tremendous size. Because it is more tolerant of low temperatures than are other members of the genus, it is an excellent plant for difficult or cool situations.

P. sodiroi, usually a vine but occasionally a rosette type, with red stems and heart-shaped leaves with silvery gray blotches.

P. squamiferum, a vine type with leaf stems covered with bright red hairs and with leaves that have 5 deep lobes.

P. Wendlandii, a rosette type with long, straplike leaves. Because it is symmetrical from all sides, it is excellent as a centerpiece. Some consider it the ideal house plant. A new cross between *P. Wendlandii* and *P. Mandaianum* has red foliage.

Close Kin to Philodendrons

Some well-known and excellent house plants closely related to the philodendrons are dieffenbachias, aglaonemas, syngoniums, and anthuriums.

Dieffenbachias have beautiful foliage and easily adapt themselves to most homes. They thrive in the dry, warm conditions of the living room, and respond best if kept on the dry side. Probably the best-known kinds are *D. picta* and its golden-yellow sport *D.* RUDOLPH ROEHRS, and the robust *D. amoena.*

The Chinese evergreen, *Aglaonema simplex,* is among the toughest of all house plants. It may be grown in soil, sand, or water, although it does best in soil. When grown in water, it is necessary to change the water every few weeks and to add a tiny pinch of some all-soluble plant food such as RAPIDGRO during the periods of active growth.

Syngoniums are dwarf climbers that are potted with tree bark or poles. Those belonging to the *S. podophyllum* group have arrow-shaped leaves. EMERALD GEM is a recent introduction, with fleshier, dull, crinkled leaves that climb more slowly. GREEN GOLD is another close relative, with yellowish-green leaves. The patented variety TRILEAF WONDER is another excellent member of this group which does especially well as a house plant. Its glaucous leaves are variegated, creamy yellow, and green.

S. Wendlandii has arrow-shaped leaves with whitish centers. It does best in warm, moist air.

Two different types of anthuriums are available: those with unusual and striking flowers and those with extremely decorative foliage. Best of the blooming kinds are *A. Andreanum* (illustration following page 96) and *A. Scherzerianum.* The two with most unusual leaves are *A. Veitchii* and *A. crystallium.* The latter has oval-pointed, mossy- or velvet-green leaves with very prominent white veins. Immature leaves have a reddish cast.

Alocasia Thibautiana also known as *A. Korthalsii* is another aroid that make a very beautiful house plant because of its rich, dark green leaves boldly marked with wide bands of white tissue.

Bromeliads

A nearly foolproof group of house plants is the pineapple family, or the bromeliads. Although some members of this group have been used as house plants in Europe for many years, they became popular in this country only recently. Incidentally, Mulford B. Foster, mentioned earlier in this chapter, is editor of the Bromeliad Society Bulletin.

The best known bromeliad is *Billbergia nutans,* whose tall green tubes grow in clusters. The flower spike rises from the tube and overhangs it gracefully.

Another member of this interesting and bizarre family is *Aechmea,* with the base of its leaves so constructed as to form a receptacle for water. Some folks use this natural cup to hold small cut flowers.

A. fasciata is an urn-shaped plant with silvery-striped, gray-green leaves, rose-pink bracts, and blue flowers. The soil in which this plant grows should not be watered until after it drys, and the natural leaf cup should be kept filled with water. With bromeliads it is more important to keep fresh water in their leaf cups than it is to water the roots. (Illustration following page 96)

A. pineliana has soft-toned leaves in shades of red brown and dusty rose. Its flower stem bears rose-colored bracts, tipped by a flower head of bristles.

A. orlandiana has pale green, saw-toothed leaves splashed with black mottlings. White flowers bloom on an orange stem in winter.

Cryptanthus lacerdae, SILVER STAR, resembles a starfish in shape, with flat, radiating, green- and silver-colored leaves. Another striking one is *Cryptanthus bromeloides,* TRICOLOR.

An unusual flowering variety of bromeliad is *Vriesia carinata,* var. MARIE, with spectacular, long-lasting bloom giving the over-all effect of a permanent flower arrangement.

The most widely known bromeliad is the cultivated pineapple, whose fruit millions of people enjoy fresh, canned, or frozen.

Few persons realize that the leafy part of a fresh pineapple can be grown as a house plant. The rosette of leaves at the top of the fruit can be cut off and the lower end inserted into a shallow tray of moist, sharp sand, where it will form roots in five to eight weeks. The rooted rosette is planted firmly in a pot containing a mixture of equal parts of sand, soil, and leaf mold to which small amounts of crushed cinders and well-rotted manure have been added.

Once the plant is well established and growing in this new medium, the gardener can force it to flower and fruit by filling the top tier of leaves with a solution containing 5 grains of calcium carbide in a quart of water. The solution should be left in the leaf cluster for twenty-four hours and then drained off by tipping the plant on its side. Blooms should appear within a month if the treatment is successful.

Dracaenas and Sansevierias

Two reliable house plant groups in the lily family are dracaena and sansevieria. Although both groups have been around for a long time, the recent revival of interest in house plants has brought these old-timers back into the limelight.

The handsomest of all dracaenas is the relatively unknown sport of *D. Warneckii, D. Bausei,* a compact-growing plant with long narrow leaves that have green margins and white midribs. (Illustration following page 96)

D. Warneckii has green and white pin-striped foliage. A beautiful specimen has thrived near the east window of my dining room for the last two years with little care except for an occasional watering.

D. Godseffiana, a native of equatorial Africa, looks unlike other members of this genus. Whereas most dracaenas have either narrow or broad leaves arising from the center of the plant and grow as a rosette, this species has oblong leaves arising mostly in pairs from the many nodes set closely along the wiry branches.

Perhaps the most easily grown of all house plants in sansevieria, commonly known as snake plant. It grows in sun or shade, dry or wet soil (although the stems will rot if the soil is kept too wet), and is quite immune to insect attack.

A modern version of the tough old snake plant is *S. nelsoni,* which forms leaves in rosettes, giving this plant that "new look." Other unique sansevierias are *S. Ehrenbergi,* which has steel-blue leaves edged with white and *S. cylindrica,* with terete leaves.

There also are low-growing forms of sansevierias, such as *S. compacta* and *S. Hahnii,* that are tough like the tall varieties but look like green rosettes.

Ivies

The ivies (*Hedera*) have long been used as house plants. They require drier soil conditions than many house plants; otherwise their stems will decay. When grown under dry conditions, however, they are more subject to spider mites. Hence one must be constantly on the watch for mites and use the remedies recommended at the end of this chapter.

There are a great number of sports of the true English ivy (*H. helix*) that make satisfactory house plants. MAPLE QUEEN is a small-leaved, slow-growing variety well adapted to small containers. WEBER'S CALIFORNIA IVY is similar but has more rounded leaves. CALIFORNIA GOLD is a golden variegated sport of WEBER'S CALIFORNIA IVY.

Two fine ivies originally introduced by Weber Nurseries of Los Angeles, California, are GLACIER and GOLD DUST. More recently this firm introduced JUBILEE, which has narrower leaves and is more self-branching than GLACIER. Besides its many variegated leaves, JUBILEE has some completely white ones of medium size.

WILLIAMSANA is a brand-new, variegated sport of GLACIER but with more uniform variegation and medium-sized leaves which curl downward. LANCELOT is still another sport of GLACIER, with clean-cut, spear-head-shaped leaves.

BIG DEAL is another unusual ivy that really does not look like an ivy. Its rounded, 2-inch-broad leaves resemble those of geraniums.

Some recent introductions of the well-known firm of Louis Hahn and Son of Pittsburgh, are GREEN RIPPLE, SHAMROCK, and IMPROVED SYLVANIA BEAUTY.

The kangaroo ivy, *Cissus antarctica,* from Australia, with leathery, notched leaves on wiry red stems, is rapidly replacing the shiny-leaved grape ivy, *Cissus rhombifolia.*

Other New or Unusual Foliage Plants

A recent introduction in the house plant line, and a close relative of the once popular artillery plant, is *Pilea cadierei,* commonly called ALUMINUM PLANT or WATERMELON PILEA. I am told some folks actually believe the silvery, metallic blotches that cover a good portion of the upper leaf surface is aluminum. Its no wonder, either, for any metallurgist would be hard put to make a paint that looks more like aluminum than these silvery leaf blotches! Actually the metallic luster is caused by a layer of air that separates the upper layer of cells, or epidermis, from the palisade layer just below. The silvery blotches, therefore, are blisters which are invisible when the leaf is viewed by transmitted light.

Fatshedera Lizei, the California ivy, whose pedigree is discussed in *Chapter 7,* is an excellent house plant for the colder parts of the country. When grown in difficult situations, and if kept a bit too dry, mites will attack and disfigure the younger leaves. In mild regions, particularly in Southern California, *F. Lizei* is used outdoors as a ground cover, a vine, a shrub, or an informal espalier.

Schefflera actinophylla, a slow-growing, treelike, shiny-leaved plant, is excellent for rooms with low humidity and low light intensity. It does best when kept on the dry side. (Illustration following page 96)

Pittosporum is a compact, slow-growing plant with neat, rounded, glossy leaves having prominent white midribs. In the North it does best in glassed-in porches; in the South it is an excellent outdoor subject.

The prayer plant, *Maranta kerchoveana,* has green leaves with unusual chocolate-colored blotches on either side of the midrib. A more striking and better variety is *Maranta leuconeura Massangeana.* Although not a new plant, *Tacca cristata* is an unusual one. It has bright shiny green foliage and sinister purple-black flowers with long thread-like bracts that give it its common name, the bat plant.

The Chinese velvet plant *Gynura aurantiaca* has thick purple hairs that make a velvety nap over the leaves. When viewed from one angle, the leaves are green; from another, they are purple. The leaf hairs are so prominent that the plant has long been used in botany classrooms to demonstrate these structures to students. Gynura is rather susceptible to pests, particularly mealy bugs, and hence must be watched more closely than most house plants. Moreover, many of the common insecticides may harm it. Be sure to test the plant spray on a single leaf and leave it for a few days before applying it to the entire plant.

The blood-red-leaved *Iresine* does well in sunny windows that receive at least four hours of sun on clear day.

Setcreasea PURPLE HEART is a Mexican plant with rich purple fleshy leaves and stout stems and resembles Tradescantia or Zebrina in growth habit. It was brought back from Mexico about ten years ago by my colleague E. J. Alexander of The New York Botanical Garden and was introduced into the trade by Alfred Graf of the Julius Roehrs Company, East Rutherford, New Jersey.

Saxifraga sarmentosa tricolor is a beautiful sport of the old strawberry "begonia." Its leaves are variegated green, pink, red, yellow, and white.

In bulbs and tubers we should remember many of the lesser known African species. *Lachenalia tricolor,* for example, with red and yellow tubular flowers, is not only a spectacular bloomer, but is also a good keeper. Many new and beautiful *Caladium* hybrids have been developed recently. ROEHRS DAWN has large glistening white leaves with red veins. (Illustration following page 96)

Ferns, too, should not be forgotten. Lately the dainty yet sturdy RABBITSFOOT FERN, trained on pillars and other forms, have arrived from Japan. These are best stood in shallow dishes containing about a ½ inch of water. The water should be changed from time to time. Similarly, the upper parts of the HAWAIIAN TREEFERN, *Cibotium Menziesii,* will grow in a dish of water. Additional species of the weird-looking STAGHORN FERN have also been introduced recently. *Platycerium diversifolium,* of upright habit, can be grown in pots. (Illustration following page 96) Much improved types of BOSTON FERNS such as *Nepholepis hillii,* with sturdy, lobed, lacy fronds that are upright and golden green, will soon be available.

The truly tropical plants should be surrounded by more humidity than is available in the average living room. Failure of many exotic plants is due primarily to the very dry atmosphere. However, these finicky subjects will thrive when planted in a glass container such as an aquarium.

Cacti and succulents, which thrive under the very dry conditions of apartments, are other favorite subjects of plant collector E. J. Alexander. Most of these, however, require very strong light, as much as six hours of sun every day. The following will flower if kept

Springtime, one of the earliest
ripening (late May) California
peaches.

Ruby, a deep red apple recently
introduced by the Ohio Agricultural
Experiment Station.

The *Ayres* pear is a fine eating
pear produced on trees virtually immune
to the fire blight disease.

Professor L. G. Schermerhorn of Rutgers University
with his most recent introduction, *Jersey* rhubarb.

The *Queens* tomato, another of Professor
Schermerhorn's famous introductions.

Anthurium Andreanum.

The Staghorn fern
Platycerium diversifolium.

Schefflera actinophylla.

Dracaena Bausei.

Aechmea fasciata is a striking member of the pineapple family.

Caladium Roehrs Dawn has large glistening white leaves with red veins.

Leaves and fruits of the *238th Street* ivy.

A bed of *Hedera Helix 238th Street* growing at The New York Botanical Gar

in a sunny east or south window: ROSE-PLAID CACTUS *Gymnocalycium Friedrichiae,* with red-pink blooms that will develop even when the plant is small; and *Notocactus mammulosis,* with golden-yellow flowers.

African Violets

Because their blooming habits are the most reliable throughout the year, African violets are the most widely grown and popular flowering house plants. They have the happy faculty of quickly adapting themselves to the light and temperature conditions of the modern home. They are among the very few flowering plants that grow as well under artificial lights as under natural lights, if not better.

African violets are not properly violets, but belong to the important Gesneriad family, which includes such well-known plants as gloxinias and episcias. The botanical name is *Saintpaulia,* after Baron Walter von Saint Paul, who first found them in Tanganyika, Africa, in 1890 and shipped them to Europe.

The intense interest in this plant arose in the 1920s when the very popular variety BLUE BOY began to produce sports. From the two original species, *ionantha* and *diplotricha,* came hundreds of doubles, supremes, miniatures, and trailing varieties with blue, purple, red, lavender, or pink flowers.

African violets do best in rooms where the day temperature is 75 degrees and the night temperature 68 to 70. When the night temperature drops below 60 degrees, already formed flowers will drop prematurely and undeveloped flowers will fail to open normally. The leaves will turn downward around the edges. The plants are very sensitive to drafts.

In midwinter, failure to flower may be due to lack of sufficient light. Winter blossoming is most profuse when the plants get fourteen to sixteen hours of slightly diffused light. This can be supplied by artificial lights, as described later in this chapter.

Small-sized flowers sometimes are the result of insufficient plant food, a condition easily remedied by using any one of several readily available special African violet plant foods. Flower production in African violets, as in many other plants, appears to be related to the supply of phosphoric acid, one of three major elements in all complete plant foods.

Mites are the most destructive pests known to attack African violets. There are aerosol plant bombs on the market specifically designed to control these and other pests on this popular plant. One

I have used with good results is ANTROL AFRICAN VIOLET INSECT BOMB.

A complete list of African violets introduced within only the last two years would cover many pages of this book. Here are a few of the newer ones and some of the older ones that are so outstanding they will be with us for a long time:

Singles. White—SNOW PRINCE; blue—BLUE MOON, MENTOR BOY; purple—PURPLE DAWN, ORCHID WONDER; pink—PINK CHEER, PINK DELIGHT; red—RED KING, RED VELVET.

Doubles. White—WHITE MADONNA, DOUBLE PURITY; blue—DOUBLE DELIGHT; dark blue—DOUBLE LADY; reddish purple—FIRE CHIEF; pink—PINK ACHIEVEMENT; white with blue and lavendar markings—ROSETTA; reddish lavender with trim white edges—EDNA FISCHER.

Supremes have larger, thicker foliage but are not so floriferous as the ordinary kinds. Purple—MENTOR BOY SUPREME, VIOLET BEAUTY SUPREME; pink—PINK BEAUTY SUPREME; blue—the du Pont hybrids.

Girls. The foliage of these kinds is serrated like fancy skirts. White—SNOW GIRL; pink—PINK GIRL; purple—ORCHID GIRL, PURPLE GIRL; red—RED GIRL; blue—MARTHA GIRL, SAILOR'S DELIGHT.

Trailers. These trailing varieties derived from the East African species *Saintpaulia Grotei* for use in hanging baskets are still rare.

A truly exciting, very recent introduction is WHITE SURPRISE, with snowy white blossoms—some single, some double, and others semi-double—above quilted foliage. ANGEL LACE has large white blooms with lilac-blue fringed edges and large leaves of the du Pont strain. PINK DRESDEN has semi-double, long-lasting, deep pink blossoms with serrated leaves. WILCOX BLUE PACIFIC, with flowers as big as pansies, is among the biggest, bluest, and most beautiful of African violets.

The first fringed pink African violet to be put on the market is PINK FRINGETTE, with beautiful, deep pink, fringed blossoms up to 1½ inches in diameter formed well above the wavy foliage.

Even leaf hairiness has been bred out of African violets. The variety HARVEY has shiny, begonia-slick leaves.

Just as this book was being readied for the printer, some brand-new varieties were shown at the annual convention of the African Violet Society held in April 1955.

Among the outstanding new kinds that are bound to please even an African violet hobbyist are:

ROSE WING, a heavy frilled white with orchid markings; FUSED PINK, a striking new shade of pink; WHITE PUFF, a double white; MOONBEAM, with an unusual combination of blue on white; and DOUBLE PINK, which is truly double and was selected as the best seedling in the show.

African violet hobbyists can get more extensive lists by writing to African violet specialists and asking for their latest lists. The African Violet Society of America is also a good source of information on new kinds. The present secretary of this organization is Mrs. James R. Jones, Route 2, Box 180, Woodstock, Illinois.

Relatives of African Violets

Two close relatives of African violets are episcias and gloxinias. The latter have been available from florists for a long time, but episcias have recently stepped into the limelight as flowering house plants.

The best-known episcia is *E. coccinea,* or FLAME VIOLET, with broad, bronzy, thick plushlike leaves and veins of emerald green. The very striking leaves alone make it a plant worth growing, but in addition it produces flaming scarlet flowers.

Episcias are even more sensitive to sharp drops in temperature and to drafts than are the African violets. Like their close relatives, they can be grown under weak natural light and under artificial lights but need higher humidity than Saintpaulias to really thrive and send out their "runners," from which young plants develop.

The most commonly available species at present is *E. fulgida,* with large velvet coppery-colored leaves veined with brilliant chartreuse. One of the most striking is *E. cupreata* SILVER SHEEN, whose cream-colored fuzzy leaves have a rusty margin. Its pale orange flowers, shading into yellow, have in the center dark speckles which extend into the throat of the flower.

Among the most recently introduced varieties of episcia—all with small red flowers—are:

CHOCOLATE SOLDIER, with chocolate brown, semi-smooth leaves and contrasting gray-green midrib stripe; FROSTY, with silvery leaves and margins and blotches of emerald green; HARLEQUIN, with shiny silvery leaves, dark raised blotches between veins, and dark brown margins; and EMERALD QUEEN, with rough emerald-green leaves, a silvery midrib, and a herringbone pattern.

The second close relative of African violets, the gloxinias, produce very unusual bell-shaped flowers. Some are 4 to 6 inches across and come in a glorious range of colors, from velvety shades of blue to pink, red and purple, depending on the variety. Some are two-toned, like the latest model automobiles.

BLUE DELIGHT has flowers with a solid blue border on a pure white background. PINK SURPRISE has 4½-inch blooms of delicate pink, speckled with a darker shade and with a narrow rim of solid deeper pink.

When grown as house plants, gloxinias like much the same conditions as episcias and African violets, and are by far the showiest bloomers as well as good keepers if kept above 60 degrees, evenly moist and protected from bright sun. Temperatures below 60 degrees are distinctly harmful, and they too resent drafty spots. The variety KISS OF FIRE is a husky, compact, late-blooming hybrid that produces large, brilliant scarlet blossoms on short erect stems.

Begonias

Begonias, all natives of warm regions of the earth, come in three types—fibrous, rhizomatous, and tuberous. The fibrous types are most numerous, the rhizomatous are easiest to grow, and the tuberous have the showiest flowers.

Plant collectors and hybridizers in recent years have introduced many new kinds. Some very recent importations from Belgium include outstanding Rex hybrids with unusual leaf designs and color combinations. Among the startling colors are lavender and purple, red and maroon, or brown and silver combined with lavender, purple, or pink—a selection certainly wide enough to blend with any home décor. MERRY CHRISTMAS has satiny red leaves framed in green, with red centers and edges.

The fibrous begonia *B. valdensianum* has broad, grass-green leaves with slightly wavy edges and prominent, light green veins.

The wax begonia CARMINE QUEEN has small double blossoms that resemble miniature full-blown roses.

Begonia boweri, a recently introduced miniature begonia from Mexico, grows about 4 inches high. It produces pale pink flowers and interesting fringed and blotched leaves. It will bloom profusely in a sunny northeast window.

Begonia IRON CROSS has olive-green, quilted leaves and a reddish-brown pattern resembling an iron cross. It will be available late in 1956.

Geraniums

Ever since grandmother's day geraniums have been one of the most popular house plants because of their bright, long-lasting flowers. In recent years many new varieties have been introduced, with colors ranging from pure white to shell pink, shrimp, salmon, coral, rose, scarlet, cerise, purple, violet, and deep crimson. One has only to see all these different shades of color in the same house at the same time to appreciate how far we have come from the standard red-flowered geranium of the good old days.

Not only has the color range in flowers vastly increased, but the foliage colors have been improved so much that modern gardeners grow some geraniums for their leaves alone. The variety JUBILEE, for example, has a wide chocolate zone on a golden background. Its single flowers are salmon pink. Other geraniums with variegated leaves are ALPHA, with red-brown zoning on a light green leaf and with vermilion flowers, and scarlet-flowered DISTINCTION, with bright, saw-toothed leaves marked by a narrow black ring. The best tri-colored leaf types are VELMA, BURDETTE COUTTS, and SKIES OF ITALY.

As with African violets, it is impossible to list here all the recent introductions. All we can hope to do is to indicate some of the old and the new that are more unsual in flower color, leaf type, and growing habit.

Among the best of the single-flowered kinds are the pure white SNOWFLAKE and the red BATTLE OF GETTYSBURG. Other excellent geraniums for window gardens are MAXINE KOVALESKI, BETTER TIMES, FIAT SUPREME, OLYMPIC RED, PINK ABUNDANCE, and MME. BUCHNER.

There are some unusual varieties with flowers resembling phlox, pansies, azaleas, and roses. Among the odd individuals in these categories are the ruffled, cut-leaved GLAUCIFOLIUM, with maroon flowers; POINSETTIA, with pink and scarlet blooms; NEW LIFE, with phloxlike flowers of red flecked with white; MORNING STAR, with shrimp-red flowers; and NEW ERA, with varied flower colors, no two of which are alike.

Among the ivy-leaved geraniums is BRIDESMAID, with large clusters and blossoms of double, soft orchid pink; THE DUCHESS, a semi-double white flushed with orchid and lined with pink around the edges of the petals; and EL GAUCHO, with showy double cerise flowers with a violet undertone.

The miniature or dwarf geraniums, with their small leaves, compact habit, and slow growth, are crowding the larger standard varieties in popularity as house plants. Most of the dwarf kinds have red flowers, a few have rose or salmon ones, and still fewer have white blossoms.

The first tricolor-leaved dwarf geranium FAIRYLAND has single scarlet flowers and small, dark, gray-green leaves with a wide ivory border that is zoned with splashes of rose or red. ELF, a golden tricolor-leaved dwarf, is somewhat similar to FAIRYLAND but even more striking.

One of the few pure white dwarf geraniums is WHITE CAP. Its petals are waved at the edges and its leaves are dark.

Perhaps the quickest growing of the dwarf geraniums is PYGMY, with its light green leaves and clusters of double scarlet-red flowers. Other varieties are LITTLE DARLING, with pink flowers, and BLACK VESUVIUS, which has bright red blossoms and a very dark, zoned leaf, the darkest leaf of all the dwarf geraniums.

The Lady Washington geraniums, botanically *Pelargonium domesticum,* have the showiest flowers of the entire geranium family. Here are some of the favorite kinds:

MARY ELIZABETH, a watermelon pink with a white throat; LUCY ANN LESLIE, deep pink, with upper petals veined red from the base to a crimson center spot; GRANDMA FISCHER, rich salmon with each petal penciled and blotched with dark brown; MARIE ROBER, with spectacular, very large magenta to black flowers; MARIE VOGEL, with large ruffled red flowers flushed with salmon and with dark blotches on the upper petals; S. A. BREEN, large silvery-pink flowers with upper petals veined purple; and GARDNER'S JOY, large white flowers with brown blotches.

Fuchsias

Some of the choicest fuchsia varieties are: BALI HI, with a blue violet corolla and ivory-rose petals; CHIQUITA, a hanging basket type with double, pale rose-orchid flowers; JAMBOREE, with double carmine flowers; PINK PARFAIT, with double corolla of strawberry pink; SAN JOSE, white corolla and rose-red sepals; and TINKER BELL, with single white corolla and red and ivory sepals.

Other Flowering Plants

Many other showy flowering plants are to be seen in florists' shops. Especially desirable during holidays are such azaleas as the durable RUTHERFORDIANAS, the fast-growing PERICATS, and the GABLE and BELTSVILLE hardy hybrids in many new colors. In hydrangeas the newer French varieties such as MERVEILLE and MADAME CAYCUX (STRAFFORD) are replacing the softer, older kinds. Cinerarias, calceolarias, and baby primroses have been much improved. Chrysanthemums in pots are now available the year round. In poinsettias, BARBARA ECKE SUPREME represents the latest in brilliant red and sturdy foliage and a good new white, ECKE'S WHITE, heralds a new fashion.

Although not as spectacular, the following are excellent, though little-known, flowering plants: *Abutilon,* the flowering maple; *Tetranema,* the Mexican foxglove; *Exacum,* the German violet; *Euphorbia splendens,* the CROWN OF THORNS; *Crossandra,* SONG OF INDIA; *Strelitzia,* the BIRD OF PARADISE; and dwarf pomegranates.

Some gardeners say orchids are good subjects for house plant culture. One reason for this report is that it takes many months before a home-grown orchid begins to show the adverse effects of its household environment. Actually, orchids will not do well for very long in homes unless special conditions such as high humidity are provided. There are a few exceptions, however.

One orchid that is almost as easy to grow as a geranium, for example, is *Phaius grandifolius,* an Asiatic species that does well in a rich mixture of loam, peat, and manure. Its beautiful brown and white flowers are star-shaped and 2 to 3 inches across. As many as 12 flowers will develop on a single tall, straight stem in winter.

Latest News on Light

Every house plant grower must understand the importance of light to healthy plant production. No green plant will grow without light. Some, of course, will stay green longer than others in dim light, but all plants must have some light. Plants that are grown for their flowers require far more light than those that are grown for foliage only. Flower production and light go hand in hand.

Natural light from the sun is not absolutely essential for growing plants. Many plants have been grown from seed to flowering with artificial lights only. In other words, ultraviolet rays are not required for good plant growth, but the red and blue portions of the spectrum are.

In December, and in the northerly parts of our country when the days are short, light conditions in the average home and apartment are especially poor. Then artificial lights can be used to supplement natural daylight and thus help to keep house plants in good condition. Such lights can also be used to supply the complete light requirements if the necessary batteries of fluorescent tubes and incandescent

(Mazda) bulbs are installed. Such light units are easy to install and relatively inexpensive to operate.

Let us look at some of the generally accepted facts concerning the effect of light on house plants.

It is better to combine fluorescent and incandescent light for growing house plants than to use either one alone. Best response comes from a combination of nine fluorescent lamp lumens to one filament lamp lumen. In non-technical language this means one 40-watt fluorescence lamp and one 25-watt incandescent bulb, or a multiple of these.

The FLORACART *has built-in fluorescent lights for growing house plants.*

As a general rule, only those plants that grow under reduced natural light in nature do well under artificial lights. African violets, for example, may do better under artificial lights than in a sunlit window.

Artificial lighting for plants can be supplied most economically late in the day, when the lights must be turned on anyway. On cloudy days they may be turned on earlier.

Regularity of use is very important; the occasional use of artificial lights will produce no beneficial effects.

With mature-foliage plants the problem is to supply enough light so they will hold their own. It does not have to be so intense as to force additional new growth, because such plants are most desirable when they make only slow growth and yet maintain their generally attractive appearance.

The amount of artificial light available to foliage plants is approximately the product of the light intensity multiplied by its daily duration. For example, ten hours of light at 30 foot-candles intensity (1 foot-candle is the amount of light cast by one candle on a surface 1 foot away) will maintain some plants about as well as fifteen hours of light at 20 foot-candles.

Inexpensive meters for measuring light intensity are available but the following figures represent the number of foot-candles of illumination usually existing in various locations and situations:

Homes—general illumination, 5; reading or writing, 20; ironing, sewing, 40; and workbench, 40. Hotels—lobby, 20; and dining room, 5 to 10. Offices—typing and accounting, 50; conference rooms, 30; and libraries, 30.

The following groups of foliage plants are divided according to the intensity of artificial light needed to maintain them for at least twelve months (based on a daily illumination of sixteen hours):

Low light requirements (15 to 25 foot-candles): *Aglaonema commutatum, Aucuba japonica, Dieffenbachia picta, Philodendron oxycardium,* sansevieria species, and *Schefflera actinophylla.*

Medium light requirements (25 to 50 foot-candles): Anthurium hybrids, various bromeliads, *Kentia Forsteriana, Peperomia obtusifolia, Pilea cadierei,* and *Pothos aureus.*

High light requirements (50 to 100 foot-candles): *Fatshedera Lizei, Ficus pandurata, Hedera helix* varieties CALI and MAPLE QUEEN, *Tolmiea Menziesii,* and *Cissus rhombifolia.*

Although the fluorescent part of the required light must be close to the plant, the incandescent light can be projected. Hence it can be placed in a position quite removed from the plant and still be effective. As a matter of fact, some very interesting effects can be produced when both kinds of lights are properly placed above house plants.

Lest the house plant enthusiast get the impression that success with house plants depends entirely on providing the proper amount of light, let's hasten to add that good light will not make up for unfavorable growing factors such as cold drafts, very low humidity, or a complete lack of plant food. House plants must have a suitable room temperature in addition to adequate light. Most of them do best in a day temperature of 70 to 75 degrees and a night temperature of 60 to 65 degrees.

To get the best out of foliage plants under artificial lights, it is wise to keep them on the dry side. Watering too frequently and in amounts that keep the soil wet not only produces soft growth and a spindly, unattractive plant, but also favors the development of root decay.

House Plant Food

As a rule, plants recently purchased from a florist do not require an immediate application of plant food. They will flourish for several months on the fertilizer applied by the commercial grower before they left his greenhouse. After this period, however, the plants must be fed if they are to thrive.

Although there is no rule of thumb to follow in feeding house plants, one important point to remember is that they should be fed just before or during the time they are growing actively. They should not be fed when they are making no growth. The inactive period varies with each plant but, as a rule, most foliage plants make least vegetative growth during the winter months.

Because house plant fertilizers are more effective when applied in solution, the best kinds to use are the high-analysis, completely soluble kinds such as RAPIDGRO, HYPONEX, MIRACLE-GRO, GRO-STUF, and GARDEN-LIFE. The amount to use varies with the brand. Therefore the manufacturer's directions should be followed carefully.

Fertilizers such as 5-10-5 or 4-12-4, commonly used on outdoor soils, can also be used for house plants. The usual amount is 1 level teaspoonful for each plant growing in a container of 6 inches or larger. Because some of its ingredients are only slightly soluble, this type of fertilizer is applied dry and then scratched lightly into the soil and watered in.

The frequency of application depends on the size of the plants, their growth status, and the season. In winter foliage plants should not be fed more than once a month. When they are growing actively they can be fed every two weeks.

Fertilizer tablets, sold under several brand names, are also available for house plants. They are most effective when dissolved in water and applied in solution rather than pressed dry into the soil.

I have observed a number of cases of root burning when the tablets were applied dry.

Some gardening publications frequently prescribe feeding house plants with liquid manure prepared by soaking cow manure in water. I see no reason for resorting to this ancient method in these days of high-analysis, quickly soluble chemical plant foods, which are clean and easy to handle.

A final word of caution: do not overdose house plants with chemical fertilizers. Follow the manufacturer's direction to the letter. Also remember that the mere application of plant food will not remedy ills that are due to poor growing conditions such as lack of light, improper soil drainage, unfavorable temperatures, and an excessively dry atmosphere.

Watering House Plants

There is no rule-of-thumb method on when and how much to water house plants. But here are a few suggestions that will help. Water sparingly when the room temperature is low, when the weather is cloudy or rainy, or when the plants are first potted. Succulents and cacti should always be watered very sparingly. On the other hand, more frequent waterings should be made on plants with heavy foliage, on those growing in a hot, dry room, when the days are sunny, and when the plants are making vigorous growth or are in flower.

Leaf-cleaning Materials

Because the leaves of house plants last for long periods, they are excellent dust collectors. To keep foliage plants looking their best, their leaves should be freed of dust periodically. Old-fashioned mild soap and water will do the trick but it does not leave the shiny bright color that is most effective.

Special leaf-cleaning and shining materials are on the market for just this purpose. Some of the better kinds contain either lanolin or a plastic as the active ingredient. Borden's LEAF GLOSS is the newest one on the market. Others are GLO-PLANT, PLANT SHINE, FLORA-GLOW, BLACK MAGIC, and WILT-PRUF.

Milk has been recommended and used for a long time, but I feel there are better uses for milk than applying it to plant leaves.

No matter which cleaner is chosen, it is important to use it only on the upper surface, because this is the surface that collects dust and is in need of cleaning and because the breathing pores, or stomates, are relatively few on this surface. Most of the stomates are on the lower surface. Hence nothing that might clog or disrupt their functioning should be used on that surface.

Insects and Other Invaders

It may sound discouraging, but the fact is that no matter how carefully the gardener watches house plants, sooner or later pests of one sort or another are bound to infest them. The pests are brought in on newly acquired plants or even on cut flowers. Others can fly in during the warmer seasons of the year. In any case, one must examine the plants periodically for telltale symptoms of insect damage or for the insects themselves.

The following are the more important insects and related pests of house plants:

Aphids, or plant lice, perhaps the commonest pests of house plants, are soft-bodied, slow-moving, small insects, green, red, brown, pink, purple, or black. They usually congregate in clusters at the growing tips of the stems or on the undersides of the leaves. Unthrifty, stunted plants with yellow leaves follow a heavy infestation. Aphids secrete a sticky substance known as "aphid honey," which in turn is soon overrun by a black sootlike fungus growth known as sooty mold. For a long time a mixture of nicotine sulfate (BLACK LEAF 40) and soap has been used to control aphids. Besides this mixture, malathion spray will also control aphids.

White flies are small, active, pure white insects which infest the lower leaves of such house plants as fuchsia, geranium, and lantana. The immature stage, pearly and motionless, is found on the lower leaf surfaces. Malathion is the latest and best control material but it must be used exactly as directed.

Mealy bugs are white, cottony, slow-moving insects that settle in the leaf axils or along the veins on the undersides of leaves to extract the plant juices. Where the infestation is light, the white masses may be effectively removed with a cotton-tipped swab dipped in rubbing alcohol. Heavy infestations can be controlled by an occasional spraying with malathion.

Scale insects are commonest on woody house plants such as citrus, gardenias, and camellias, and on palms and ferns. Malathion is perhaps the most satisfactory control, especially when applied to young scales. An oil-nicotine sulfate mixture will also control these pests.

Thrips are tiny, narrow, fast-moving insects of yellow, brown, or black color. Their scraping and sucking mouth parts produce white, irregular patches on the leaves. Malathion or DDT in liquid or dust form will control them.

Spider mites are not true insects but they are the most destructive pests of house plants, especially on plants like ivy growing in warm dry spots. When present in large numbers, they cause the leaves to turn yellow or appear bleached, sometimes even killing them.

Fine dusting sulfur applied evenly to the upper and lower leaf surfaces will help. Even forceful syringing of the leaves and stems with water will keep them down somewhat. Best control, however, follows spraying with a solution prepared by dissolving 1 teaspoon of 15 per cent ARAMITE powder in a gallon of water. Malathion is also effective.

Cyclamen mites also cause serious damage to African violets, begonias, cyclamen, ivy, and Fatshedera by deforming young leaves and shoots, and sometimes severely stunting the plants. These pests are rarely seen by gardeners because of their tiny size. Malathion gives good control if applied early in the infestation.

Several excellent aerosol house plant bombs on the market contain relatively safe ingredients, so far as the householder is concerned, and are very effective in combating most of the house plant pests. The ordinary household pest bombs injure plants; hence one must be sure that the label states clearly that the bomb can be used on house plants. It is also well to read carefully what plants may be safely sprayed with the house plant bomb selected. Following are a few of the house plant aerosol bombs on the market: ACME, ANTROL, BOSTWICK, D-X, KILL-OGEN, and RED ARROW.

A number of insects and lower forms of animal life frequently infest soil in which house plants are growing. Among these are fungus gnats, sowbugs, slugs, springtails, and symphalids.

Fungus gnats are small white worms, in their larval stage, which come to the soil surface when the pots are watered. Some persons confuse these with nematodes. But nematodes are much tinier and cannot be seen without a hand lens. The adult gnats are very small, black, mosquito-like flies that do no harm to plants.

Sow bugs and **slugs** usually hide under flowerpots or inside the drainage holes, emerging mostly at night to feed on the leaves. Sow bugs also attack the roots of plants. Both pests can be controlled by spreading around the pots or on the soil special baits obtainable in seed stores.

Springtails are tiny, fast-moving insects also seen on the soil surface after the soil is watered.

Symphalids, or greenhouse centipedes, although not true insects, do some damage to plants by feeding on the smaller roots.

The larval stage of fungus gnats, springtails, symphalids, and, in fact, almost any soil-infesting pest can easily be controlled by dusting the soil surface lightly with 5 per cent chlordane or 1 per cent lindane and then lightly watering it in.

Diseases also Attack Plants

Fungus and bacterial diseases of leaves are not common on house plants because they can develop extensively only when the leaves are wetted frequently and remain wet for long periods.

Powdery mildew diseases are the exception, since these can develop in the absence of prolonged wetting. Tuberous begonias, African violets, and Kalanchoe are a few susceptible plants. MILDEX, discussed in greater detail in *Chapter 13,* is the best material for controlling mildews.

Far more serious than leaf diseases are certain fungus diseases of the roots and lower stems. Root and stem rots are aggravated by wet, heavy soils. Hence some of these diseases can be avoided by providing good soil drainage and by not overwatering or overcrowding the plants. Plants with root diseases rarely recover.

Chapter 7

HOW NEW VARIETIES OF PLANTS ARISE

Most amateur gardeners are not aware that new varieties of plants arise in a number of different ways. In nature these include bud mutation (sporting), cross-pollination of unlike kinds (hybridization), and natural selection among plants that do not breed "true." Plant breeders also use special means to hasten and control the development of new varieties.

Let's see what is meant by sporting, hybridization, and natural selection.

Once in a blue moon flower buds on a single branch of a tree or shrub will bear flowers and fruits quite different from those produced on other branches of that same tree or shrub. The new flowers may be of a different color, larger, or more nearly double; the new fruits may be larger or smaller, earlier or later maturing, or seedless. Such a branch is known as a bud sport or a mutant. The Washington navel orange and the pink grapefruit, for example, arose through mutation.

A mutation is caused by a hereditary, or so-called genetic, change taking place in a cell of the plant, the cell being so strategically located that it gives rise to a flower or a whole branch of this new constitution. The change being hereditary, any seeds produced in the fruits on the mutated branch can potentially transmit the new character or characters.

On the branch in question not only are the flower buds different, but also the leaf buds. A leaf bud can be removed and inserted, or budded, into the bark of another tree of the same species. This leaf bud will eventually produce a branch with fruit and flowers identical with those of the original bud sport.

Bud sporting or mutations of flower color are rather common in ornamental plants. Many of our finest camellias, carnations, gardenias, and roses arose as bud sports. With certain plants we can even forecast the shade of color that will appear in bud sporting. White chrysanthemums, for instance, invariably produce yellow sports, and pink chrysanthemums frequently produce white ones.

No one really knows how or why bud sports or mutations arise in nature. All we know is that they start in the meristematic, or actively growing, tissue of the bud.

Back in 1945, for example, Carl Frey, a florist of Lima, Ohio, while tending a large planting of HAHN'S SELF-BRANCHING IVY noticed one plant with two extra-large leaves at the tip of a branch. His curiosity piqued, he set this plant aside and later made leaf cuttings from the two abnormal leaves. When the cuttings were rooted, Mr. Frey found that the new plants produced leaves of the same unusual form and, instead of growing in the loose-leaf arrangement common to ivies, they overlapped one another so that the plant looked like wide plaited garlands. GARLAND seemed to be a natural name for the new plant. It has since proved to be an unusually "tough" ivy for difficult situations. Incidentally, SPOTLIGHT, the very latest sport of GARLAND, is so new that not enough plants have yet been propagated to make it generally available. Its form is even more unusual than that of GARLAND.

When a change occurs early in the development of the bud, virtually all cells will be altered. The branch developing from these cells will also be different and we will have a normal bud sport or mutation.

On the other hand, if the change occurs late in the bud development, only a part of the cells will be different and a part keep their original character. A branch arising from such a bud will thus contain some tissues that are changed and some that are like the original. A branch containing two different kinds of tissue is known as a chimera. Some natural chimeras are the variegated black elderberry (*Sambucus nigra aureo-variegata*) and the Japanese spindle tree (*Euonymous japonica argenteo-variegata*). The former has leaves variegated with yellow, and the latter leaves edged and marked with white.

Chimeras can also be artificially produced. This is done by cutting back a vigorously growing stem of one species and inserting a stem of another species into the tissue thus exposed. When the two tissues have grown together at their point of contact, the upper part, or the scion, as it's called, is cut back and the new buds, or so-called adventitious shoots, will arise at the point where the two tissues united. Such buds will contain tissues of both species of plants and hence form a chimera. A goodly number of chimeras have been formed by this method.

One of the earliest was a tomato-eggplant chimera produced in

1910 having characteristics of both parents on the same branch. A few other artificial chimeras and the original species used to form them include: purple laburnum, *Laburnocytisus Adamii* from *Cytisus purpureus* and *Laburnum anagyroides,* with purplish flowers of *C. purpureus* and growth habit of *L. anagyroides;* and a peach-almond chimera, *Prunus Amygdalo-persica,* from *Amygdalus communis* and *A. persica,* with leaves similar to almond but more sharply serrate, and large pink flowers and fruits more closely resembling peaches than almonds.

Another way new varieties arise is by cross-pollination, already mentioned in the discussion of how a new rose is developed. In nature insects, wind, and other agents do much of the cross-pollinating. Some of our best-known fruits, like the CONCORD grape and the ELBERTA peach resulted from such natural hybridization without man's assistance.

Cross-pollination played a part too in the unusual history of the MORAINE LOCUST (Plant Patent 836), one of our best shade trees. Its development, however, did not just happen, but was helped along by a farsighted individual, John Siebenthaler of Dayton, Ohio. In the late 1920s he began to look for a substitute for the American elm, which was dying from a mysterious malady then known as the "Dayton Jitters" and now known to be a virus-caused disease called phloem necrosis.

Mr. Siebenthaler looked especially carefully at the genus *Gleditsia,* the honey locust, because he knew this tree thrived over a wide range of environmental conditions, including the polluted air of our larger cities. Moreover, he knew it was not particular whether its soil was acid or alkaline.

John Siebenthaler and his brother George began to collect seeds from thornless honey locusts with desirable forms. Included was one large, old tree[1] in Dayton, then listed in "The Hall of Fame for Trees" and which the late Dr. E. H. (Chinese) Wilson of the Arnold Arboretum suggested in 1929 might well be used as a parent for the development of an even more desirable shade tree.

By 1930 the Siebenthalers had several thousand seedlings ready for transplanting. Those which developed thorns were ruthlessly discarded. Some young, seemingly thornless seedlings did not develop thorns until their fifth or sixth year. These, too, were discarded. Trees that produced fruits were also discarded because the Siebenthalers

---

[1] This tree has since died. It showed 327 annual rings when cut down.

considered pod production an undesirable characteristic for their "ideal" tree for lawns and for planting along city streets.

Only thirty of the original thousands were left by 1940, and by 1945 only five trees remained which conformed to the rigid standards set up by the Siebenthalers. The oldest of these five trees was fifteen years old and none produced either thorns or fruits.

In 1947, twenty years after the hunt began, the shapeliest of the five survivors was named the MORAINE LOCUST, and in May 1949 it was granted a U.S. plant patent. Here was a honey locust that was thornless, bore only male flowers and hence could not produce pods, and had a desirable shape for use on lawns or for planting along city streets.

Columbus Day 1954 was a memorable day for me because it was on that day that George Siebenthaler showed me the parent MORAINE LOCUST tree growing in all its majesty on a front lawn in a residential section of Dayton. (Illustration following page 64)

This parent, termed by one writer "Mother of Millions," is no longer used to supply budwood. It can now rest on its laurels, thanks to the keen eyes and persistence of the Siebenthalers. Today the budwood needed for producing more trees is taken from some of its offspring and is then budded into the upper parts of thornless honey locust rootstocks grown from seed.

Though the Siebenthalers depended on natural crossing or hybridization to form new plants and then proceeded to save only the most desirable individuals thus formed, the professional plant breeder can manipulate certain crosses at will to produce new individuals. But before anyone, whether professional or amateur gardener, embarks on a plant-hybridizing project, in which pollen from one flower is applied to the pistil of another of the same species, he must know something about flowers and pollen production.

Some vegetables, like corn, and a few ornamentals, like fibrous-rooted begonias, produce separate male and female flowers. But most ornamental plants carry both sexes in the same flowers. The petunia, for example, has flowers with 5 male stamens, their anthers containing white or bluish pollen, surrounding the female pistil, which is topped by its sticky stigma. The ovary containing tiny ovules, which become seeds, is located at its base.

The pollen from a flower may reach the stigma of its own pistil or the stigma of some other flower on the same plant. But in hybridizing, the gardener may apply the pollen to the pistil of an entirely different variety of petunia. The seed that forms is known as F_1—or first filial generation—seed, and plants raised from such seed are called F_1 hybrids.

To be sure that true F_1 hybrids will form, several precautions must be taken. The larger petunia flower buds must be opened carefully and the pollen-bearing anthers removed before the pollen matures and accidentally fertilizes the pistil in the same flower. Moreover, after the pistil has been hand-pollinated from a different species, it should be covered with a small paper bag or glassine envelope to prevent wind and insects from bringing unwanted pollen to the stigma.

The very large, fluffy, double petunias that have become such garden favorites in recent years are F_1 hybrids that have been produced by using pollen from a special type of full-petaled double petunia on the pistil of a single-flowered variety.

Next time you start to complain about the high price of F_1 hybrid petunia, snapdragon, tomato, or cucumber seeds, stop and think what must be done to produce them.

F_1 hybrids do not breed true. Because of this, one should not expect all seeds from such hybrids to produce plants resembling their parent. Rather such seeds will make plants that resemble one grandparent or the other, or intermediate forms of the two grandparents, or some which even resemble the F_1 parent.

These offspring of the F_1 are called the F_2 generation. From F_2 hybrids, however, the plant breeder can often fix the new combinations of desirable inherited characters so that they are retained permanently.

Where the male and female flowers are distinctly separate, as on corn plants, the job of producing hybrids is much simpler. All the plant breeder needs to do is to cut off the tassels, which are the pollen-bearing organs at the top of the plant, before the pollen ripens. This will prevent the corn plant from pollinating its own flowers via the corn silks at the upper end of each ear. Such pollenless plants can then be pollinated from a pollen-bearing variety selected by the plant hybridizer.

Professional plant breeders and many commercial growers of flowers and vegetables are always on the lookout for new color breaks, new flower forms, or more vigorous plants.

The chance discovery of a new flower color may give rise to a whole new group of plants. Once again the petunia serves an excellent example. In 1938 a salmon-pink petunia, SALMON SUPREME, was introduced to gardeners. Plants of this variety were weak and produced few seeds, but the color was unusual. Today at least a dozen well-known and improved varieties trace part of their parentage to it. Among the descendants of SALMON SUPREME are CHEERFUL, GYPSY, SILVER MEDAL, TANGO, FIRE CHIEF, and COMANCHE.

Marigolds, too, have been greatly improved in recent years because of the sudden appearance of an individual that differed from its neighbors. A marigold with chrysanthemum-like flowers was introduced in 1930 under the name DIXIE SUNSHINE. It could be grown only in the South because it required a very long growing season to produce flowers. But soon an early-flowering form with the same kind of flowers was found. Neither of these varieties is available today, but both were the forerunners of the large-flowered marigolds now on the market which include such popular kinds as GOLDSMITH, LIMESTONE, YELLOWSTONE, and GLITTERS.

Because a new color may crop up at any time, the W. Atlee Burpee Seed Company several years ago offered a $10,000 prize to anyone who finds a pure white flower on a plant of MAN-IN-THE-MOON. (Illustration following page 64) This strain of marigold normally produces creamy white flowers and it is entirely possible that a pure white individual will be discovered some day. Up to the present writing, however, no one has come forth to claim the $10,000 prize.

Drugs Help in Plant Breeding

There are times when the plant breeder cannot obtain seeds from a plant with which he is working because the plant is sterile. Any plant that fails to set seeds with its own pollen is said to be self-sterile, and one that will not set seeds with the pollen from another plant of the same kind is said to be cross-sterile. The plant breeder is hard put to make use of such sterile plants unless he finds a way to overcome their inability to set seeds. One way he can do this in some plants is to use certain plant hormones. In the self-sterile Easter lily, for example, breeders have produced seeds by applying an ointment of 1 per cent naphthalene acetamide to the stigma.

Plant hormones have also been used successfully to cross two plants belonging to different species. Scientists at the John Innes Horticultural Institute in England produced the first sexual hybrids between pears and apples by this method. They first removed the stamens from the flowers of a pear tree, variety FERTILITY, and then brushed the pistil in each flower with a dilute solution of beta-naphthoxy-acetic acid at the rate of 40 parts per million parts of water. Next they placed pollen from the apple variety CRAWLEY BEAUTY on the pistil, and twenty-four hours later made another treatment with the hormone.

The young plants grown from seeds produced by this treatment were found to have characters midway between pears and apples. So far as I know, no fruits have yet been produced by this unusual cross because not enough time has elapsed for fruit production. Apple trees usually require seven to nine years to produce fruits from seed, and pears three years or so.

Occasionally it is possible to cross two plants belonging to different genera without the use of plant hormones or any special techniques. These are known as intergeneric crosses and are rather common in the orchid family.

Among the commonly available ornamental plants, perhaps the most famous offspring of two different genera is *Fatshedera Lizei*, popularly known as California ivy, even though it was not developed in California nor is it an ivy. *F. Lizei* is a natural hybrid between the half-hardy shrub, a variety of the Japanese Fatsia, *Fatsia japonica moseri*, and the Irish ivy, *Hedera Helix hibernica*. It is known as a bigeneric hybrid, that is, its parents belong to two distinctly different genera, whereas the ordinary hybrid is a cross between two species within the same genus.

Man can also produce plant mutations with X rays, with heat, and with such drugs as colchicine. These methods usually double the number of chromosomes, that is, the materials inside living cells which harbor the hereditary characters that are passed from one generation to the next. Plants with double the normal number of chromosomes are known as tetraploids or "tetras." As a rule they are larger and have larger flowers than their parents. Tetra marigolds and snapdragons are listed in many seed catalogues today.

Pretesting New Plants

All over America in hundreds of seed trial gardens new varieties of flowers and vegetables, as well as many of the older sorts, are tested each year. Some are at state agricultural colleges and experiment stations, others are on farms operated by seed-producing firms, and still others are in municipal and privately owned parks.

Many of these trial gardens are also official All-America test gardens, where new flowers and vegetables are carefully judged by experts under all kinds of growing conditions. Best known and most widely publicized are the twenty or so All-America Rose Gardens in different parts of the country. For test of any new rose variety four plants are submitted to each of the official gardens, grown for two years, and then judged by qualified rose experts. Roses that receive a favorable rating from at least two thirds of the judges automatically become All-America selections. Such roses must be superior to roses already commercially available, in color, growth habit, vigor, hardiness, or other points of garden performance.

Forty-three roses received the All-America Award from the start of the All-America rose testing in 1939 to 1955. No award was made in 1951 because no rose was considered good enough to merit it.

All-America testing of certain flower and vegetable varieties started in 1932. The most recent flowers to be included in the tests are gladioli in 1953 and camellias in 1951. Eventually almost all the new kinds of horticultural plants will probably be pretested and rated before they are offered to farmers and gardeners.

Of course, many seeds and plants offered to gardeners each year are neither pretested in trial gardens nor patented. This does not mean they are inferior. In fact, many non-patented plants are superior to similar kinds to which patents have been issued.

Growers of certain plants, such as gladioli, begonias, or chrysanthemums, who do not wish to obtain patents may register the names of their new introductions with their respective national societies. Once the name is duly registered, there is less likelihood that it will be used for the same kind of plant by another person. Although registration does not eliminate this possibility, it is a strong moral deterrent.

The Section of Plant Introduction, formerly called the Division of Plant Exploration and Introduction, of the United States Department of Agriculture, is another important agency that has brought brand-new plants to farmers and gardeners and also has introduced plants with "new blood" to improve yields and quality, and to increase disease resistance in our older, established plants.

Directly under the supervision of this section are four Plant Introduction Gardens at Glen Dale, Maryland; Savannah, Georgia; Coconut Grove, Florida; and Chico, California. In these gardens new plants are held in quarantine for two years after their arrival. To be sure that no new insect pests are brought into this country, many of the new plants are grown in completely screened greenhouses or outdoor areas.

More recently four regional plant introduction stations servicing twelve states have been set up at Geneva, New York; Experiment, Georgia; Pullman, Washington; and Ames, Iowa. These stations work closely with the United States Department of Agriculture's Section of Plant Introduction.

Nearly all crops introduced by the federal division are first tested at the regional garden where the plant appears most likely to succeed. The first step is to evaluate the plant as to adaptation and resistance to diseases and insects. Once an introduced plant is found to have possibilities—for example, if a new wheat shows high resistance to the destructive rust disease and appears to have something to offer in a breeding program—then a supply of seeds from this variety is gathered and placed in storage to fill orders from wheat plant breeders.

Perhaps the most important function of the plant introduction stations is to help develop new strains and varieties of crops already established, because disease resistance and higher yields are the two characters that can easily be bred into old, established crops. The introduction of the fusarium disease-resistant, little wild tomato of Peru, *Lycopersicon pimpinellifolium,* for example, has enabled plant breeders to transfer this resistance to a half dozen commercial tomato varieties.

The chances of introducing new kinds of crops are less favorable, although such widely planted forage crops as soybeans, sorghum, and Sudan grass were originally introduced by such agencies from other parts of the world.

The introduction of new varieties of plants, whether developed by sporting, hybridization, or natural selection, is a source of ever increasing pleasure to American gardeners.

Chapter 8

PLANT PROPAGATION

Because most varieties of ornamental and fruit trees do not come true from seed they must be propagated vegetatively, that is, from cuttings, by budding or grafting, or by soil or air-layering. Plants propagated in this way will have the same characteristics as the parent plant, whereas those grown from seed might or might not have them.

Although cuttings, buds, and grafts have been used in many ways since ancient times, new aids and refinements in recent years assure more successful rooting and make the job much easier than formerly.

Plant hormones in powdered or liquid form applied to the lower end of difficult-to-root cuttings not only speed root development but increase the number and size of roots as well. Plant-propagating boxes have automatic heat and light controls that require little attention once the cuttings are inserted and the electric switch is turned on. New and more effective rooting and seed-sowing media assure speedy and healthy root development. Electric cables embedded in the propagating medium provide bottom heat to speed root development in cuttings. Automatic mist sprayers permit the rooting of softwood cuttings in direct sunlight. Finally, and perhaps most interesting of all, plastic sheets make it possible for the novice to get roots on plants heretofore propagated only with difficulty by professional growers with years of experience.

Root-Inducing Hormones

The use of plant-growth substances to speed the rooting of cuttings is now an accepted practice among gardeners. Commercial preparations containing the effective ingredients, indolebutyric acid or naphthalene acetic acid, are now widely available. Two that I have used over the past five years are sold under names HORMODIN and ROOTONE. HORMODIN comes in three strengths: No. 1 is a general-purpose powder for rooting carnations, geraniums, and many other house plants; No. 2 is a bit stronger and is used on woody and semi-woody plants; No. 3 is the strongest powder, for rooting many evergreen and dormant leafless cuttings.

Application of the rooting powders is simple. All the gardener needs to do is wet the lower end of the cutting momentarily in water and then dip it in the hormone powder and shake off the excess. The cutting is then stuck into the rooting medium in the regular way. (Illustration following page 160) Where there is a chance that the rooting medium is fungus-infested, it is wise to mix a small quantity of the rooting powder with an equal amount of some fungicide like ARASAN, FERMATE, or PHYGON XL before applying it to the cuttings.

Additional details on the use of hormone rooting powders come with the package. The gardener must not expect the use of these powders to take the place of good, long-established propagating practices. The cuttings must still be handled with care and must be watched until they have rooted and are ready for transplanting.

Another way, I have found, of speeding root development is to dip the whole cutting in a nutrient solution.

Several years ago while working on tests made to determine certain facts about feeding plants through the leaves, I decided to see what would happen to cuttings if they were dipped in a nutrient solution before they were placed in a rooting medium.

I made tip cuttings of a wide variety of plants. Some I dipped for a minute or two in a dilute solution of RAPIDGRO. Then I stuck them in sand or a mixture of sand and peat. Others I dipped in plain water for the same length of time and then stuck them into the same kind of rooting material.

To my surprise, the cuttings dipped in RAPIDGRO solution rooted faster and in greater numbers than the untreated cuttings. Moreover, the treated cuttings made additional growth sooner.

The strength of the solution used as a dip was 1 ounce of RAPIDGRO in 6 quarts of water.

Among plants that responded favorably to the prerooting dip were: *Arabis,* LADY MAC begonia, boxwood, *Fuchsia,* geranium, heliotrope, Baltic ivy, English ivy, *Lantana,* and several species of *Euonymous.*

Although I did not combine this treatment with the hormone powder treatment of the lower end of the cutting, I see no reason why the two treatments cannot be combined. Adventurous gardeners might like to try dipping the cuttings first in a nutrient solution for a few moments and then dipping the lower end into a rooting powder prior to inserting it in the rooting medium. I believe the combined treatment ought to work better than either one alone.

Rooting and Seed-Starting Media

The up-to-date gardener no longer has to depend on sand or a mixture of sand and peat to root cuttings or on soil to start seedlings. Disease-free or disease-preventing materials are now widely available for these purposes.

One of the best materials for rooting cuttings is mica that has been puffed up under extremely high temperatures much as puffed wheat is "exploded." This "exploded" mica was first sold under the name VERMICULITE and is now also available as TERRA-LITE VER-MICULITE and MICA-GRO. The material comes in several sizes for specific uses, such as rooting cuttings and sowing seeds.

The newest material for use as a rooting medium is a white multi-cellular plastic sold as STYROFOAM by the Dow Chemical Company, Midland, Michigan.

A natural or nonsynthetic material excellent for starting seedlings is sphagnum moss. How to use it to avoid damping-off disease of seedings has already been described at the beginning of *Chapter 2,* on ANNUALS, PERENNIALS, AND BULBS.

Glen Dale Plant Propagator

When Dr. Vernon T. Stoutemyer, at present head of the Department of Floriculture and Ornamental Horticulture at the University of California in Los Angeles, was employed by the United States Department of Agriculture, he developed a remarkable contrivance for propagating plants in the average home. First known as the Glen Dale Plant Propagator, this is a box on stilts with fluorescent lights built in the lid. Unlike a regular green house, it has no glass and requires no adjustments of lighting, ventilation, or watering.

Here is how it operates. Standard-size greenhouse flats are filled with VERMICULITE or some other suitable rooting medium, which is thoroughly wetted. The flats are placed in the propagator, the cuttings are inserted in the rooting medium, the lights are turned on, and the lid is closed. If all goes well, the cuttings will be rooted within a few weeks.

The most critical aspect of operating these miniature greenhouses is correct watering. Usually, if the VERMICULITE or other rooting medium has been wetted down thoroughly at the start, there is no need for further watering until the cuttings have been rooted. Aside from occasional examination to see whether water is needed, the plant propagator is left to itself if it stands in the cellar or some other place in which the temperature stays around 70 to 75 degrees in summer and does not fall below 50 degrees in winter.

The heat which the fluorescent tubes give off is negligible, but if the surrounding temperature goes much above 80 degrees, even the small amount of heat from the lights may be critical. Under such conditions the box will have to be opened from time to time.

The Glen Dale Propagator is now available as a factory-made unit under the name START-A-PLANT. (Illustration following page 192)

Rooting Cuttings under Mist

An extremely effective way to root softwood cuttings is by use of either continuous mist or interrupted mist over the cuttings during the rooting period. The method is now widely used by many professional plant growers and even by a few home gardeners who like to root their own cuttings.

The mist method substitutes a fine spray of water for shade, thus permitting the rooting of softwood cuttings in full sunlight. The cool, fine mist prevents wilting and burning of the cuttings and, because of the greater amount of light, enables the cuttings to form roots more quickly. Some of the more difficult-to-root varieties and even some that cannot be rooted by ordinary methods are now being rooted under mist. Surprising as it may seem, leaf diseases do not develop under the constantly wet conditions. On the other hand, rots and leaf spots are common in the old-fashioned sweatboxes that require heavy shade and glass enclosures.

The earliest records of rooting cuttings in open beds under constant mist were made in 1936 by G. E. L. Spencer at the Imperial College of Tropical Agriculture, Trinidad. He successfully rooted cacao cuttings.

One of the first reports of open-frame mist propagation of a northern woody plant was made by Edgar S. Diehl, who rooted 90 per cent of five thousand American holly cuttings in 1951. The late Dr. David Fairchild, author of *The World Was My Garden,* also was an early user of this method.

In using the new open mist method, gardeners must abandon most of their old ideas on rooting cuttings. The spot where the propagating bed is to be set up should be the hottest and sunniest available. Moreover, the water source must be completely dependable, because if the water supply fails for as little as fifteen minutes, the cuttings may be lost.

More recently a number of investigators have found that constant mist is not necessary and that cuttings root faster and have a better root system when subjected to an interrupted mist, such as one minute of mist then two or three minutes with none.

The interrupted mist method is said to be superior to continuous mist because less water is used and the temperature of the rooting medium is higher and thus more favorable for rooting.

Another advantage of the interrupted mist is that the cuttings can be hardened off more easily simply by spacing the off-and-on periods of mist at wider intervals, a procedure not possible under the continuous mist method.

Less water means a lower water cost and a simpler drainage problem.

Perhaps the ultimate in a fully automatic, interrupted mist system is the PHYTOTEKTOR, developed by Harvey Templeton, Jr., of Winchester, Tennessee, which roots softwood cuttings directly in the soil. (Illustration following page 160)

The PHYTOTEKTOR unit consists of a wire frame covered with a large sheet of polyethylene plastic film, the shape resembling a miniature quonset hut. The plastic film provides temporary protection to the cuttings from sun and wind while roots are forming. Beneath the plastic covering nozzles are operated automatically by a so-called electronic "leaf," which turns on the mistlike spray when the leaves are dry and turns it off when they are wet. The electronic "leaf" is merely a small piece of plastic with two contact points. As long as there is a continuous film of water between the two points, no mist flows from the nozzles. As soon as the film dries, contact is broken and the current is turned on automatically to form mist. An almost constant film of moisture is thus maintained on the leaves of the cuttings with this relatively simple apparatus. The electronic leaf, by the way, is sold by Electronic Mist Control Company, Ithaca, New York.

After the cuttings are rooted, the entire PHYTOTEKTOR unit is lifted and moved to a new location to start a new batch of cuttings. The rooted cuttings are left in the open in full sun to continue growth and to "harden off" until they are ready for transplanting to a nursery row or a permanent location.

The manufacturers of PHYTOTEKTOR also make the MISTIC BUBBLE, a small, inexpensive model for home gardeners.

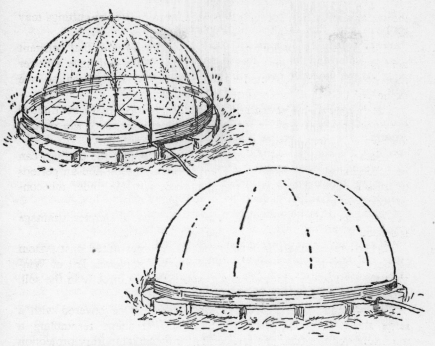

The MISTIC BUBBLE *is of great help to gardeners who root cuttings: The apparatus is sketched as it appears just before cuttings are inserted into the rooting medium; and after the cuttings are inserted and the mist is turned on, the* MISTIC BUBBLE *is covered with a plastic film which is left on until the cuttings form roots.*

A simpler propagating unit, for amateur gardeners, has been developed by L. F. Lipp formerly of the Arnold Arboretum. Following, in Mr. Lipp's own words, is the way to set up the unit:

"A deep greenhouse flat is filled with sand, vermiculite, or a mixture of sand, peat moss and 'Styrofoam.' For cuttings which root easily, sharp sand or vermiculite will do. For more difficult material a mixture is made up of seventy per cent peat, ten per cent sharp clean sand and twenty per cent 'Styrofoam.' This styrene plastic comes finely shredded from a florist supply house. The hard or soft wood cuttings are treated with a hormone powder and set in the flat. The cuttings then should be watered well. Next a wire frame is made over the flat for a frame-work to support a damp cheesecloth covering. Over the cheesecloth is placed a sheet of the semi-transparent polyethylene film large enough to tuck under the sides, ends and bottom of the flat. This plastic has the unexpected quality of checking loss of water and yet permits the cuttings to 'breathe.' The cheesecloth spreads the moisture evenly in the flat and adds a little shade for the cuttings.

"When completed, the propagation unit can be placed on a green-house bench or in a window of a dwelling. During the late spring and summer the unit can be placed under a tree or in the shade of a building. With this method, the unit does not need to be watered for weeks or even months if well sealed; in fact, more than one watering may even be harmful! If placed in a greenhouse or sunny window it should be shaded by a newspaper during hot sunny days of summer. It is incredible how 'domesticated' the cuttings become, growing green and turgid in what seems a natural habitat.

"Once the cuttings are adequately rooted, care must be taken, for they must not be subjected to extreme changes in atmosphere. Remove framework of wires and cheesecloth, then replace the plastic film over the cuttings and during excessive hot days place a newspaper shade over the film to prevent burning of cuttings. Perhaps it was a coinci-dence, but we are highly pleased to find by leaving the plastic on for a considerable time, azaleas and rhododendrons will break dormancy earlier. This alone has been a disturbing factor for many nurserymen. When the cuttings are well hardened, they can be planted in a cold-frame, lath house or nursery. The use of 'Styrofoam' gives the essen-tial insurance of air in the rooting mixture over a long period. These small particles of plastic help eliminate the problem of over-watering the cuttings. Cuttings may be left in the peat mixture to develop into rugged plants. A dilute nutrient solution should be added to this mixture for some species, to prevent chlorosis, since corrections are exceedingly slow once the deficiency appears. Many propagators have had considerable experience with decay of soft wood cuttings due to fungus growth. A good rule to safeguard cuttings is to add a small amount of 'Fermate' to the rooting powder. With this principle and worthwhile precaution, a never-ending list of difficult plants has been rooted by the writer. Over and above the scores of plants that have been rooted, apples, *Betula pumila, Cotinus coggygria atropurpurea, Taxus baccata fructu-luteo,* and *Daphne altaica* have also been grown from cuttings with this method. And along with this, we are receiving gratifying letters from amateur propagators who have also had remark-able results."

Propagation by Layering

Layering is another method to propagate difficult-to-root plants. The method is based on the fact that roots will develop on woody stems if the stem is first wounded and the wounded portion is kept moist and free from infections.

In soil-layering, a wounded section of a stem while still attached to the parent plant is bent below the soil surface for a long enough time to allow roots to form in the wounded area. Once roots are formed, the rooted stem is detached from the parent and planted in another location.

Air-layering, in which the roots are forced to develop above-ground, is more popular and easier to carry out than is soil-layering. The practice of air-layering is far from new. The Chinese used the method more than two thousand years ago, but the practice has been greatly simplified and the chances of success greatly increased by the development of Krene plastic film, sold under the trade name AIR-WRAP. AIRWRAP kits, available in seed and horticultural supply stores, contain all the materials needed to air-layer woody stems and even to root herbaceous cuttings.

The use of plastic film for air-layering was first developed by the late Colonel William R. Grove of Laurel, Florida. The method has been further improved by DeWitt Eaton of Sarasota, Florida, who holds the patent on the use of plastic film for air-layering. Mr. Eaton has combined rooting hormones, plant nutrients, and pesticides into a water-soluble "ink" which is dyed green and printed in green strips on the Krene plastic film.

As with most newly introduced products, plastic film for air-layering has been improperly used at times and, consequently, has failed to produce roots. At other times the failure has been due to the use of excessively thick stems, to improper slitting or girdling of the stem, or to the use of overwet sphagnum.

It is possible to air-layer any woody plant grown indoors in the North, or such difficult-to-root outdoor plants as hybrid camellias, crotons, hibiscus, and gardenias in the South.

I have successfully air-layered woody stems of both indoor and outdoor plants and would like to pass on these experiences to my readers.

But first let me say that it is far simpler to air-layer plants indoors than outdoors. I'll give the reasons for this later.

How to Air-Layer Indoors

Among the house plants most commonly air-layered are dracaenas, philodendrons, dieffenbachias, and rubber plants—those which have reached the ceiling or have become leggy or unsightly.

After the plant to be air-layered is selected, the first step is to wound the stem at the point where roots are desired. This is done with a sharp knife, either by making a longitudinal cut upward for an inch or so into the center of the branch, or by removing a complete circle of bark about ½ inch wide from the stem. The slit portion or the barkless area is then rubbed with the green-striped plastic. In slit stems a wooden matchstick or a small bit of moistened sphagnum moss should be inserted between the cut surfaces to prevent closing and healing of the cut. (Illustration following page 160)

The whole area, including an inch or so of the stem on both sides of the wound is then wrapped with a handful of moistened, but not dripping wet, sphagnum moss. Squeeze out all excess moisture of the moss beforehand.

Finally, a sheet of AIRWRAP plastic film is wrapped carefully over the ball of sphagnum with the upper and lower ends twisted around the stem and securely tied. In wrapping and tying the plastic, see that the moss is well contained and that no openings remain in the film.

The wound made on the stem interrupts the downward movement of plant foods and hormones formed by the plant. This sets up a stimulus which leads to formation of callus tissue and development of roots at the upper zone of injury.

The several ingredients incorporated in the green stripes on the plastic film are believed to be helpful in initiating root development and in providing raw food elements and some prophylactic aid. The green stripes, by the way, are soluble and will stain the fingers if gloves are not worn. But it is easy to remove the dye by dipping the fingers in a mixture of 1 part CLOROX and 2 parts of water and then washing them in soapy water.

The purpose of the sphagnum is to keep the atmosphere around the wound moist and otherwise favorable for root development.

Finally, the Krene plastic film keeps the moisture sealed in and eliminates the need for ever wetting the moss. At the same time it allows gases to move freely in and out of the air-layer.

It is easy to see when roots have formed because the plastic covering is fairly transparent.

Once the roots have formed on the stem, the job of producing the new plant is only half done. The stem must be cut from the parent plant just below the rooted area and then potted. The new plant must be set in the shade and away from drafts for at least two weeks to allow the roots to become accustomed to the new medium.

Air-Layering Outdoor Plants

Late spring and early summer are the best times to air-layer stems of trees and shrubs outdoors. Not only do roots develop more quickly and more abundantly at these seasons, but the rooted stems have ample time to become established as plants long before cool weather arrives.

The first step is to select a healthy branch ¼ to ½ inch in diameter that will make a shapely plant. Side shoots, leaves, twigs, thorns, or other appendages should be removed for 3 inches above and below the point where roots are desired. This will allow ample space for the air-layer. Wound the stem and apply sphagnum and the AIRWRAP plastic cover in the same way as for indoor plants.

Air-layering of outdoor plants is frequently less successful, however, for several reasons. Appreciation of this fact and the reasons for it may help gardeners avoid failures.

The temperature and humidity outdoors fluctuate far more than they do indoors, particularly around air-layers that are exposed to direct sunlight.

The sphagnum moss is more likely to become waterlogged outdoors, especially if the ends of the plastic cover are not closed tight. A heavy rain will force water between the twisted ends of the wrap. Excessive moisture in the sphagnum, particularly early in the rooting stage, is decidedly detrimental to root formation. To minimize the chances of getting excessive amounts of water into the air-layer, I have successfully used SCOTCH ELECTRICAL TAPE, which, according to Dr. Donald Wyman of the Arnold Arboretum, was originally suggested by James M. Rooney of Attleboro, Massachusetts. This tape, which sticks well and is waterproof, should be attached to the bare branch above the upper end of the plastic wrap and then gradually spiraled downward to completely close the top end of the wrap.

One disadvantage of using an inflexible tie, such as tape, is that it may girdle a rapidly expanding stem if it is left in place for more than a few months.

In addition to water seepage into the sphagnum ball during heavy rains, some failures are caused by the use of overwet sphagnum at the time the air-layer is made. Let me say again that the sphagnum moss must be moist but not dripping wet when the air-layer is prepared.

Slitting the stem of outdoor trees or shrubs prior to applying the sphagnum and its plastic cover frequently weakens the distal portion of the branch. To reduce the possibility of breakage by wind, it is wise to apply a splint as a support.

Once the roots are well developed and are visible through the transparent plastic cover, detach the rooted stem at once, or the sphagnum will dry out. If a delay is unavoidable, loosen the upper end of the plastic cover and add water. Once the roots are formed, an excess of water in the sphagnum does not appear to be harmful.

I cannot overemphasize the fact that even when the roots are well developed on the stem the job of producing a new tree or shrub is only half done! Extreme care must be exercised from this point on far more than the plants that are air-layered indoors and kept indoors after they are detached from the parent plant.

Before severing the newly rooted stem from the parent, it is wise to remove half of its leaves. This step will increase its chances of survival. As with air-layered stems of indoor plants, the newly rooted stem is severed just below the rooted zone and the plastic cover is removed. The new plant is then put in a pot of soil or in a moist but not wet spot in the garden. In either case, the new plant must be kept away from direct sunlight and from drafts for several weeks, or long enough to allow the roots to become accustomed to the soil and to make more growth.

In addition to removing half of the leaves after roots have formed and before the rooted stem is severed, I have found that wilting can be prevented and the chances of successful transplanting increased by spraying the leaves or dipping them in a diluted solution of WILT-PRUF, a water-miscible plastic especially developed for reducing water loss in newly transplanted trees and shrubs.

Despite all the precautions that must be taken, air-layering is lots of fun and is remarkably rewarding. In my work on this method I found that the London plane, *Platanus acerifolia,* New York City's most widely planted street tree, is one of the easiest trees to root by air-layers. Well-developed roots form on stems up to ¾ inch in diameter two to three weeks after the stems are wounded and the moss and AIRWRAP plastic are applied.

Other woody plants my assistant John Walther or I rooted easily during the late spring and summer of 1954 by means of air-layers included *Abelia, Albizzia,* arborvitae, azaleas, barberries, *Callicarpa, Camellia, Colutea,* cotoneasters, *Deutzia, Forsythia, Gardenia,* hollies, *Itea,* lilac, *Mahonia, Magnolia,* mulberry, *Philadelphus, Pieris, Pyracantha,* pussywillow, *Rhododendron,* roses, Russian olive, *Staphylea, Symphoricarpus, Tamarix,* viburnums, *Weigela,* Winesap apple, and yews.

Lest some of my readers conclude that we no longer have any plant propagation problems, may I point out that we were not successful in rooting every branch we air-layered. Some of our outstanding failures were with *Cryptomeria japonica;* climbing hydrangea, *Hydrangea petiolaris;* and pink dogwood, *Cornus florida rubra.* But even though we failed to get roots on these plants, Dr. Donald Wyman, horticulturist at the Arnold Arboretum, reported that he was successful with some of these and many others as well.

Incidentally, anyone interested in becoming a real expert at propagating plants might consider joining the Plant Propagators Society. Edward H. Scanlon of Olmstead Falls, Ohio, is Secretary-Treasurer.

Other Ways to Use Plastic Sheets

Another interesting adaptation of plastic sheeting in plant propagation is called the PLASTIC PLANT WIGWAM by Victor J. McNitt of Sherburne, New York, its inventor.

This method differs from the others already described in that it permits the grafting of choice, difficult-to-root plants either out in the open or indoors. The proper grade of plastic sheeting capable of confining moisture but allowing gases to move in and out is used to completely cover and confine the grafted portions. No grafting wax is necessary over the area where the two kinds of plants are joined. It is necessary only to tie the two parts securely with plastic tape before covering with the "wigwam."

The old-fashioned way of increasing the supply of valuable evergreens that could not be rooted from cuttings involves, first, potting and growing the understock plants; second, forcing them into growth out of season, usually in February; third, grafting and waxing the desirable kinds of plants, or the scion, on these. Then the grafted plants are placed in relatively confined benches until the two parts have united. Finally the upper part of the understock is "snagged" or cut off to permit the scion to grow into the desired tree. All of these steps are beset with such dangers as failure to "knit," fungus infections, and drying out. Only a person with long experience and proper facilities can successfully graft a large portion of the plants so handled.

The PLASTIC PLANT WIGWAM eliminates most of these pitfalls and assures a goodly percentage of successful grafts even in the hands of a novice. The stock plant can be grown outdoors in the usual manner, in the garden or even on the lawn. A small piece of the desired variety is then grafted on this stock plant by any of the standard techniques. If the stock plant is very small, the PLASTIC WIGWAM is placed over both the stock and scion and securely fastened at the ground level to prevent moisture loss. If the stock plant is too large, the PLASTIC WIGWAM is placed over the scion and that part of the understock branch to which it is joined. It is then securely tied and closed on the stock but below the graft. A piece of muslin is placed over the PLASTIC WIGWAM to reduce the light and to keep the atmosphere cool inside the wigwam.

After the union takes place, the PLASTIC WIGWAM is opened gradually to introduce more air and to harden the growth. The procedure from this point on is the same as with the ordinary methods. With this method, Mr. McNitt has succeeded in grafting a number of plants that are considered extremely difficult, if not impossible, to propagate by any other known methods.

Dr. Henry Teuscher of the Montreal Botanic Garden has successfully grafted conifers on small potted trees outdoors by the so-called "approach grafting" technique. He, too, made use of plastic sheeting, but in a different way. To keep the young understock trees moist, the pots in which they were growing were first covered with sphagnum moss, then thoroughly watered, and finally completely wrapped in plastic sheeting. Stock trees handled in this way required no further care until after the graft unions had joined.

Using Plastics for Seed Germination

Where plants come true from seed, the easiest and cheapest way obviously is to grow them from seed. Plastics also play an important part where trees are grown from seed.

Some seeds like those of the CORK tree and the KATSURA tree require no special handling or pretreatment and hence can be planted immediately after they mature. Other seeds, like those of maples and hornbeams, must pass through a dormant period, just like potatoes, before they sprout. Such seed is mixed in a 50-50 mixture of moist sand and peat, placed in a polyethylene plastic bag, and put in a refrigerator at 41 degrees for three months.

Still other seeds, like those of certain cotoneasters, mountain ashes, and viburnums, must be pretreated before being placed under refrigeration. The seeds are mixed with the 50-50 sand-peat mixture and then placed in the polyethylene bags for three months at room temperature, where the day and night temperatures fluctuate from 60 to 80 degrees. After that period the bags are placed in the refrigerator again at 41 degrees for another three months. Then they are removed and planted in flats of soil. This procedure speeds the germination of certain seeds. For example, Roger G. Coggeshall, plant propagator at the Arnold Arboretum, germinated JAPANESE MOUNTAIN ASH, *Sorbus japonica,* by this method in six months, whereas the same kind of seed handled in the old-fashioned way required a year to a year and a half to sprout.

Preplanting Dips for Bulbs, Seeds, Corms, and Roots

Earlier in this chapter I described how I obtained better rooting of tip cuttings by presoaking them in a RAPIDGRO solution prior to inserting them into the rooting medium.

I also found in the same type of tests that I could get quicker come-up and more vigorous plants if I soaked certain bulbs, tubers, corms, and seeds in a complete nutrient solution just prior to planting them. (Illustration following page 160)

For example, the plants arising from dahlia tubers, gladiolus corms, lily and tulip bulbs presoaked for three hours in a solution containing 1 ounce of RAPIDGRO in a gallon of water emerged from the soil sooner and were more vigorous than plants growing from dormant parts that were merely soaked in water or not soaked at all.

Soaking seeds like tomato and pepper for several hours prior to planting them produced the same beneficial response.

I have also obtained similar striking differences with grass seed soaked in RAPIDGRO solution. The seed must be dried before it is sown. A few years ago a new section of my lawn sown with treated seed came up quicker and thicker than an adjoining area sown with untreated seed. Watering down a newly seeded lawn with a dilute nutrient solution, without presoaking the seed, will have the same beneficial effect.

I am told that wheat, corn, and oats treated with RAPIDGRO in the Pacific Northwest show a similar response. Merely soaking the wheat seeds in the solution before sowing, for example, increased yields five to seven bushels an acre.

Along the same lines a British research worker, W. O. Roberts, during World War II developed a method for economizing on fertilizers used on nutrient-deficient soils. He soaked cereal seeds in nutrient solutions containing the soil-deficient element at a sufficiently high concentration to supply most of the total requirements of the plants.

Other new developments on plant foods are presented in *Chapter 11*.

Perhaps it would be well to close this chapter with a word of caution. The gardener should bear in mind that though plastic sheeting and the other new aids described here make plant propagation easier and more rewarding, they are not a substitute for knowledge and skill in handling plant material.

Chapter 9

LAWNS AND LAWN MANAGEMENT

Every home owner takes great pride in having an attractive lawn for his house. But in the whole field of gardening nothing is more difficult to grow than a fine lawn. The reason is that millions of tiny plants crowd a confined area; this naturally makes them more susceptible to all kinds of enemies, both plant and animal.

Above and beyond these limiting factors are the widely varying conditions in different parts of the country, so that no one set of recommendations will hold for all. Take the kind of grass seed, for example; I know of no one kind that will do well in all parts of the country. It is extremely important for the gardener to use the grass varieties best adapted to his general area, for the farther a grass is removed from its native habitat, the more troubles it will have. Later in this chapter I will point out the good and bad features of the more commonly used grass varieties in the country. The gardener can get information on which of these he should plant from his state agricultural experiment station or his county agricultural agent, usually located in the county seat.

There are so many publications available on the basic steps in lawn preparation that I feel I need devote little space to this phase. I would, however, draw attention to the following precautions:

The wise lawnmaker always plants the best grades of clean, weed-free seeds. Even though they cost more per pound, they are cheapest in the long run. Bear in mind that the most expensive grass seed available rarely exceeds a tenth of the cost of making a new lawn or renovating an old one. The better grades of grass seed contain a large percentage of permanent varieties like MERION or Kentucky blue-grass, fescues, and bents rather than a lot of annual grasses.

When starting a new lawn, don't use too much seed. Some home owners have the impression that sowing large amounts of seed will make a thicker lawn, which will be free of weeds. Actually, heavy

135

seeding produces overcrowded, spindly plants that not only cannot prevent weeds from getting started but are also more subject to disease.

New Ideas on Feeding Lawns

One of the most widely abused maintenance practices is that of feeding the lawn. The fault does not lie with the home owner so much, perhaps, as with the advertisers of lawn foods and their conflicting claims.

Until recently lawn experts were agreed that a single spring feeding was not enough to maintain a healthy, vigorous lawn for an entire season. The reason was that such plant foods could supply the nitrogen for short periods only. Hence the recommendation to apply dry fertilizers like 5-10-5 in the spring and fall, or a high-analysis plant food like FOLIUM, GRO-STUF, or RAPIDGRO four or more times at periodic intervals throughout the season.

With the advent in 1955 of so-called urea-form fertilizers like BORDEN'S 38, GOLDEN VIGORO, and URAMITE (discussed in considerable detail in *Chapter 11*), which supply nitrogen to lawns over a three-month period, the whole situation may change. At this writing no one knows for sure whether or not a one-shot treatment for lawns will become standard practice.

With the older kinds of fertilizers, lawn experts are in agreement about the best time to fed the lawn. The general rule, of course, is to apply such plant foods at the time the grass can make best use of them. According to this rule, therefore, bluegrasses, fescues, and bents, which grow most during the cool parts of the season, should be fed in early spring and early fall. Bermuda, St. Augustine, and zoysia, which are most active at the higher temperatures, are best fed in summer.

Liming May Be Needed

Do not apply lime every spring just out of habit. It may be harmful to the desirable grasses and beneficial to crabgrass. The perennial grasses need a slightly acid soil, one that tests between pH 6.0 and 6.5, whereas crabgrass grows well in a neutral or alkaline soil.

The only way to be sure that the soil needs lime is to test it. Gardeners can do this themselves with any of the soil-testing kits on the market, or they can call in their county agricultural agent, the state university's soil-testing department, or a private testing service. Under average conditions in nonlimestone areas, limestone

When applying lime, fertilizer or grass seed use a Spreader for a more even and economical distribution of material.

at the rate of 5 pounds per 100 square feet should be applied once every three years.

Rolling Can Be Abused

Avoid rolling the lawn excessively. A very light rolling in spring may be worth while to press down grass plants that have heaved during the winter, but never roll the lawn to correct faults in grading. Ruts and other surface irregularities should be repaired by raising the turf and then adding to or removing some of the soil below. The light rolling should be done when the soil is just dry enough so that it crumbles easily in the fingers, never when it is wet or soggy.

Water Deep or Not at All

A top lawn expert has wisely said that watering with a hose or sprinkler is the most abused and misused lawn maintenance practice. A good lawn can be ruined within a few weeks by careless watering.

Artificial watering must be deep and thorough, rather than light and frequent. Frequent light sprinklings in hot weather benefit summer weeds more than they do the desirable grasses. Two or three deeply penetrating waterings during the summer should keep the lawn fairly green even through a period of extended drought.

But don't apply so much water that it floods the soil surface. This will mat the grass and make it more susceptible to fungus parasites. Red fescues, for example, are easily killed by overwatering.

Don't Cut Too Short

If it is to remain in good condition, a lawn must be cut properly. This requires a sharp, properly adjusted mower. The grass must be clipped, not torn off. There is less danger of leaf decay in cleanly cut grass blades than in torn ones.

Never cut the grass too short—to less than an inch. A closely shorn lawn may look neater, but it will not be so healthy as one cut to 2 inches when needed. Moreover, crab grass and other hot weather weeds become established more quickly in closely clipped lawns.

Aerating

In recent years, thanks to golf course turf experts, we have come to appreciate the importance of a well-aerated soil in maintaining a vigorous stand of grass. The soil in old lawns and even that in heavily traveled new lawns becomes so compacted that it ceases to be a good growing medium for turf grasses.

In addition to soil compaction, some lawns suffer from excessive matting. This prevents water from entering the soil during rains or when it is applied with the hose or sprinkler.

Aerification will increase the air and water intake of compacted or grass-matted soils. Either a spading fork or special aerifying tools are easy to handle. The best time to do the job is when the soil is moist enough to allow the aerifying tool to penetrate readily. Never tackle it when the soil is muddy.

When using a spading fork, insert the tines at least 3 inches deep and wiggle the work handle back and forth so that slender holes remain in the soil after the tines are withdrawn. Repeat the operation every foot or so until the entire lawn is literally poked full of holes. Specially made aerifying tools do an even better and quicker job. These are sold or rented by lawn and garden supply stores.

Grass Varieties

The most widely publicized grass variety introduced in recent years is a strain of Kentucky bluegrass known as MERION bluegrass. This was discovered in 1936 by Joseph Valentine on the Merion Golf Course, Ardmore, Pennsylvania.

MERION grows well throughout the area adapted to Kentucky bluegrass and seems to do best in the more southern sections of the region. This is especially fortunate because it is the area where bluegrass is difficult to maintain properly. MERION also does well on the west coast.

MERION bluegrass has several qualities that make it superior to ordinary Kentucky bluegrass. It is more resistant to drought and does not go dormant so quickly in midsummer as the usual Kentucky. MERION goes dormant when the temperatures reach the upper 90s, whereas ordinary Kentucky bluegrass tends to go dormant as soon as the temperatures reach the low 80s.

MERION is less susceptible to the leaf spot disease that sometimes plays havoc in a Kentucky bluegrass lawn and is somewhat more resistant to weed and crab grass infestations. It can be cut shorter than is advisable for the usual Kentucky bluegrass. It also has the remarkable quality of combining with warm season grasses like zoysias and U-3 BERMUDA grass, which do not turn brown in hot weather, to produce a lawn that stays green in both winter and summer.

For new lawns, MERION bluegrass is better sown a little earlier in fall than is usually recommended. When sown as early as August 15 it makes the best turf. The soil must be prepared especially carefully for this superior grass. The soil acidity must be at the neutral point. If necessary, add lime. Organic matter must be liberally worked into heavy soils, and feeding must be done at more frequent intervals than with other lawn grasses.

Lest my readers conclude that we have at long last found the perfect grass, let me hasten to add that MERION does have some undesirable properties.

It does not do well in light, sandy soils. Both fescues and zoysias are better for such situations. Insect pests attack it just as readily as other lawn grasses. It is sensitive to phenyl mercury compounds used to control certain diseases. Finally, in some sections of the country, it is very susceptible to the rust fungus *Puccinia graminis* though the fungicides sold as PHYGON XL, DITHANE Z-78, MANZATE, and sodium sulfanilate all are reported capable of controlling this fungus on MERION bluegrass.

A second grass, widely publicized in the last few years, is zoysia. One species, MANILA GRASS, *Z. Matrella,* has been used as a lawn grass in the southern states and California for some time.

Perhaps the best known of the zoysias is a fine-leaved strain of the KOREAN LAWN-GRASS, *Zoysia japonica,* known as MEYER Z-52, It makes a fine, heat-resisting, tough lawn on a wide variety of soils in the milder parts of the country. It does well in sandy seashore areas, where most other grasses fail. Salt air does not seem to harm it, and it is unusually resistant to insect pests and diseases. Like all zoysias, it must be fed regularly with liberal quantities of high nitrogen fertilizers.

Although the zoysias make good turf in dry weather and stay green in midsummer, in winter they turn brown for nearly six months of the year in the colder parts of the country. Hence in the colder areas where they can be grown, as for example along the east coast, their best use is for summer lawns at seashore resorts, where other varieties are difficult to maintain and where the brown color in the colder months of the year is of little concern. In a suitable climate like Florida, zoysias will stay green all year, and in many other southeastern states for most of the year. It does best south of a line extending from Delaware and Maryland west to St. Louis.

Besides their poor color in the more northerly regions during the winter, zoysias have another drawback, slow spring starting. Not until well after cool-season weeds like chickweed have been growing for some time do the zoysias get started. This places them at a competitive disadvantage with early-growing weeds.

Zoysias start very slowly from seeds. In fact, some kinds produce few to no seeds. For these reasons they are grown from so-called plugs, which are clumps of grass 1 or 2 inches in diameter, or sprigs, grown in turf nurseries or turf grass farms. The plugs contain a pure stand of the desired species with the soil still adhering to the roots. The sprigs contain roots and stolons with no soil. Directions for planting zoysias come with the plants, and the procedure to follow will depend on whether plug or sprig material is used.

Recently it was reported that maleic hydrazide, discussed in detail in the chapter on plant-growth regulators *(Chapter 12),* can be put

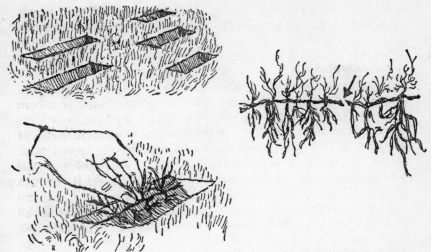

Steps in planting sprigs of zoysia grass: Remove V-shaped pieces of soil with a spade; separate single runners by hand, or cut longer runners into 3-inch lengths; place one sprig into each V-shaped trench so that the green blades are above-ground. Cover runner and roots with soil, pour a small amount of Rapidgro solution onto the sprig and press it firmly into the soil.

to good use in getting zoysia plugs started in an already established lawn. The idea is to spray the established lawn with maleic hydrazide to throw the grasses temporarily into a dormant condition. Then the zoysia plugs or sprigs are planted and can grow for a while, at least, with little competition from the regular lawn grasses.

Another strain of zoysia, EMERALD, was recently released to nurserymen by the Georgia Crop Improvement Association of Athens, Georgia. It is said to be a superior strain well adapted to the Southeast. It may do well in some areas farther north as well. Plugs and sprigs should be generally available from turf nurseries by the spring of 1957.

Another widely publicized plant for lawns is Dichondra. This is not a grass but is used as a lawn cover in the South and West. It is a low-growing perennial with kidney-shaped leaves of velvety dark green color like that of lawn clover. One reason for its popularity in areas where it can be grown is that it needs mowing only two or three times a year! It is not hardy in the northern parts of the country.

Other New or Unusual Grasses

PENNLAWN is a new grass for all-around general turf use which is to be made available to home gardeners in 1956. A variety of creeping red fescue developed at the Pennsylvania Agricultural Experiment Station, PENNLAWN will be useful for home lawns, athletic fields, cemeteries, parks, and golf fairways. It is said to have greater tolerance to leaf spot disease, better foliage density, faster rate of spread by underground rootstocks, and greater ability to withstand closer clippings than any of the turf grasses with which it has been compared.

Two new creeping bent grasses, PENNCROSS and PENNLU, will also be available in 1956 for use on golf course putting greens. The former is propagated from seeds, and the latter must be grown vegetatively, or from stolons.

POLYCROSS CREEPING BENT is a new hybrid said to be superior to SEASIDE and COLONIAL BENT. It grows from seed and produces a turf that is equal or superior to turf produced by the best vegetative strains. It has a greater disease tolerance than SEASIDE BENT and will produce a fine quality turf under a wider range of conditions. Bent grasses, of course, are used primarily on golf greens and other special areas where the very finest quality turf is required. They are, however, more generally subject to fungus diseases and insect pests than other kinds of grasses.

Another relatively new introduction is U-3 BERMUDA grass, which makes a good dense sod that stays green in summer but turns straw-colored in winter. It does best in warm to hot climates and usually does not survive heavy freezes. It is a heavy feeder and hence must be fertilized often to keep it in good vigor.

Weed Control in Lawns

Weeds are probably the major cause of lawn failures in most parts of the country. Hence weed control is a problem to be faced by all who want to maintain a fairly presentable lawn.

On large lawns or heavily infested small ones, hand weeding is not only exhausting and time-consuming but frequently futile because at certain seasons weeds come up so rapidly that the gardener cannot keep ahead of them.

Dandelions, plantain, and certain other broad-leaved weeds are quickly and economically destroyed with a single timely spray of 2,4-D solution. This is possible because of the selective action of this chemical, which destroys broad-leaved plants but leaves the desirable, narrow-leaved lawn grasses relatively unharmed. Gardeners must take several important precautions when using weed killers containing 2,4-D. They should not use them on windy days or under excessive spray pressures lest the material drift to nearby trees, shrubs, or vegetables and play havoc with them. Moreover, they should not apply them to new lawns until the grass is at least 2 inches high, or to lawns in which there is a considerable percentage of bent grass. Other precautions are listed on the container together with directions for use. (Illustration following page 160)

The latest method of packaging 2,4-D for controlling dandelions and plaintain in lawns is in aerosol bombs. The du Pont Company has included an inert white pigment which leaves a residue on the sprayed plants and thus avoids re-treating an area. To use such a bomb one need only shake the can well, invert it, direct the nozzle toward the weeds, and press the button!

Crab grass is perhaps the commonest and most troublesome lawn weed in many areas. It starts anew each year from seeds which germinate in spring to early summer. Crab grass makes its most vigorous growth in soil temperatures above 80 degrees, when the desirable grasses, like Kentucky blue, make little or no growth.

There are two ways to attack the crab grass problem: by cultural practices and with chemicals. Greatest success is achieved when these two methods are combined.

First, everything should be done to encourage the desirable grasses to make vigorous growth and to discourage the crab grass. Light, frequent waterings in midsummer, summer fertilization, and close mowing, therefore, should be avoided, since these practices encourage crab grass. The desirable grasses can be encouraged by proper use of plant foods and lime and by high mowing. Plant foods should be applied in early spring and early fall, when the desirable grasses can make best use of them. I do not favor their application in midsummer when the crab grass is growing vigorously and the desirable grasses are dormant. I mentioned the importance of proper liming and mowing practices earlier in this chapter.

Insofar as high mowing is concerned, I have seen some fine Kentucky bluegrass lawns mowed at 2 to 3 inches. A tall cut like this provides such a heavy shade to germinating crab grass seeds that few are able to survive.

The chemical approach to crab grass control should be utilized only after due attention has been given to the cultural requirements.

In recent years agricultural chemists have spent a goodly portion of their time in the quest for crab grass-controlling chemicals. As a result, we now have a number of remarkable and effective crab grass killers.

Crab grass can be attacked at two stages: before the seeds germinate or while the seedlings are still tiny, and when the plants are large.

Materials used to prevent germination or kill tiny seedlings are known as pre-emergence weed killers. Among the better-known, widely available ones in this category are CRAG HERBICIDE I, a close relative of 2,4-D; ALANAP, a chemical first developed as a selective weed killer for use in melon and related crops; and IMPROVED WEED-ONE, which contains a mixture of 2,4-D and 2,4-5 T.

All three materials will kill crab grass seedlings just as they start to sprout. Because some crab grass seeds start to germinate in spring and others continue to sprout through midsummer, it is necessary to make two to four applications over the germinating period to achieve control.

As with 2,4-D, gardeners must take a number of precautions when using pre-emergence weed killers. For best results directions on containers should be followed to the letter.

For summer and early fall treatments where no pre-emergence chemicals were used and where crab grass is well established, the gardener has a number of effective materials.

Perhaps the latest and best of these is disodium methyl arsonate, for which the name SODAR has been proposed by one authority and which is also sold under such trade names as ARTOX, CRAB-E-RAD, DIMET, and WEEDONE CRAB GRASS KILLER L-850.

Although this chemical has not yet been tested under all sorts of conditions, it has done such a remarkable job that it is worthy of more than passing mention.

First of all, it works as a contact killer. That is why it can be applied only when the crab grass is well developed. It works almost as well when applied during cool weather, at 50 degrees, as at temperatures of 90 degrees or above. Most other contact weed killers are erratic in this respect.

A single application destroys small crab grass plants, and two will kill larger ones. The interval between the two applications is five to seven days. Most important of all, of course, is that it really kills the crab grass, not just cripples it, as do some less effective chemicals. Treated crab grass begins to show injury less than three days after the first application and is completely dead within two weeks.

Thus far it has done the best job of crab grass control in lawns containing Kentucky or MERION bluegrass, fescues, and bents. It is said to injure zoysias in the Deep South.

Disodium methyl arsonate is noncorrosive and hence can be applied with a sprayer, sprinkling can, or syphoning devices. Although it contains an arsenical, it is considered relatively nontoxic.

Directions for use come with the package. The dosage will vary with the weather conditions; less is needed at high temperatures than at low temperatures. For moderate temperatures, at least 1 pound of active ingredient is required for 5,000 square feet of lawn.

Disodium methyl arsonate, then, whether purchased under the name of ARTOX, CRAB-E-RAD, DIMET, SODAR, and WEEDONE CRAB GRASS KILLER L-850, seems at this writing to be one of the most effective crab grass killers, with the fewest undesirable properties, yet to appear on the market.

Two other types of crab grass eradicators that also kill by contact are the phenyl mercury acetates, or PMA, and potassium cyanate, or KOCN. The former are more effective early in the season, during June and early July, when the crab grass plants are small. The latter work best in late July and August, when the plants are large and have begun to root at the nodes. Fescues and bents are rather sensitive to the cyanates. Details on how to use the phenyl mercuries and the potassium cyanates come with the packages. Follow directions carefully for best results.

Clover in Lawns

Clover in lawns may be a highly desirable plant or a weed, depending on what the home owner wants. If he wants to get rid of it because it forms a poor sod and makes the lawn muddy and slippery when walked on in winter, then it is a weed. If he likes nice green color in summer and does not mind if the clover chokes out some of the desirable grasses, then it is a good lawn plant.

Where the home owner considers it a weed, the best way for him to get rid of it is to spray the lawn with 2,4-5 T at one third the manufacturer's recommendation for brush control. The 2,4-5 T should be applied in enough water to wet all the foliage without excessive run-off. The lawn should be cut to its regular height before applying the chemical.

Home owners who want to encourage growth of clover should apply liberal amounts of lime and phosphate fertilizers and should water frequently. Clover likes an alkaline soil and a plant food high in phosphates like 5-10-5 or 4-12-4.

Renovating Old Lawns

But what can the home owner do if his lawn has grown up to weeds so that it is more weeds than grass? Should he spade it over and start from scratch? If he spades up the whole lawn and carries off all the crab grass plants, will that pesky weed reappear next year?

Many home owners faced with this problem want to know whether there is some way to renovate an old lawn without digging it all up. There is one way that works very well, if the home owner is willing to follow directions to the letter.

The method involves the use of the chemical calcium cyanamid sold as LAWN AND GARDEN CYANAMID, which is unique in that it destroys seeds and young weeds and at the same time supplies nitrogen and lime to the soil.

The way cyanamid works is not really mysterious. It has been well established that heavy applications of calcium cyanamid will severely burn and consequently kill weed seeds near or at the soil surface. Once the cyanamid is added to the soil and is moistened, "free" cyanamid, which is toxic to seeds as well as to growing plants, forms. It is this "free" cyanamid that kills both germinated and ungerminated weed seeds. It is unstable and soon breaks down to ammonia and nitrate nitrogen, which the new lawn grasses then use as plant food.

According to technical representatives of the manufacturer of LAWN AND GARDEN CYANAMID, the following procedure can be used on an old lawn without turning over the soil and sod:

Measure the area carefully. Mow the lawn closely and then water well to a depth of 4 inches. Rake off the old growth and scratch the surface well. Scatter the cyanamid evenly at the rate of 5 pounds for each 100 square feet of surface. Then use an iron rake to bring the cyanamid into close contact with the soil. Allow to stand for three weeks, watering occasionally to keep the soil moist.

In the interim undesirable grasses and weeds (as well as what remains of desirable grasses) are burned off, and nitrogen and lime are supplied. The nitrogen supplied by cyanamid is sufficient for the lawn for the fall season. Each 1,000 square feet should also receive

20 pounds of 20 per cent superphosphate or, if this is not readily available, 15 pounds of 5-10-5 to encourage root growth. The latter, of course, will provide additional nitrogen. For each 100 pounds used, cyanamid also supplies the equivalent of 70 pounds of lime.

After the three-week waiting period soak the soil surface well, then rake the surface lightly and seed the area in the standard manner. Rake or roll to put the seed into intimate contact with the soil, and water until the grass is established.

Because of the three-week period that must elapse before the lawn is reseeded, the best time to use cyanamid is in early August. The lawn can then be seeded in early September and become well established before winter. Once the grass is flourishing, weeds are less of a problem because they cannot compete with the resulting thick, vigorous stand of grass.

Much of the same method can be used also to kill weeds and weed seeds prior to starting a new lawn. As in renovating an old lawn, the job must be done in early fall in the northern parts of the country.

To produce a weed-free seedbed for lawn grasses, the ground must be thoroughly prepared about a month before seeding is scheduled. This should include complete grading and leveling so that further cultivation is not required after the cyanamid is applied.

The granular cyanamid is then evenly applied to the smooth surface of the soil at the same rate as in renovating an old lawn— 5 pounds per 100 square feet. On level areas it is left undisturbed, but on slopes it should be lightly raked in together with the additional fertilizer needed. Again allow three weeks for the cyanamid to kill the weed seeds and to lose its toxic effects. Because water is necessary for the proper action of the material, the soil should be kept moist by frequent sprinklings, particularly if no rains fall in the interim.

After the three-week waiting period, seed the area. Because only the weeds in the top inch of the soil are destroyed, soil below this level should not be disturbed. In fact, it is best to disturb the soil surface as little as possible while seeding.

LAWN AND GARDEN CYANAMID is available for lawn and other garden uses in 10-, 25-, and 50-pound packages. Additional details on its use are supplied with each package.

Control of Insects

Besides weeds, another common cause of lawn failure in many parts of the country is invasion by insects. Lawns damaged by insects

An old lawn can be renovated without turning it over completely. First mow lawn, then rake off the old growth and scratch the surface well; scatter LAWN AND GARDEN CYANAMID evenly at the recommended rate and rake it lightly to bring it into intimate contact with soil. Then wait three weeks, keeping the soil moist. Water the area thoroughly and finally rake again, but no deeper than ½ inch, to remove dead weeds and grasses and to break up any crust that has formed. Finally sow the grass seed in the usual way.

are brown, thinned out, or ragged. Of course, the only way to be absolutely sure that insects are responsible for such damage is to find them at work.

Grubs of various kinds, including those of the Japanese beetle, chew off grass roots. They can be found in late May and June and again in late August and September beneath rootless, dry sod, which can be easily lifted. The grubs, creamy white with brown heads and three pairs of legs, are usually curled in the shape of the letter C.

Cutworms, chinch bugs, and webworms feed on the stems and leaves of grasses rather than the roots. These, too, can be detected only by examining carefully the browned grass.

In recent years both chlordane and dieldrin (pronounced deel-drin) have proved far more effective for controlling lawn-infesting pests than the long-popular arsenate of lead or the more recent DDT.

If the lawn has not been grubproofed within the last five years, *one* of the following should be applied evenly over each 1,000 square feet. Where a powder is used, it should be lightly watered in after application. The percentages, by the way, are for products most commonly available on the market under various brand names.

Chlordane—5 per cent dust, 5 pounds per 1,000 square feet; or, 40 per cent wettable powder, 10 ounces in 20 gallons of water as a spray; or 75 per cent emulsion, 4 ounces in 20 gallons of water as a spray. Dieldrin—1 per cent dust or granulated, 8 pounds; or 25 per cent wettable powder, 5 ounces in 20 gallons of water as a spray; or 18.6 per cent emulsion, 6 ounces in 20 gallons as a spray.

Both chlordane and dieldrin are poisonous and must be handled with care. Avoid inhaling the dust or the wettable powder. Be sure to read the directions on the package. The insecticides are now being sold also adsorbed on granules of inert materials such as vermiculite, talc, and tobacco stems. This should increase their popularity because they can be applied with a lime or fertilizer spreader. LAWNTROL is a popular mixture containing dieldrin on a granular carrier.

Diseases

Unless a lawn contains lots of bent grasses, our most destructive fungus diseases are rarely a problem. The materials sold as CADMI-NATE, CRAG 531, and PURATURF 177 will prevent such well-known diseases as dollar spot, copper spot, and pink patch. Either CALO-CHLOR or CALOCURE is excellent for diseases like brown patch and snow molds.

Lawns containing bluegrasses and fescues, however, are subject to one or more of the so-called "out triplets": "going-out," "melting-out," and "fading-out." These names have been given to destructive diseases caused by the fungi known as *Helminthosporium* and *Curvularia,* which have become very prevalent in lawns in the eastern United States in recent years. All three of the "out" diseases start as small, more or less circular, dead spots scattered here and there in the lawn. With heavy rains or frequent sprinkling of the lawn, the spots enlarge and coalesce until most of the lawn is affected.

In the Northeast, Kentucky bluegrass may be attacked by the "going-out" disease at any time from mid-April to late May. MERION bluegrass appears to be markedly resistant to the disease. The "melting-out" disease may strike Kentucky bluegrass, fescue, and even bent grass between early spring and the arrival of hot weather. The "fading-out" disease attacks nearly all species of grasses after the advent of hot weather.

Unfortunately no single chemical treatment will control all the fungus diseases to which lawns are subject.

FERRATED ACTI-DIONE gives good control of both "going-out" and "fading-out." Fungicides containing phenyl mercury, the same kind mentioned under crab grass control, will protect lawns against the three "out" diseases. These are sold under such trade names as PMAS, CARAC PMAS, PURATIZED, and TAG.

Scientists are attempting to develop a so-called "broad-spectrum" fungicide which will control all the important diseases of turf. Dr. Frank Howard at the Rhode Island Experiment Station, an outstanding authority on turf diseases, feels that such a material will soon be available to home gardeners. Until one is developed, however, the home gardener can find out from his state plant pathologist or local county agricultural agent which of the currently available fungicides is most effective in his particular area and whether an annual treatment is advisable.

If home owners follow these suggestions on lawn care, I feel sure their lawns will be greener and more attractive next year.

Chapter 10

LANDSCAPING

This chapter will not teach anyone how to do the job of a landscape architect or a landscape gardener. Such a course would need far more than a chapter. Rather, in these few pages, I shall point out some fundamental facts about landscape planning and planting and tell of some of the more recent developments in the field.

Good landscaping increases the resale value of a home as much as 15 or 20 per cent. Even big business realizes that well-landscaped industrial areas are worth while because they inspire most employees to do better work. One of the oldest and perhaps one of the best landscaped industrial areas I have ever seen is that surrounding the National Cash Register Company's buildings in Dayton, Ohio. Another beautifully designed and executed landscape planting is that surrounding the main office of the General Foods Corporation in White Plains, New York.

A Few Fundamentals

I believe everyone agrees that simplicity in landscape plantings is the mark of true beauty as we see it today. Simplicity is also basic to the design of the modern home, the modern school, and even the modern factory.

The ranch-type homes now being built so extensively all over America have also changed our concept of good landscaping. Because many of these homes are more spreading and the property less expansive than formerly, trees and shrubs which attain smaller size at maturity are required. No longer are trees that grow 100 or more feet high being selected as part of home landscape design. Such trees, of course, have their place, but let's keep them in the forest. Trees whose ultimate height reaches 20 or 30 feet are preferred because their size and shape are far more appropriate for the modern home.

The factor of economy also enters the picture. Home owners have found that the taller-growing trees are more expensive to maintain. It costs more to spray and prune them, and should they die from disease or other causes, they are far more expensive to remove.

The type of foundation planting to have will depend on the way the house is placed on the foundation wall.

The sprawling, low, ranch-type home requires low-growing, spreading plants primarily to accent the entrance and to soften the angle of wall and grade at the corners.

Unless properly landscaped, split-level houses built on flat ground present a "grain elevator" appearance. To avoid this effect, the landscape gardener must try to cut the height by breaking vertical lines and introducing horizontal ones. Use of trees with horizontal branches helps to cut the height in such situations.

Because the proper arrangement of trees and shrubs is an art, it cannot easily be taught by the printed word. Nevertheless, there are certain fundamentals that can be passed on to those who plan to do their own landscaping. Here is a list of "do's and don'ts" suggested by experts in the Department of Floriculture and Ornamental Horticulture at Cornell University.

DO PLANT:

1. Only low-growing shrubs underneath windows. Flowers or ground covers may be used to advantage, or these places may be left unplanted except for extending a lawn to the foundation wall.

2. Low-growing shrubs around porches except in situations where porch furniture is to be used. Part of a large porch may be shaded by a vine or a tree-form shrub.

3. Dwarf- to medium-sized plants at the sides of small entrances and steps. This shrub planting sometimes may be supplemented by planting a vine that can be supported at the side of a doorway.

4. Medium- to tall-growing shrubs at the corner of the house except where a driveway or walk is close to the side of a house. Here a vine may be used instead of a shrub. Where windows are at the corners, a tree-form shrub may be used to shade this corner window, or dwarf shrubs may be used as suggested in item I.

5. Medium-sized shrubs or vines in spaces along the foundation where the windows are far apart.

6. Vines on a chimney unless the chimney is small. A shrub also may be used near a chimney.

7. With some duplication of material to avoid the appearance of a botanical collection.

DO NOT PLANT:

1. Tall-growing trees in the foundation planting.
2. A straight row of one variety of plant around the house.
3. Tall-growing shrubs in front of windows. They darken the room and block the view toward the outside.
4. Too great a variety of plants. Such plantings may look like a botanical collection. Plants with brightly colored foliage should be used with caution.

Appropriate Small-Growing Trees and Shrubs

Perhaps the best group of small trees for modern type homes are the Oriental flowering crab apples. These are hardy wherever apples are grown, and most of them are less than 25 feet tall at maturity. They are available in a wide range of sizes, habits, and colors of flowers and fruits. In addition to those described in *Chapter 4*, the following slow-growing flowering crab apples are suitable for small properties:

CUTLEAF CRAB, from western China, with white flowers in late May and small, yellow, pear-shaped fruits with a red blush in fall; grows to about 20 feet.

SARGENT CRAB, from Japan, with small white flowers in mid-May and dark red fruits in fall; rarely exceeds 8 feet in height.

Of the many kinds of hawthorns grown in this country, one of the very best is without doubt the WASHINGTON THORN, *Crataegus phaenopyrum*. Although its single white flowers are not so striking as those of PAUL'S SCARLET THORN, another nice hawthorn, its bright red fruits, which last from fall through the winter, provide colorful food for the birds.

The star magnolia, *Magnolia stellata*, described in some detail in *Chapter 4*, is one of the earliest flowering of the small-growing trees. In addition, it is the hardiest of all the magnolias, a characteristic that greatly increases its range of usefulness.

Some other flowering small trees or large shrubs suitable for small properties are the white fringe tree, *Chionanthus virginicus;* Scotch laburnum, *Laburnum alpinum;* Japanese snowbell, *Styrax japonica;* and the Korean, Japanese, mountain, and showy mountain stewartias, *Stewartia koreana, S. pseudocamellia, S. ovata,* and *S. ovata grandiflora,* respectively.

The evodias, *E. danielli* and *E. hupehensis,* are also excellent small trees which are valued for their late summer flowers and their red and black fruits in early fall.

I like the silk tree or pink mimosa, *Albizzia julibrissin,* very much. This is a slender tree with fernlike foliage and with flowers that resemble pink tassels appearing in July. It is a low-growing tree that quickly reaches a height of 20 feet or so. The variety *rosea* is a bit more hardy than the one found commonly in the South. It is hardy along the east coast as far north as Boston. Incidentally, anyone who wants to grow it from its beanlike seeds will find that puncturing the seed coat once or twice with a needle will assure better germination.

SOURWOOD, or SORREL TREE, *Oxydendron arboreum,* with drooping clusters of white flowers in late summer, is another striking low-growing tree. On trees growing in full sun, the leaves turn a vivid scarlet color in the fall.

The PEKIN LILAC, *Syringa pekinensis,* is a vigorous small-growing tree with cherrylike bark and large pyramidal clusters of creamy white flowers that appear in late June. Its dense foliage also qualifies it for use as a shade tree.

Other low-growing trees suitable for small properties are described in *Chapter 4.*

Following is a list of plants that ordinarily do not exceed 3 feet in height or that can be kept under 3 feet by regular pruning:

Deciduous Shrubs. Alpine Japanese flowering quince, *Chaenomeles japonica alpina;* Beans broom, *Cytisus beanii;* cranberry *cotoneaster, Cotoneaster apiculata;* creeping cotoneaster, *C. adpressa;* dwarf Japanese barberry, *Berberis Thunbergii minor;* early creeping cotoneaster, *C. adpressa praecox;* dwarf flowering quinces, *Chaenomeles lagenaria* varieties *nana* and *pygmaea;* glossy abelia, *Abelia grandiflora;* Jersey tea Ceanothus, *Ceanothus americanus;* Kew broom, *Cytisus kewensis;* purple broom, *C. purpureus;* roseus ceanothus, *Ceanothus pallidus roseus;* and spike broom, *Cytisus nigricans.*

Narrow-Leaved Evergreens. Canby pachistima, *Pachistima canbyi;* compact Hinoki false-cypress, *Chamaecyparis obtusa compacta;* creeping juniper, *Juniperus horizontalis;* cushion Japanese yew, *Taxus cuspidata densa;* dwarf cryptomeria, *Cryptomeria japonica nana;* dwarf Hinoki false-cypress, *Chamaecyparis obtusa nana;* Japgarden juniper, *Juniperus procumbens;* mountain Chinese juniper, *Juniperus communis saxatilis;* mugho Swiss pine, *Pinus Mugo mughus;* prostrate single-seed juniper, *Juniperus squamata prostrata;* pygmy Hinoki false-cypress, *Chamaecyparis obtusa pygmaea;* Sargent Chinese juniper, *Juniperus chinensis Sargentii;* shore juniper, *Juniperus conferta;* and spreading English yew, *Taxus baccata repandens.*

Subshrubs. Blueridge St. Johnswort, *Hypericum Buckleyi;* cypress lavender-cotton, *Santolina chamaecyparissus;* evergreen candytuft, *Iberis sempervirens;* goldencup St. Johnswort, *Hypericum patulum;* Henry St. Johnswort, *Hypericum patulum Henryi;* Kalm St. Johnswort, *Hypericum kalmianum;* true lavender, *Lavandula officinalis* varieties; and variegated St. Johnswort, *Hypericum Moserianum.*

Other Shrubs. Mock orange varieties ARGENTINE, AVALANCHE, and MONT BLANC, with fragrant white flowers in June, rarely exceed 4 feet in height.

Potentilla fruticosa, considered by some as a lowly native plant, is being rediscovered by many home gardeners as a worth-while shrub for foundation plantings. Although its yellow or white flowers are not particularly showy, their presence throughout the summer and the relatively little care the plant requires make it worth looking into.

The SUWANNEE RIVER privet, discussed in *Chapter 3,* is ideally suited for use in foundation plantings in front of the modern, ranch-type home because of its low, spreading growth habit. It is equally useful as a low hedge or a border plant in the milder parts of the country.

For home owners who like forsythia but have little room for the ordinary kind, which grows so large, I suggest the variety *Bronxensis,* introduced by The New York Botanical Garden's horticulturist, Mr. T. H. Everett, several years ago. Although this variety does not flower as profusely as the standard kind, it is a slow grower and hence keeps within bounds for many years without pruning.

Uses for Tall-Growing Shrubs

Tall-growing shrubs cannot be planted beneath windows because they, too, will soon screen out the view. They are best used in corner plantings to help break the vertical lines of the house. As a rule, at least three specimens of the same kind make a pleasant landscape "clump." Individual specimens should be planted at least 3 feet from the foundation wall, 6 feet apart, and about 4 feet from a border.

Among the desirable kinds which grow 6 to 8 feet high, together with their cultural requirements or special attributes, are:

BEAUTY BUSH, *Kolkwitzia amabilis,* which is not reliably hardy in the colder parts of the country. It has graceful foliage, and white-throated pink flowers.

BRIDALWREATH, *Spirea Vanhouttei,* which is easy to grow and has white lacelike flowers in May.

BORDER FORSYTHIA, *Forsythia intermedia spectabilis,* which tolerates shade and has showy golden flowers in early spring.

RED-STEM DOGWOOD, *Cornus alba,* which prefers a moist soil and tolerates shade.

SUMMER SWEET, *Clethra alnifolia,* which requires an acid, moist soil and has fragrant spikes of white or pink flowers.

WINGED EUONYMOUS, *Euonymous alata,* whose branches have corked wings, and red foliage in fall.

WINTER HONEYSUCKLE, *Lonicera fragrantissima,* which is not quite hardy in exposed situations, in the Northeast, and has yellow to white flowers in April and May and semi-evergreen leaves.

WINTERBERRY, *Ilex verticillata,* which prefers a moist soil. Both male and female plants must be planted in clumps to assure production of scarlet berries. Like many of the trees mentioned later in this chapter, it tolerates salt-laden air and hence does well in seashore plantings.

A New Ground Cover

A ground cover of one kind or another is to be found in almost every proper landscape planting. Ground covers are used frequently in areas where little else will grow, or at times they are used to produce some special effect.

The commonest ground covers are pachysandra or Japanese spurge, *Pachysandra terminalis;* myrtle, *Vinca minor;* EUONYMOUS, *Euonymous radicans;* and English ivy, *Hedera helix,* or a variety known as Baltic ivy, *Hedera helix* var. *baltica.*

Each of these has certain desirable characteristics that make it more suitable than the others for some particular spots. But each one also has some undesirable characteristic. For example, pachysandra and euonymous are extremely susceptible to scale insects, and myrtle is subject to a fungus disease of its stems. English ivy makes an excellent ground and wall cover, but unfortunately it does not hold its attractive green color throughout the winter. When grown in sunny spots or in wind-swept area, the leaves turn brown or become badly blotched. In some winters the branch tips or the entire plant may be killed. Although the Baltic ivy withstands unfavorable conditions a bit better, it too becomes unsightly in some winters.

A welcome addition to the group of ground covers is another strain of English ivy recently named by horticulturist Everett HEDERA HELIX 238TH STREET. It begins to make new growth earlier in spring than ordinary English ivy; in fact, it is actually weeks ahead of the parent strain. Moreover, it keeps its bright green color all through the winter, is extremely winterhardy, and has a number of other highly desirable attributes. The viny shoots of 238TH STREET are vigorous, stiff, and spread laterally, producing a pleasing effect. Umbels of light green flowers appear in late fall on the fruiting branches. The fruits are large and are carried in globular umbels. At first they are green, but as the winter advances they darken, so that by March they are deep olive brown with a black cap. (Illustration following page 96)

I have grown 238TH STREET for about six years now on a sunny wall near my home in New York and in a wind-swept, sunny cemetery plot in central Westchester County. In both places it has come through the winters unscathed.

One of the first recommendations I made when I was appointed Consultant on Landscape Maintenance for the United Nations headquarters in New York was that an experimental planting of several hundred 238TH STREET ivies be set out. This planting will be compared with literally acres of English ivy now growing around the United Nations headquarters. If it holds up as it has in the past, I am sure more and more of the United Nations ground cover plantings will be made up of 238TH STREET. In March and April, then, visitors and employees of the United Nations no longer will have to look at browned, dead-looking English ivy.

By spring of 1955 gardeners of The New York Botanical Garden had rooted about thirty thousand cuttings of 238TH STREET. At this writing rooted cuttings have been placed on sale by the Garden's administrator, Mr. A. C. Pfander. Within a year or two many nurserymen will no doubt carry ample stocks of this highly desirable ivy.

Middle Westerners will be especially interested in another ivy, the Bulgarian, *Hedera helix* var. *bulgaria,* introduced by Dr. Edgar Anderson, director of the Missouri Botanical Garden at St. Louis. Bulgarian ivy is most hardy and vigorous and is evergreen throughout the year. It has larger leaves than 238TH STREET IVY.

A special strain of the English ivy known as THORNDALE is unusually resistant to low temperatures. It is said to have withstood twenty-seven Chicago winters without protection.

Roses as Ground Covers

Occasionally certain kinds of roses are used as ground covers. The following are considered superior for this purpose: *Rosa wichuriana,* white; MAX GRAF, pink; CARPET OF GOLD, yellow; CORAL CREEPER, apricot; and LITTLE COMPTON CREEPER, deep pink.

A Plant for Crevices in Stone Walks

In POPULAR GARDENING magazine for June 1955, Sally Wright of Perkasie, Pennsylvania, says that *Arenaria verna caespitosa* is the *"one and only"* plant for growing in crevices of stone walks. This, the most dwarf member of the SANDWORT genus, is long-lived, undemanding, and seldom requires clipping. It is very tolerant of foot traffic and of being overrun by garden furniture and equipment. It does well in any kind of soil except poorly drained heavy clays. *Arenaria verna caespitosa* is propagated either from seed or plant division. Seeds are obtainable from Rex Pearce of Moorestown, New Jersey.

Seashore Plantings

In recent years an increasing number of city folks have bought beach-front properties somewhere along the east coast. Invariably the problem of what to plant arises, a problem not solved so easily as are those in ordinary gardens. The two main aspects of the problem are the strong prevailing winds and the salt spray.

Among the trees and shrubs that can survive under such conditions and that actually help to break the force of the ocean breezes are American holly, beach plum, wild cherry, tamarisk, Jack pine, Japanese black pine, and California privet. The London plane tree and the ailanthus, two of the toughest trees for use in large cities, also can withstand the wind and salt air of the seashore.

Problems of Newly Landscaped Sites

Many new home sites are chosen because of the fine trees on the properties. Unless these trees are protected by every known means during house construction and grading, they will not continue to flourish and many even die.

Frequently home owners call on me to explain the poor vigor and dying of fine old trees around recently built houses and to suggest a remedy. Unfortunately I can do little to help them. The damage was done anywhere from one to five years earlier, and precautionary measures should have been taken at the very beginning of house construction.

Changing the grade around old trees, especially by adding soil over the original level, is perhaps the most frequent cause of premature death.

Some precautions to take are: Do not construct the house too close to large trees. Not only will important roots be cut, but the water table in the soil may change so drastically as to impair the health of the trees.

Avoid purchasing properties covered with old tree stumps, because the cost of removing these stumps is tremendous. To my knowledge, there is no effective, quick-acting chemical for removing them.

Finally, it is advisable to call in a reliable tree man to advise on which trees are worth saving and to suggest where the cellar excavation should be dug to cause least harm to the trees that are to remain.

In addition, I like the following six specifications for protecting existing plant materials suggested by Ralph Synnestvedt, Jr., landscape architect of Glenview, Illinois:

1. All trees and shrubs should be properly protected with planks, frames, and fences.

2. Soil and building materials should not be stockpiled on root systems or against tree trunks.

3. The promiscuous cutting of interfering branches by building mechanics should be prohibited.   ·

4. Excessive amounts of water, such as from excavations, should not be pumped on existing plant material.

5. Trucks, cars, and heavy equipment should not be moved across root systems, especially those of maples and beeches.

6. No fires should be built near enough to existing plants to cause damage.

Lack of space prohibits my going into greater detail, but for those interested in finding out more about this subject I suggest referring to my book *Maintenance of Shade and Ornamental Trees,* published by Oxford University Press, New York.

Garden Lighting

What was once only fit for a king—illuminated gardens at night—is now easily within the budget of the average home owner. An investment of a few dollars for some well-placed garden lights extends the usability of the garden well into the evening hours, when most of the members of the family are at home.

Two developments are largely responsible for the increased interest in the use of lights in the garden: the availability of a waterproof extension cord with moistureproof connections and the use of either insecticides or insect light traps to reduce the insect nuisance after dark.

The relatively inexpensive waterproof extension cords are attached to electrical outlets and laid on the ground in out-of-the-way places.

Steps in air layering with plastics:
1. The bark is removed (or slit) and the wounded portion rubbed with the green striped material.

2. The wounded area is then wrapped with moistened sphagnum moss.

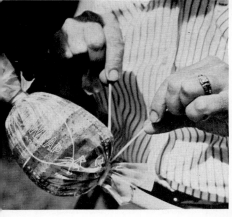

3. The moss is tightly covered with the Air-Wrap plastic film with the ends well secured.

4. The plastic sheeting is removed to show root development.

The chrysanthemum cuttings on the left were treated with a root hormone *Rooto* Cuttings on the right are untreated.

The tulip bulbs at the right were given a preplanting soak in *Rapidgro* solution; those on the left were soaked in plain water. Photo taken two months after planting.

The *Phytotektor* is completely automatic and roots softwood cuttings directly in soil.

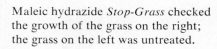

Maleic hydrazide *Stop-Grass* checked the growth of the grass on the right; the grass on the left was untreated.

Foliage feeding. The Golden Muscat grape on the extreme right was leaf sprayed daily with *Rapidgro* for several weeks. Plant on the extreme left received normal root feeding.

Tomatoes on a plant grown in the usual way.

A plant sprayed at flowering time with *Blossom-Set* hormone.

A dandelion plant before and after being treated
with a weed killer *Improved Weedone.*

Weeds have nearly choked out the row of cucumber plants
on the left, whereas in the photo at right a pre-emergence
weed killer (*Alanap*) has controlled the weeds.

The lighting fixtures are then placed in the desired spots and the cords plugged into them.

Engineers have designed a complete line of electrical fixtures and accessories solely for outdoor use. Included are such simple things as floodlights and such complicated apparatus as projectors with lenses to control the quality of the light.

The portable floodlights are so constructed that they can be spiked into the turf or the ground and their lights projected to some interesting tree, shrub, or flower border. Other floodlights are available for attaching to the house or trees.

An important rule to follow is to place the lights and adjust them so that the lighted bulb cannot be seen from the gardener's house, the path, or a neighbor's house.

Using the right kind of light in the right place thus transforms the garden into a live and charming place at night.

Vertical Gardening

I would like to close this chapter on new landscaping developments by describing an idea of mine which I developed about a dozen years ago. I realize, of course, that a twelve-year-old idea is not exactly new, but I am sure it will be new to the great majority of the readers of this book and hence I feel justified in presenting it.

This idea should have particular appeal for gardeners with limited back yard space, or to those with gardens whose beauty is marred by an unsightly wall of a building, shed, or garage. I was faced with both of these problems a dozen years ago when I lived in Highland Park, New Jersey. As on most city properties, my garage occupied an important part of a small back yard. By utilizing the sunny side of the garage wall, however, I was able to transform a bare, unsightly spot into a mass of bloom during summer and fall. Moreover, I increased more than fourfold the cultivable area along the garage wall.

Some secondhand lumber, some nails, and a few hours of carpentry were all I needed to create this vertical garden.

Building Directions. My aerial garden consisted of five adjacently placed units projecting about 2 feet from the side of the garage.

Each unit of four removable boxes was supported on a frame. Here's how each unit was built: I collected enough 1-inch lumber to construct four flower boxes, each 36 inches long, 8 inches wide, and 6 inches deep. Into the bottom and along one side of each box I bored three ½-inch drainage holes equal distances apart. To prevent rapid

decay of the boxes, I painted the inside of each with copper naph-thenate, one of the best wood preservatives for greenhouse flats and for other plant-growing containers.

To help support the boxes in each unit, I used two 6-foot lengths of two-by-fours. These were placed parallel and just a little more than 36 inches apart. The two adjacent lower ends were connected by nailing a piece of one-by-four, forming a three-sided frame. The frame was then placed upright, the one-by-four serving as a base, about a foot from the garage wall. The top of each two-by-four upright was nailed firmly to a one-by-two brace extending to the wall. Finally, four 7-inch lengths of two-by-one-inch wood, 14 inches apart, were nailed along the inside of each upright and almost at right angles to it, but sloping backward slightly. The ends of the boxes were placed on these supporting strips, with the drainage holes in the back. The top box was placed farthest back (nearest the wall), and each lower one was allowed to extend farther out front to avoid having drainage water splash on the box beneath.

In the same way, I built four similar units, utilizing the unused side of the two-by-four of the first unit to help support part of the second unit, and so on.

The outside parts of each box, as well as all supporting frames, were painted with outside white paint. The whole aerial garden was 18 feet long and about 6 feet high, with a total of twenty flower boxes.

Ready for Planting. Once the boxes were in place and the paint dry, they were ready to receive the soil. I used a new batch of good rich garden soil every year. After the soil was in, the boxes were left fallow for a few weeks to allow weed seeds to sprout, and were then weeded by shallow cultivation.

About the middle of May, as soon as all danger of frost was past, the boxes were ready for planting. I always used stocky young plants. These were gently tapped out of the pots to preserve the soil ball and were then planted in the flower boxes.

The number of plants set in each box was governed by the type of plant and its size at maturity. For example, I found that four or five balcony-type petunias were sufficient for one box.

When several kinds of flowers were planted in a box, the taller-growing kinds were placed toward the back, and the smaller-growing ones were set toward the front.

Once the young plants were set in place, the soil was watered thoroughly. When the soil had settled, an inch or more of space remained between the soil surface and the top of the box. I filled this space with moistened peat moss for two purposes. First, it greatly reduced the germination of weed seeds in the soil beneath and, even more important, it helped to prevent excessive evaporation of moisture from the soil and kept the soil cool.

When the plants began to grow, all subsequent treatments were the same as those for any garden except for one practice—that of

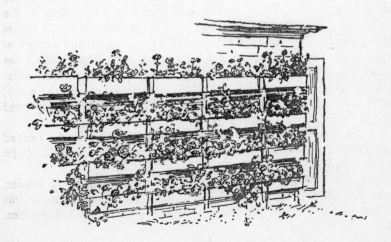

watering. During dry spells the soil in the boxes tended to dry out rather quickly, even under the layer of peat moss. Hence it was necessary to soak the soil thoroughly about twice a week.

To prevent rain water draining off the garage roof from pouring into the boxes, I built a little trough along the roof edge.

Best Plants to Grow. Among the plants I used in my aerial garden over the years were blue lobelia, STAR OF TEXAS, mixed verbenas, signet and dwarf marigolds, scabiosa, begonia, annual phlox, ageratum, linaria, and plain and giant ruffled petunias. I found that balcony-type petunias of various colors were the showiest as well as the most reliable plants. These also required the least care.

By midsummer, in some years, the petunias would become "leggy" or scraggly. To remedy this, I pruned back the plants drastically, leaving 4- to 5-inch stems with 3 or 4 pairs of leaves on each. New stems soon broke forth along the older stems, and within a few weeks a new crop of blooms appeared. The reinvigorated plants then continued to bloom well into the autumn.

The unsightly aspect of the supporting two-by-fours was hidden by twining morning glories, clematis, or flowering beans around the supports. The plants or seeds of these were, of course, planted directly in the garden soil at the base of the aerial garden. Incidentally, the remaining soil at the base also was planted with flowers to add to the charming effect of the garden.

Chapter 11

SOILS, SOIL CONDITIONERS, AND PLANT FOODS

Literally and figuratively soil is the foundation of all gardening. Soil serves as a storehouse for plant nutrients, an abode for microorganisms, and a reservoir of water for the plant's growth. It also provides anchorage for the plant.

The average garden soil is composed largely of elements that plants do not need or cannot use. The greater portion is made up of silicon, aluminum, and iron. In regions where rainfall has been plentiful over the past thousands of years, most of the elements that are soluble in water have been leached out. Because many of these are needed by plants, the job is to recover such materials and put them back in the garden. The whole commercial plant food industry is based on this premise.

Besides putting back what the rainfall has taken away, gardeners may need to change the physical condition of their soil to make it more favorable for plant growth. They may have to change it, for instance, from a heavy or at times sandy body to one that is porous and spongy—one that will not bake hard or dry out excessively during dry spells. Further on I shall describe how both natural and synthetic soil conditioners can be used to achieve a friable soil.

Most garden soils in urban areas are not the natural ones found there when our country was settled. They are remade or relocated soils. Many around recently built houses consist largely of subsoil taken from the cellar excavation. Such soils may have a layer of hauled-in topsoil which covers rocks, tin cans, bricks, plaster, cinders, and other debris. They may be productive on the surface but highly unproductive below. Something can be done to improve them, nevertheless.

In some areas the original topsoil has been scraped off and sold, or at best was mixed with the underlying infertile material when the lot was graded. The quickest, though not the cheapest, way to remedy such a situation is to buy good topsoil and have it spread over the poorer subsoil.

If the subsoil is sandy, gardeners can reduce the amount of topsoil required by "doctoring" the subsoil with organic matter such as peat moss and manures to increase the water-holding capacity of the whole soil.

Where the subsoil is very clayey, a different procedure is needed because far more organic matter is necessary to make any appreciable improvement. It is more practical to "cut" the clayey subsoil with sifted hard-coal ashes and, where lawns and vegetables are to be grown, with liberal amounts of ground limestone. This is best done by spading or rototilling a 2- to 3-inch layer of ashes into the top 8 inches of subsoil, along with limestone, where lime-loving plants are to be grown. The incorporation of small amounts of organic matter will also help.

These procedures are suggested for improving the physical condition of subsoils prior to placing good topsoil over them. The great majority of gardeners, however, are primarily interested in improving both the physical and chemical structure of the topsoil they now have rather than the subsoil.

No matter what the present condition of the topsoil, the proper requirements for good plant growth can be supplied by certain practices. Incidentally, one cannot tell from the color of the soil just how fertile it is. Sometimes light-colored soils are more fertile than dark ones. Some black forest soils, thought to be very rich, are actually of low fertility and will not grow a good crop unless fertilizers are added.

Lime, if Necessary

A soil test will reveal how acid the soil actually is. If quite acid, and unless acid-loving plants are to be grown, then lime should be added to improve growing conditions. Lime not only sweetens the soil, and thus frees many nutrients otherwise unavailable, but it also supplies much needed calcium and magnesium. In some soils the physical condition as well will be improved by its use.

For lime-loving plants, which include most of those grown in gardens, the soil should be limed so that it is nearly alkaline, or to a soil reaction of pH 6.5. Do not add more than 30 pounds of hydrated lime or more than 50 pounds of pulverized limestone to 1,000 square feet of garden at any one time. County agricultural agents or agricultural experiment stations will test soil and advise on the amount and type of liming materials to apply. If they suggest pulverized limestone, you will get best results from working it deeply into the soil. Hydrated lime can be applied in the upper 3 inches.

Among the plants that can be grown in alkaline or only slightly acid soils are American and Japanese holly, barberry, boxwood, euonymous, firethorn, mahonia, pines, hemlocks, all shade trees (except possibly pin oak and scarlet oak because of their susceptibility to chlorosis), all annuals, chrysanthemum, dahlia, delphinium, gladiolus, iris, peony, rose, leatherleaf viburnum, and most lawn grasses.

Where the test indicates that the soil is not acid enough for best growth of some plants, it can be made more acid by incorporating either sulfur or aluminum sulfate. The amount to be added will depend on the acidity of the soil at the start and the degree of acidity required. Local county agricultural agents and experiment station horticulturists can also advise on this point.

Some of the trees, shrubs, and flowers that prefer distinctly acid soil are *Leucothoe, Pieris japonica,* Carolina rhododendron, catawbiense hybrid rhododendrons, azalea, blueberry, *Gordonia,* witchhazel, silver bell, sourwood, yellowwood, *Aconitum, Lobelia, Shortia,* and dog-tooth violet.

Improving the Structure of Soil

As already mentioned, the physical structure of a sandy soil can be improved by incorporating goodly quantities of organic matter such as peat moss or animal manures. These natural materials will improve the structure of heavy soils also, but larger quantities are needed.

In addition to improving the physical structure, organic matter is a valuable storehouse of nutrients not immediately needed by the plants. It releases them at the time the plants can use them.

Perhaps the most widely publicized gardening development in recent years has been the advent of the synthetic soil conditioners. The Monsanto Chemical Company was the first to develop them, and KRILIUM is the trade-marked name of its synthetic soil conditioner.

As with other new products, some unscrupulous manufacturers marketed so-called "conditioners" without adequate testing. As a result, thousands of gardeners spent their money for worthless materials when the conditioners were first offered for sale.

Gardeners who use synthetic conditioners now, however, have a better chance of succeeding with them. The reason is that only reliable conditioners are left on the market; the manufacturers of those of doubtful value have either gone bankrupt or are compelled by the Federal Trade Commission to cease making false claims about their products.

But even where a gardener uses a bona fide soil conditioner he must follow certain precautions and procedures to ensure the desired results.

First of all, the gardener must understand that synthetic conditioners will not improve all soils. They will do nothing for a sandy soil that contains no clay, for example. Nor will they improve poor drainage caused by subsoil hardpans, rock ledges, or seepage.

Is there any way, then, to determine what soil can be improved by the use of a synthetic soil conditioner? The following simple three-minute test will answer this question:

Fill a cup of dry soil from the garden or lawn area that you suspect may be in need of a soil conditioner. Add 4 or 5 drops of water to a small handful of this soil, mix thoroughly in the palm of the hand, and stir with a finger until every tiny granule of soil crumbles and the soil feels silky-smooth. Then roll this soil into the shape of a cigarette. If it retains its shape, the soil can definitely be improved with a conditioner; and if it does not hold its shape but flops over, it too might be improved. But if the soil cannot be rolled into the shape of a cigarette and remains granular, its structure probably cannot be improved with a conditioner.

Here are a few basic facts and suggestions that will help gardeners get the best out of the new synthetic soil conditioners:

(1) Before the structure of any clayey or silty problem soil can be improved, the conditioner must be thoroughly mixed with the soil particles. The only way to do this is to turn the soil over beforehand. *Chemical conditioners cannot work miracles—they will only preserve the physical structure existing at the time they are added.*

(2) Allow the soil to dry a bit on top before applying a powdered or flaked soil conditioner. The conditioner will turn gummy and fail to mix properly if applied to a wet soil.

(3) Once applied, powdered conditioners should be worked immediately to the proper depth with a spading fork, rake, or other suitable tool. They work only to the depth incorporated and no deeper.

(4) A light to moderate sprinkling after mixing is absolutely necessary. When the water is added, the molecules of the soil conditioner with their many electric charges attract the clay soil particles like a magnet and form many small lumps or crumbs. Don't flood the soil

or the crumbly structure will break down before the conditioner can do its work. A heavy cloudburst will do the same kind of damage, so be sure not to treat soils just before an impending rainstorm.

(5) Use only the amount recommended and no more. Research workers at the Connecticut Agricultural Experiment Station found that chemical conditioners applied in excessive amounts (far beyond the manufacturers' recommendations) retarded germination, repressed plant growth, and produced lower yields of certain crops.

Soil conditioners can effect amazing improvements in certain soils, but there are things they will *not* do. Gardeners will experience fewer disappointments if they keep the following facts in mind:

Chemical conditioners will not work by themselves. That is, they just cannot be scattered or poured over a body of unspaded soil and be expected to put the soil into better physical condition.

Chemical conditioners do not supply any plant nutrients unless, of course, such nutrients have been specially added. Moreover, they will not completely replace organic matter. The manufacturer of the most popular synthetic conditioner on the market says that although relatively small amounts of his product will create excellent physical structure in clay and silt soils, he does not recommend his product as a substitute for composts, manures, straw, and other organic matter. Unlike organic matter, synthetic conditioners do not stimulate the growth of soil microorganisms.

Finally, synthetic conditioners do not increase the moisture-retaining properties of all soils, nor do they always increase yields in all crops. Most of the crops thus far grown on chemically conditioned soils, however, have outyielded those grown on untreated soils.

Now that we know what the new conditioners will not do, let's examine some of their advantages over natural conditioners derived from organic matter.

First, synthetic conditioners "fix" the soil into the desired crumbs or, as they are called, aggregates within a day or so of their application. Organic matter takes much longer because it must first be acted upon by soil organisms to produce the natural conditioning materials known as polyuronides.

Second, the crumbs or aggregates formed by the chemical conditioners last much longer because they are not subject to decomposition by soil organisms. Some clay soils treated with the first synthetic conditioners in Ohio retained good porous structure for at least four years.

Plants grown on soils treated with chemical conditioners utilize added fertilizer to better advantage. In some recent tests, for example, the yield of corn was lowest in a soil receiving neither conditioner nor fertilizer. The highest yield was obtained where both a conditioner and fertilizer were added to the same kind of soil. Soils receiving only conditioner or only fertilizer gave yields between these two extremes.

Because of their more porous structure, chemically treated soils dry out faster in spring and hence warm up earlier. This makes early-spring plowing and planting more feasible.

The quicker-drying character of such soils means they must be watched more carefully, particularly at seeding time. Unless treated soils are watered regularly, small seeds planted in the upper ½ inch may germinate poorly. But once the seedlings and plants are well established, less frequent watering is necessary because conditioner-treated soil stimulates a spreading root growth. This greater root system helps the plant resist drought.

Finally, transplants grown in conditioned soil become established more quickly. Plants can be lifted more easily and will begin growth sooner in their new location because damage to the fine absorbing roots is kept at a minimum. Some recent tests with chrysanthemums in California established these points.

Are Conditioners Expensive?

The initial cost of a good chemical conditioner may seem high. But the cost is not prohibitive when one considers the ease of handling and the many years of improved soil structure resulting from their use. Increased manufacturing facilities and greater production have already resulted in a considerable reduction over the original price of four years ago.

Many landscape men have found lawn building with a synthetic soil conditioner to be substantially cheaper than using sod or topsoil. Where topsoil costs about five cents a square foot, for instance, a synthetic soil conditioner costs about half of this. Usually sod costs about forty cents a square yard, whereas the conditioner's cost is twenty-two and one half cents plus the cost of grass seed.

Use of chemical soil conditioners is definitely economical on so-called problem soils where the value of the plant material is high and the amount of the conditioner necessary to do the job is relatively low. In other words, there is a definite place for such conditioners on soils for lawns, for the greenhouse, and for establishing trees and shrubs.

Conditioners also have been found practical in certain farming operations. For example, a narrow band of the conditioner placed over the seed row at planting time reduces soil crusting after rains and increases seedling emergence.

Even in a vegetable garden the grower can limit his use of synthetic conditioners to the hills or strips where the crops are to be grown instead of applying them over the whole garden. This will reduce by nearly two thirds the quantity of soil conditioner needed. Increased yields of such crops as broccoli, lettuce, cabbage, and tomatoes are possible where heavy clay soils are treated by the hill or row method.

In the final analysis no one can predict with certainty just how well synthetic soil conditioners will do in any particular lot of soil. In general, they do improve the structure of most problem soils that are clayey. But sometimes, even when the structure is thus improved, the plants grown are not necessarily superior. Conversely, there are cases where a synthetic conditioner used on a soil considered to be in excellent condition at the start produced still more vigorous plants!

Gardeners faced with the problem of improving the structure of heavy problem soils are advised to try the synthetic conditioners on a small scale to determine the effect on their particular soils before embarking on any large-scale treatment.

We have not learned all there is to know about soil-improving materials by a long shot. Every day something new turns up. Take, for example, a recent discovery by Rhode Island Experiment Station scientists about the use of sawdust around certain plants. They found that there is a soluble "something" in sawdust that improves growth of certain plants. When sawdust was leached with water and the resulting solution was applied to the soil around blueberries, it doubled the growth of the plants. Use of a thick sawdust mulch tripled the growth rate. When the leachate was boiled before application, growth showed no increase whatever. These results strongly suggest that wood fragments contain a soluble, heat-sensitive material that is beneficial to blueberries independent of the physical improvements brought about by the mulch.

Worms and Soil Improvement

The value of earthworms as soil improvers has been highly over-rated, I believe. Work at Ohio State University some years ago revealed that although worm castings are beneficial when added directly to potted plants, the mere presence of large numbers of worms in a soil did nothing to increase plant production.

The normal habitats of one species, *Eisenia foetida,* commonly sold as a soil improver, are manures and composts. This kind, therefore, soon dies if placed in loamy soils of farms and gardens, and any improvement following introduction of such worms is due to their decomposition rather than to their activity.

William C. Grant, Jr., of the Department of Biology at William and Mary College, summarized the whole problem in the January 21, 1955, issue of *Science* so well that I am taking the liberty of quoting him directly. "In general it can be said that worms are abundant in well-aerated soils of high organic content, but it is doubtful whether they actually improve poor soil conditions because their action is most likely effective only in the maintenance of good soil properties already present. The organic gardener should look with some skepticism on the claims for the benefits derived from the introduction of worms into soil and at least should be certain that worms supplied by the earthworm farmers are of a species known to inhabit the type of soil into which they are to be introduced."

Dyed-in-the-wool organic gardeners frequently insist that synthetic chemicals do not grow plants as good as those derived from natural sources. I doubt this very much. At the University of California's Citrus Experiment Station, for example, orange trees have been growing continuously for more than fourteen years in nutrient solutions, without any organic matter. The trees continue to yield good crops of fruits, are green and healthy, and the quality of the oranges produced, so far as can be measured, is as good as that of oranges grown in soil.

Another oft-quoted saying is that a well-fed plant is less subject to disease. This too must be taken with the proverbial grain of salt. It is well known, for example, that fire blight, the highly infectious bacterial disease of pears, is always more destructive on trees fed heartily with nitrogen than on low-nitrogen or starved trees.

Scientists of the United States Department of Agriculture have unearthed some evidence that high levels of nutrition can increase the virulence of a fungus disease of gladiolus known as curvularia leaf spot. A number of gladiolus plants were exposed to the causal fungus. One plant supplied only with water showed no disease; another, given nitrogen, phosphorus, and potash (NPK) was lightly infected. When five times as much NPK was given, the plant became heavily infected, and when twenty-five times as much NPK was supplied, the fungus killed the plant!

When we learn more about diseases and nutrition we may be able to control some plant diseases by the judicious use of plant foods.

PLANT FOODS

Besides correct acidity and good physical structure of soil, plants must have a properly balanced diet to make sturdy growth and produce an abundance of flowers, fruits, and vegetables.

At the moment scientists believe that sixteen elements, of which nitrogen, phosphorus, and potash are the chief ones, are necessary for good plant nutrition. The three numbers separated by dashes on all fertilizer packages indicate, always in the same order, the percentage of these three major nutrients in the mixture. For example, a 5-10-10 fertilizer is one that contains 5 per cent nitrogen, 10 per cent phosphorus, and 10 per cent potash. The thirteen other essential elements are carbon, hydrogen, oxygen, calcium, magnesium, sulfur, copper, iron, manganese, boron, zinc, molybdenum, and vanadium.

Sixteen elements, then, form the backbone of all green life on this earth, and when available in proper form, in the correct amounts, and at the right time, produce strong, healthy trees, shrubs, and flowers.

The standard way to supply plants with many of these elements is to incorporate the raw food elements, in the form of dry fertilizer, in the soil in which plants grow. As every gardener knows, this is frequently a back-breaking job, for to get the best results from this type of chemical fertilizer he must mix it thoroughly into the soil.

At times the essential elements are not readily available to roots even when these nutrients are present in the soil. For example, in early spring when the soil is wet and cold, roots do not readily absorb nitrogen. Thus, many plants, particularly trees, are denied this major nutrient at a time when they need it most. On the other hand, during periods of drought plants cannot use chemical fertilizers applied in dry form. The fertilizers must first be dissolved in water.

These are but a few of many situations in which it is wise to use the newer, high-analysis, completely soluble plant foods now available to every back yard gardener. I refer, of course, to materials like RAPIDGRO, with which I have worked for the last seven years and which was the first high-analysis fertilizer available for use in foliage sprays. I'll say more about leaf feeding later. Other well-known brands of high-analysis, all-soluble fertilizers are FOLIUM, SWIFT'S INSTANT VIGORO, DU PONT'S SOLUBLE PLANT FOOD, HY-GRO, and GRO-STUF.

I believe that the following factors, in addition to extensive advertising, have been responsible for widespread use of such fertilizers in the last few years:

They are quickly available to plants through roots, bark, or leaves, depending on how they are applied. Plants respond more quickly, thus enabling the gardener to see improvements sooner.

They are easy and pleasant to handle. Most of them are sold in dry form, a few as concentrated liquids, but they all must either be dissolved or diluted in water before use. They are virtually odorless— and those of us who have worked with animal manures really appreciate this characteristic.

They are more efficient and hence there is less waste. Working with radioactive tracers, Dr. H. C. Wittwer of Michigan State College found that the leaves are efficient organs for the absorption of phosphorus.

Some studies at the Rothamsted Experimental Station in England revealed that nutrients applied to the leaves of sugar beets are taken up about twice as efficiently as when applied to the soil. The nutrient absorption from the soil is affected by the amount taken in by the leaves. Plants whose leaves were sprayed with nitrogen alone absorbed more phosphorus and potassium from the soil than check plants did. Plants sprayed with potassium absorbed more phosphorus via the roots.

They can be distributed more evenly than dry fertilizers and can be applied at times when the size of the crops or the season prevents applications of dry fertilizers.

In short, their use fits in more closely with our modern way of doing things—of getting more done with less drudgery.

High-analysis fertilizers are more expensive, but that's because some of the ingredients, particularly the instantly soluble phosphates, are costlier than the ingredients used in low-analysis fertilizers. Moreover, virtually every particle in them is usable. They contain no fillers like sand, lime, or other inert materials. Packaging them in neat, easily handled containers also adds to their cost. To compare a fertilizer like 5-10-5 with a concentrated one on the basis of nutrient content alone does not give a true picture of the relative values. After all, it's not so much the amount of nutrients applied that counts as how much is absorbed and used to produce more vigorous plants, greater yields, or larger flowers. For example, even though identical amounts of nutrients are applied, only 10 per cent of those in the dry fertilizer may be absorbed by the roots, whereas 80 or 90 per cent of those in the concentrate, dissolved or diluted in water, may be absorbed through the leaves, the bark, or the roots.

How to Use Concentrates

At the proper season the concentrates, when dissolved or diluted in water, can be used to great advantage in any of several ways:

(1) As a transplanting solution around newly set plants. The usual dilution is a tablespoon of the concentrated salts dissolved in each gallon of water. Pour a cupful of the dilute solution around each newly set tomato, pepper, celery, or annual or perennial flowering plant. Larger plants like trees and shrubs may need several gallons of the nutrient solution. Treated plants survive transplanting shock better and go on to make vigorous growth more quickly.

(2) As a starter solution for seeds as sown. This is two or three times as strong as the transplanting solution. Use a cupful for each foot of row before filling the soil over the seeds. When pouring the liquid, be careful not to wash light seeds out of the furrow.

(3) As a booster solution over the soil around already established, partly grown plants to boost their growth or hasten their maturity and increase yields. This is the same strength as the starter solution, or 2 to 3 tablespoonfuls per gallon of water. The number of applications varies with the crop. Long-season vegetables like tomatoes and eggplants and certain flowers and shrubs require two to three applications, say, two, five, and eight weeks after the plants are set out.

(4) As a foliage spray. For this use the solution is weaker than most of the others, the exact amount varying with the brand used. The usual dilution is a level tablespoonful in a gallon of water, or a pound in 44 gallons of water. The number of applications, again, varies with the crop; long-season ones requiring more. One spraying about every three weeks for three or four times is usually recommended. (Illustration following page 160)

Foliage-nutrient sprays should be applied either with a pressure sprayer or with one of the specially designed fertilizer spray guns available in seed stores. The latter have siphoning devices and are attached to the garden hose. For best results, apply the nutrient sprays in the morning and thoroughly drench the leaves, particularly their lower surfaces, with the spray.

As already mentioned, the amount of high-analysis plant food to use will vary with the grade or formula. Generally speaking, no more than the following amounts should be dissolved in each 10 gallons of water used: 5 ounces of a 12-12-12, 13-13-13, or a 13-26-13; 4 ounces of a 15-15-15, 15-30-15, or a 16-16-16; 3 ounces of an 18-18-18, 20-20-20, or a 23-21-17. Ten gallons of diluted fertilizer prepared from any of these are sufficient to cover at least 40 square feet of garden or lawn. Two to four applications per season should supply enough plant food for most garden crops and lawns.

Gardeners are cautioned that not all fertilizers which are quickly soluble in water are safe to spray on leaves. On the other hand, all those recommended as foliage sprays can safely be used around the roots. The manufacturer will indicate clearly on the label whether his product can be used in foliage sprays.

Most of the concentrates that are safe to use as foliage sprays can be combined with the newer organic pesticides, such as ferbam and DDT, thus enabling the gardener to feed his plants and control pests in one operation. Here, too, the manufacturer of the plant food can advise the gardener as to which pesticides are compatible with his product.

More nutrients will enter leaves when cane sugar is added to fertilizers applied as foliar sprays. This interesting observation was reported by F. G. Gustafson of the University of Michigan, who used radioactive tracer techniques in his studies. Foliar sprays with added sugar are also absorbed by the leaves in the dark when plant activity is usually at its lowest ebb.

The same investigator also studied how fast materials are absorbed by way of the leaves. Cobalt 60 in the form of cobalt chloride was applied to the primary leaf of three-week-old bean plants. Cobalt was found in all parts of the plant two hours after application.

Large-Scale Uses of Concentrates

In some communities fuel oil dealers are putting their idle oil trucks to good use during late spring and summer by carting and applying soluble plant foods to lawns and other plants.

The tanks on the trucks are thoroughly cleaned with a detergent and then with steam to remove all traces of oil before the nutrient solutions are added. The oil hoses, too, are replaced with special spray hoses and nozzles.

Any one of the better-known concentrates like RAPIDGRO, FOLIUM, or GRO-STUF can be applied from the tanks. In some cases crab grass killers or pesticides, or both, are included in the sprays.

Because of the speed of application and the volume of material handled, the cost to the home owner is nominal.

One company has gone a step further, so that fuel trucks are not needed. The Fertilene Corporation of America, New York City, sells the so-called FERTILENE 300 TANKERETTE, an auto trailer-like tank of 300-gallon capacity with a pressure pump, a reel with 150 feet of hose, and a nozzle for spraying. The unit is exceptionally mobile, since it can be pulled anywhere by an automobile or a small truck and it is inexpensive to operate.

Minor-Element Deficiencies

Plants, like humans, are subject to so-called deficiency diseases, and such diseases can be cured by supplying the patient with the deficient element. Among the minor elements required by plants, iron is perhaps the one most often deficient.

The so-called chelates are the latest chemicals for preventing and curing certain deficiency diseases in plants. SEQUESTRENE OF IRON, also known as SEQUESTRENE NaFe, the first of several iron chelates on the market, has proved to be more efficient than such chemicals as iron sulfate and iron ammonium citrate in preventing and curing chlorosis (leaf-yellowing) caused by a deficiency or unavailability of iron.

Oddly enough, iron chlorosis does not necessarily signify a shortage of iron in the soil. It may occur in soils containing sufficient amounts of iron for plant growth but the iron may be either unavailable to the plant or the plant may be unable to utilize it effectively.

Chlorosis due to iron deficiency is usually found in crops growing under two widely different sets of environmental conditions: on lime soils and on acid soils.

About a dozen years ago I found a severe case of iron deficiency in hundreds of pin oak trees growing in an area formerly filled in with coal ashes and therefore definitely alkaline. In such a situation the iron is removed from solution and is in a form unavailable to the trees. I succeeded in curing the leaf chlorosis by injecting iron phosphate directly into the tree trunks. The iron thus injected was transported to the leaves, where it was used to make up for the deficiency.

We now know that iron in chelate form stays in solution despite alkaline conditions and thus can be assimilated directly from the soil. Iron chelates are applied, therefore, in either of two ways: in powdered form directly to the soil, or dissolved in water and sprayed on the leaves.

For best results with soil applications, the iron chelate should be distributed uniformly over the soil surface beneath the plant and then thoroughly watered to a depth of at least 6 inches. To assure an even distribution, the proper amount of chelated iron powder should be mixed with fertilizer or with some inert material such as sand, or the required amount should be dissolved in water and sprayed or sprinkled over the soil.

Leaf sprays should be applied as thorough cover sprays. This means that sufficient liquid should be applied to wet all leaf surfaces thoroughly. On outdoor plants such sprays are best applied during the middle third of the growing season, when there is little chance of harming the crop. Foliage sprays should not be applied to crops in blossom or in fruit.

One brand of iron chelate, IRON TETRINE, used at the rate of 1 pound in 100 gallons of water per acre of crop as a foliage spray, was definitely beneficial to celery, corn, cabbage, beans, watermelon, cantaloupe, eggplant, turnips, broccoli, peas, cauliflower, cucumber, pepper, tomato, squash, and radishes.

The same concentration and rate of application were also found to be beneficial to the following ornamentals: gardenias, chrysanthemums, roses, rhododendrons, gladioli, azaleas, and snapdragons.

Some of the newer hydrangea varieties appear to be more susceptible to iron chlorosis than the older kinds. Saturating the soil with a solution of SEQUESTRENE OF IRON fully restored the green color of some chlorotic hydrangeas within five days. In other hydrangeas the normal color was restored after two or three weekly applications.

The chart on page 179 gives details on the amount of SEQUESTRENE OF IRON to use in the soil or in foliage sprays to cure chlorosis in some ornamental trees and shrubs.

In addition to SEQUESTRENE OF IRON (NaFe) and IRON TETRINE, iron chelates are also available under the proprietary names VERSENE, VERSENOL and PERMA GREEN IRON 135. No doubt additional brands of essentially the same product will eventually appear on the market.

Not All Yellowing Due to Iron Deficiency

Gardeners must not jump to the conclusion that all yellowing of leaves is caused by a deficiency of iron. Chlorotic leaves may also result from fungus, virus, insect, or mite attack; low temperatures; toxic materials in the air or soil; excessive soil moisture; or surpluses or deficiencies of copper, manganese, zinc, or other metals. Correct diagnosis is therefore essential to ensure the preventive or curative results desired with the metallic chelates.

SEQUESTRENE OF IRON APPLICATION CHART

For Ornamentals			
Plant	Soil Applications		Foliage Sprays
	tablespoons per plant	ounces per 1,000 sq. ft.	ounces per 25 gallons water
Azaleas	½ to 1	12	16
Chrysanthemums	½	4	4
Gardenias	1	6	4
Hydrangeas	1	12	4
Pieris	½	12	8
Rhododendrons	1	12	8
Roses	½ to 1	6	4

FOR TREES AND LARGE SHRUBS			
Plant	Soil Applications		Foliage Sprays
	ounces per plant	ounces per 1,000 sq. ft.	ounces per 25 gallons water
Camellias	8	40	. . . . . .
Magnolias	2	. . . . . .	. . . . . .
Pin Oak	12 (small trees)	. . . . . .	8
	24 (large trees)	. . . . . .	. . . . . .
Spruce	8	. . . . . .	. . . . . .
Tree Box	32 (large trees)	. . . . . .	. . . . . .

Other Materials Correct Minor-Element Deficiency

Several other products are available to correct deficiencies of the minor or trace elements. One is so-called agricultural frit, or FTE (fritted trace elements). This material consists of small pieces of specially prepared glass that are relatively insoluble but still release sufficient amounts of the minor elements to enable the plant to grow normally. To absorb minor elements like iron, manganese, boron, copper, zinc, and molybdenum, plant roots must be in direct contact with the frit particles. Hence for best results it is essential to thoroughly incorporate the frit through the entire zone. FTE comes in 1- and 5-pound packages for home garden use. One pound will treat about 400 square feet.

Another way to overcome minor-element deficiencies is to use ES-MIN-EL (Essential Mineral Elements). This is available in liquid form for use as a foliage spray and in dust form for soil treatment wherever a deficiency of trace elements is indicated.

Testing for Plants' Needs

In the past the fertilizer needs of trees and shrubs were supplied largely by rule of thumb, by guesswork, or from diagnoses based on long years of experience with plants.

A machine called the spectrograph has revolutionized the whole picture because it leaves no room for guesses and long experience with plants is unnecessary. It provides a quick answer to whether the plant is suffering from a deficiency or an overdose of some nutrient.

The procedure is to collect, in July or August, some leaves from a tree suspected of having a nutritional disorder, dry them, and then grind them to a fine powder and reduce them to ashes at a temperature of 500-600 degrees. The ash is then dissolved and the solution placed on an electrode and burned with a high-voltage electric spark or arc. Each of the elements present will emit its own characteristic light, which is passed through a prism and recorded on a photographic plate as a series of dark lines or bands. These bands indicate the amounts of the various elements present. The spectrograph can determine how much calcium, phosphorus, magnesium, manganese, copper, boron, iron, and zinc are in the leaves. Potassium is determined with a flame photometer and nitrogen by chemical methods.

Using these modern methods, the Department of Horticulture at Michigan State College has set up a Leaf Analysis Service for Michigan orchardists, and plans are under way to analyze leaves for nurserymen, park superintendents, and others entrusted with the care of trees. The department records the results of its tests on a nutrient-element balance chart, which is easy to understand. The service may be available to home gardeners someday if interest warrants and funds are available.

Many nutritional problems have been solved through this service. For example, young Taxus with yellowed leaves suggestive of an iron deficiency were submitted to the Leaf Analysis Service. The analysis revealed not an iron deficiency but an acute potassium deficiency, which was also limiting nitrogen absorption. Application of potassium corrected the yellowing and overcame the nitrogen deficiency.

In another instance a peach grower who assumed that his trees were suffering from a deficiency of magnesium submitted a leaf sample. The test revealed that the trees were suffering from a severe potassium deficiency. Had he applied dolomitic lime, which is used to overcome a magnesium deficiency, he would have made the deficiency worse!

In a large number of leaf samples analyzed in 1954, the Michigan Leaf Analysis Service found relatively few cases of acute deficiencies or toxicities. It did find "hidden" deficiencies of boron or manganese, or both, in more than half of the samples submitted.

Someday all state colleges of agriculture will probably have facilities for making leaf analyses to aid gardeners in calculating the fertilizer needs of plants.

New Synthetic Nitrogen Fertilizer

Perhaps the most striking development in the plant food field in recent years is a form of synthetic fertilizer that supplies nitrogen to plants safely, at a uniform rate, and over a far longer period than was possible ever before even with natural organic fertilizers. In fact, the new product, a combination of urea and formaldehyde, bids fair to replace many of the natural organic materials as the source of slowly available nitrogen. Urea-form is the name given to this unusual chemical, which has the desirable characteristics of both the natural organics and the synthetic chemical nitrogen fertilizers. It can be prepared so as to make nitrogen available to plants almost as rapidly as that from urea, or to make it available over a two- to three-year period.

This controlled availability of nitrogen constitutes a major advance in agriculture. Heretofore, maintenance of a uniform nitrogen level has always been difficult because the high solubility of this nutrient in water caused the plant food to disappear very rapidly from soils in rainy areas.

The usual chemical sources of nitrogen (ammonia, ammonium salts, nitrates, urea, and cyanamide) all are readily soluble in water. In normal soils the nitrogen from these materials is directly available to growing plants or rapidly convertible to available form.

Nitrogen is also present in many kinds of organic matter such as tankage, cottonseed meal, and sewage sludge, but before it can become available to plants it must go through the process of nitrification, that is, it must be changed into a form usable by the plants, either as nitrate nitrogen, or to a lesser extent, as ammonia nitrogen.

Although the nitrification of natural organic fertilizers is commonly thought to proceed slowly, it takes place much more rapidly than most persons realize. Under favorable conditions 80 to 85 per cent of the organic nitrogen becomes available to the plant during the first three weeks after application. As a matter of fact, when temperatures and moisture conditions are relatively high, natural organic fertilizers will break down and release their nitrogen almost as rapidly as urea does. The ordinary chemical nitrogen compounds release their nitrogen even more rapidly than do the organics.

By comparison the nitrogen in urea-form is converted to its usable form much more slowly. Although the peak is reached during the third to fifth week after application, a high rate of release continues for more than another month. In other words, the urea-form fertilizers ration the amount of nitrogen automatically and thus avoid supplying large amounts at any one time.

But even with urea-form, the rate at which nitrogen is made available to plants drops to a low level within three and one half to four months. Hence, to maintain nitrogen in good supply, urea-form fertilizers would have to be added twice a year to outdoor soils and three times a year to greenhouse soils.

Another important advantage of urea-form over the highly soluble chemical nitrogen fertilizers, and even over the organic nitrogen kinds, is that it won't "burn" plants.

The older kinds of dry fertilizers, even some that contain a high proportion of natural organic materials, will "burn" grass unless they are watered in immediately after application. The "burning" is caused by the withdrawal of moisture from the grass blades by particles of plant food that remain lodged on the blades. These particles, dissolved in water, make a highly concentrated solution, or one with what is known as a high osmotic value, as compared with the sap inside the grass blades. By the process called osmosis the solution of low concentration moves from inside the grass to the more concentrated plant food solution outside, causing the grass blades to collapse, brown, and "burn."

On the other hand, a water solution of urea-form has a low osmotic concentration. It cannot form concentrated solutions even on wet grass because the constituents dissolve only sparingly and the resulting solution has a weaker osmotic "pull" than the cell sap. Hence no water is drawn out of the grass and no "burning" results. When urea-form products are watered into the soil—either by rain or with a hose—the nutrients are taken up by the roots as needed.

Urea-form has been applied at rates containing as high as 800 pounds of nitrogen per acre without burning. This is equivalent to 2 tons of ammonium sulfate. On the other hand, severe "burning" of vegetation will occur with as little as 400 pounds of nitrogen per acre applied as urea.

Another advantage of the urea-form fertilizers is that their properties and composition can be standardized. There is no variation as with natural organic fertilizers.

Early tests by a number of turf experts, including Professor H. B. Musser at Pennsylvania State University and Dr. Fred V. Grau of the West Point Products Corporation, Pennsylvania, showed that the desirable slow, uniform nitrogen response for turf can be obtained with a single application of a suitable urea-form product. Ordinary turf can get sufficient nitrogen for satisfactory growth for an entire season with 4 pounds of nitrogen applied as urea-form per 1,000 square feet. In actual tests 20 to 40 pounds of nitrogen in this form have been applied to turf at one time without causing injury.

Professors O. R. Lunt and R. H. Scarioni, of the University of California at Los Angeles, recently tested urea-form mixtures on greenhouse ornamentals. They reported that 5 to 6 pounds of URAMITE (a trade-marked urea-form product made by the du Pont Company) per 100 square feet broadcast as a top-dressing produced no injury to greenhouse azaleas, carnations, roses, and snapdragons. In some of their experiments they repeated the treatments every three months with no harmful effects. Top-dressing 1½ to 2 teaspoonfuls to each 6-inch pot containing Croft lily, chrysanthemum, cyclamen or hydrangea caused no damage. The two professors reported that all plants grown with URAMITE were of excellent quality, and the quality of the carnations, chrysanthemums, and hydrangeas was the best in their experience.

At this writing Long Island florists are testing URAMITE on such long-season crops as carnations, hydrangeas, and several kinds of lilies.

Among the urea-form fertilizers now available are BORDEN'S 38, GOLDEN VIGORO, and URAMITE. The first is made by the Borden Company of New York City, the second by Swift and Company of Chicago, and the third by E. I. du Pont de Nemours & Company of Wilmington, Delaware. GOLDEN VIGORO contains other major nutrients in addition to urea-form nitrogen.

Urea-form products release their nitrogen much more quickly in the presence of the other major plant nutrients, phosphoric acid and potash, and more rapidly at pH 6.0 than at pH 5.0 or 8.0. Those that seem to be best sources of nitrogen for plant growth usually contain 37 to 39 per cent nitrogen. With these compounds, as with natural organics, the rate of nitrogen availability is governed by the rate at which the nitrogen is changed to nitrates by soil microorganisms.

The cost per unit of nitrogen in urea-form fertilizers is higher than that of standard chemical nitrogen because urea, itself a source of nitrogen, is one of the ingredients. The nitrogen in natural organic materials such as tankage is usually three to five times as expensive as an equivalent amount in chemically made nitrogen materials. Once the urea-form fertilizers are mass-produced, however, the price of their nitrogen, unit for unit, will approximate or be cheaper than that in natural organics.

The advantages, then, of the new urea-form fertilizers are: They can release nitrogen in small amounts over a long period; because of their low solubility they are safe to apply even in relatively heavy doses; they are odorless and hence do not attract flies, and when used as top-dressings they do not encourage growth of algae, or green scum, on the soil surface.

Chapter 12

GROWTH REGULATORS AND WEED KILLERS

Of all the subjects discussed in this book, none is more intriguing than growth regulators. Some of these substances are made by plants and are called hormones, others are synthetic chemicals concocted by man in the laboratory, but both kinds have the property of inhibiting or otherwise modifying the normal physiological processes in plants. Scientists have put some of the unusual properties to good use in the field of horticulture. Age-old practices are being set aside, and quicker and cheaper ways of doing things horticultural are the result.

Some of these hormone or hormone-like substances have the power of speeding up the plant's growth rate or of slowing it down; some speed root development on cuttings or prevent sprout formation in stored potatoes and onions; others increase the set of fruits on trees or vines; still others will prevent the development of unwanted or undesirable fruits. Some are so specific and selective that they kill certain weeds without harming desirable plants growing near by.

My reason for including a discussion of weed killers in this chapter is that many weeds can be controlled with hormones and hormone-like substances. There are, of course, the so-called general weed killers that are nonselective and kill all vegetation, whether good or bad. These, too, will be mentioned briefly.

The agricultural scientist has only scratched the surface so far as growth regulators are concerned. At the rate new ones are being found, it would not be amiss to forecast that even more startling properties will be discovered.

For example, man may soon be able to make tender plants resistant to low temperatures merely by spraying them with the proper hormone. This prediction may seem farfetched, but actually it is based on a recent report by a Canadian research worker, W. G. Corns, of the University of Alberta. Dr. Corns discovered that the parsnip, *Pastinaca sativa* var. HOLLOW CROWN, was far more resistant to frosts where the tops of the plants had been sprayed with proprietary plant hormones APP-L-SET or COLOR-SET. When the first hard frosts arrived in early October, Dr. Corns noted that the hormone-sprayed plants were erect and green, whereas the leaves of the untreated plants were collapsed and darkened. The tops of the treated plants remained erect and green until more severe frosts occurred in late November.

Flowering in some plants can be hastened by the application of certain hormones. Professors Wildon and Hamner of Michigan State College recently reported that the material designated as TIBA, chemically 2-3-5 triodobenzoic acid, hastened flowering in petunias and zinnias from ten to twenty days ahead of untreated plants. In one test petunias flowered and set seed before untreated plants of the same kind even started to flower.

Even more intriguing is the possibility that man may be able to produce flowers and fruits at will, and although the hormone has not yet been found that will change vegetative buds to floral ones, the possibilities of accomplishing this are bright indeed. Enough research has been done to suggest that such a hormone (florigen) exists, that it originates in the leaves, and that it moves to the point where the flowers are to develop. Just picture what this discovery will mean to the world's food supply!

But enough of this daydreaming! Let's get down to realities and see where presently available hormones and similar substances can be used to make gardening more successful and more pleasant.

Fruit-Setting Hormones

When the temperature at flowering time falls below 59 or 60 degrees, many plants, particularly tomatoes, will not set fruits. As a matter of fact, this is one reason why the first flower cluster rarely produces many fruits. When properly applied to the tomato flower, even under adverse conditions of low temperatures and poor pollinating weather, these hormones will help to produce ripe tomatoes three weeks earlier than untreated flowers, and in addition produce more, larger, and meatier fruits. (Illustration following page 160)

One of the most widely used of the tomato hormones is BLOSSOM-SET, sold by Science Products Company, Chicago 37. BLOSSOM-SET comes as a liquid that needs only dilution with water and then is sprayed on the blossom clusters. It also comes in a convenient aerosol can, which merely requires pressing the button and directing the spray at the tomato flowers. Other fruit-setting hormones are sold under such names as HORMEX, SEED-LESS-SET, SURE-SET, and FRUITONE.

The fruit-setting hormone must be sprayed carefully into the face and not the back of the flowers. Occasionally, where an excess of nitrogen has been used on the tomato plants, the use of these hormones may cause premature softening of the fruit and puffiness or large hollow spaces in the fruit. These are the exceptions rather than the rule, however.

One of the newest materials for increasing fruit set, particularly on lima beans, is N-meta-tolyl phthalamic acid, sold under the name of DURASET. When used on this crop under adverse growing conditions, yields have been doubled over those from untreated plants.

I have used DURASET on tomatoes and obtained nearly twice as many fruits from plants sprayed several times with it as from untreated plants.

Although the way DURASET works is still obscure, the hormone is known to be systemic; that is, it travels through the plant and retards so-called abscission formation. The formation of an abscission layer at the base of the flower stem causes the flower to drop off before the fruit is set. DURASET looks promising for increasing fruit set on other fruits and vegetables as well.

Another fruit-setting hormone is sold under the trade name BERRY-SET. This increases the size of strawberry, raspberry, and blackberry fruits. It is easy to use. Simply dissolve the BERRY-SET powder in water as directed and spray the berry plants fourteen to sixteen days after blooming, when most of the flowers are open and small whitish berries are visible. Repeat the spray five days later. Strawberries average 20 per cent larger and blackberries 100 per cent larger than those on untreated plants.

Female American holly trees, which ordinarily produce berries only if a male tree is growing near by, can be induced to form berries by spraying the open flowers in spring with the proper hormone. BERRY-SET and FRUITONE are two products which not only will help berries to set on hollies but will help to hold leaves on cut evergreens for several weeks longer than normal.

Fruit Prevention

There are situations where the reverse effect of that just described is desired. I refer to the prevention, on certain trees, of fruits that are unwanted for one reason or other. The female ginkgo, for example, produces foul-smelling fruits; some mulberries produce fruits that stain the walks and garden structures; and horse chestnuts form fruits that are overly attractive to playful boys.

Both hormone and nonhormone chemicals have been found capable of preventing fruit formation. Applied as sprays at blooming time or immediately after blooming, they either destroy the fruit-forming capabilities of the tree or kill the flowers on very young fruits with little to no damage to the leaves and branches.

Satisfactory results can be obtained by using the following materials at the concentrations given and taking any precautions supplied by the manufacturer:

American elm, *Ulmus americana:* APP-L-SET, 60 parts in a million parts of water (ppm) at full bloom, when the pollen is being discharged.

Carolina poplar, *Populus canadensis:* 1 quart of DN-289 and 1 pint of summer oil in 100 gallons of water, at full-bloom stage.

Catalpa, *Catalpa speciosa:* APP-L-SET, 60 ppm in full bloom.

Crab Apple, *Malus purpurea:* PARMONE, 7 ounces in 100 gallons of water when the fruit is very small.

Eastern poplar, *Populus deltoides,* ELGETOL, 2 quarts to 100 gallons of water at full bloom.

Ginkgo, *Ginkgo biloba:* CHLORO-IPC, 500 ppm about twelve days after blooming. Professional arborists and other shade tree maintenance workers, who are likely to have mist blowers, can use either of the following on female ginkgo at blooming time: 1 pint of MH-30 in 8 gallons of water, 1 gallon of this dilution for each large tree; or 1 pound of MH-40 in 8 gallons of water plus 8 ounces of glycerine, 1 gallon of this mixture per tree.

Honey locust (thornless), *Gleditsia triancanthos inermis:* APP-L-SET, 100 ppm when the fruit is 1 to 2 inches long.

Horse Chestnut, *Aesculus hippocastanum:* APP-L-SET, 30–60 ppm at blooming time.

Red maple, *Acer rubrum:* APP-L-SET, 40 ppm in full bloom.

Silver maple, *Acer saccharinum:* APP-L-SET, 40 ppm in full bloom.

Tree of Heaven, *Ailanthus altissima:* APP-L-SET, 200 ppm in full bloom.

The material APP-L-SET, listed so frequently here, is now being tested to determine its ability to delay blossom opening for several weeks on plants such as flowering cherries. Later-blooming plants are less likely to be injured by early-spring frosts.

Along similar lines, many of the materials mentioned here can be used also to thin out the blossoms of fruit trees instead of killing all of them. Commercial orchardists use such materials as the dinitro sprays (DN) and hormones like AMID-THIN to reduce heavy fruit stand and thus increase the size and quality of the fruits that do form. The materials are used at much weaker concentrations to thin the blossoms than are needed to kill all the flowers and prevent fruit formation.

Cornell scientists recently reported that NPA, or N-1-naphthyl phthalmic acid, effectively reduced fruit set in peach trees when applied at blooming time. This material appears to have several advantages over others presently used to thin peaches.

Prevention of Fruit Drop

Hormone materials are available for preventing the premature dropping of fruits, especially apples. One of the most effective is COLOR-SET. The fruit, however, must be harvested as soon as the proper maturity is reached, otherwise the apples will hang on tenaciously and may then become overripe. This is particularly true with summer and fall varieties, like MC INTOSH.

COLOR-SET is available in one-fourth pint bottles, and each bottle, when added to 100 gallons of water, makes a 20-parts-per-million concentration.

Other proprietary materials that also can be used to prevent premature fruit drop are APPLE-LOK, APP-L-SET, FRUITONE, and PARMONE. As noted earlier, when used at stronger doses at flowering time, most of these same materials are capable of completely preventing fruit formation.

Sprout Inhibitors

Several materials are commercially available which will prevent or sharply reduce sprouting of potatoes, onions, and other root crops in storage. Some, like maleic hydrazide, discussed later in this chapter, must be applied to the growing plants in the field just before harvest time. Others like DORMATONE and FUSAREX are applied as the potatoes and other crops are put into storage.

These sprout inhibitors obviously should not be used on crops that later are to be used for seed, because treated plant material would be useless for such a purpose.

Rooting Cuttings

Quicker and better rooting of cuttings is obtainable with certain hormone preparations containing indolebutyric acid, as for example

HORMODIN, and naphthalene acetic acid and chemically related compounds like ROOTONE. The amount of active ingredient varies with the material, hence one must be guided by the manufacturer's directions. Use of too much of the preparation or use on plants other than those for which the product is recommended may damage or kill the cuttings. Hence the admonition to use these rooting hormones exactly as recommended.

Maleic Hydrazide

Maleic hydrazide, better known as MH or MH-40, is such an unusual chemical that I feel it merits special mention. To me it is the most versatile of all the growth-regulating substances yet discovered. I believe it will hold that rating until scientists discover the flower-inducing hormone, florigen, mentioned earlier in this chapter.

Originally dscovered in 1895 by two German scientists, MH was rediscovered in 1947 by chemists of the Naugatuck Chemical Division of the United States Rubber Company, who also uncovered some of its extremely interesting properties.

Maleic hydrazide has the very unsual ability of temporarily retarding plant growth without impairing the health of the plant. The degree of the retardation is directly proportional to the dosage sprayed on the plants.

Maleic hydrazide is now being marketed under a half dozen different trade names for use on lawns and for several other purposes. Properly treated grass grows much more slowly and thus requires less frequent mowings. In fact, in some experimental plots only a single mowing a season was necessary. (Illustration following page 160)

It is not recommended for lawns subject to heavy traffic because such grass makes slow to poor growth anyway. But it can be used to retard grass around the edge of the lawn, in areas adjacent to flower beds, under trees, and along fences. In other words, it is to be used in little-traveled areas that are difficult to get at with the mower.

How MH Works. MH works in the growing tips, in the so-called apical cells of the plant's stem, where it retards the division of cells. Slowing down cell division, in turn, results in retarding stem growth.

The chemical is absorbed by green grass for about twenty-four hours after it is applied. Once inside, it moves downward for about a week. Its effect is less pronounced if heavy rains fall within a few hours of application.

Retarding the growth rate takes place slowly. Gardeners should not expect results overnight. The effect of a summer treatment, for example, will not be readily apparent for nearly a month, but a spring treatment works faster and its effect is apparent within two or three weeks.

The best times to treat for optimum results are in the fall while the grass is still green (just prior to the dormant period) and in April or early May.

MH can also be applied during the summer, but the period of growth check is shorter than with spring or fall applications. To permit maximum absorption, the grass should not be cut for a week after treatment.

The dosage for late summer treatment, after vigorous regrowth begins, is 4 to 5 ounces of 40 per cent maleic hydrazide (MH-40) powder dissolved in 2 gallons of water for each 1,000 square feet of lawn. A 3-gallon knapsack compressed-air sprayer is best for applying the solution.

Experimental Work Extensive. Most of the experimental work with maleic hydrazide was done along the Connecticut parkways, where more than 12 million square feet of turf have been treated. The basic grasses in these tests were REDTOP, CHEWINGS NEW ZEALAND FESCUE, and KENTUCKY BLUEGRASS. Tests in the Deep South were made on BERMUDA, CARPET, and ST. AUGUSTINE grasses. Slowing down of the growth rate was also noted in these grasses.

Specially designed nozzles on hydraulic sprayers operated at 200 pounds' pressure are used to apply MH to large turf areas along parkways and on golf courses.

MH Safe to Use. Toxicological tests show that MH is a safe chemical to use, almost as safe as common table salt. Cows fed on MH-treated grass eliminated all the chemical—none appeared in the milk.

There are no drift and sprayer contamination problems. In other words, MH will not drift, as do some formulations of 2,4-D, to damage trees and shrubs growing near by. Then, too, the sprayer used for MH treatments can be used for insecticides following a thorough rinsing of the tank and hose.

Precautions. Only a few precautions are necessary with MH. It should not be used on newly planted grass areas. Nor should it be used more than twice in the same season even on well-established lawns. Re-treatment during the same season should be made only after normal grass growth has resumed. Treatments must always be made on green, growing grass. Finally, excessive doses will produce a temporary browning of the grass.

For retarding growth of grass, maleic hydrazide is sold under such trade names as STOP-GRASS, SLO-GRO, KEM-KUT, and TRIMTONE.

Other Uses for MH. Maleic hydrazide also checks the growth of several kinds of hedge plants. Several years ago I found that two applications of a ½ per cent solution at three-week intervals starting in late spring would slow down the growth of California privet and thus reduce the need for frequent clipping. I applied the solution with a pressure sprayer until it dripped from the leaves.

I'm sure many owners of privet hedges will be interested in trying such a chemical. They will agree that it is a lot easier to spray the hedge a few times during the growing season than to wield hedge clippers every few weeks.

The use of maleic hydrazide, however, will not make clippers obsolete. They still will be needed to shape up hedges, even MH-treated ones.

The following hedges have been successfully sprayed with MH by other research workers to slow the growth rate: NEPAL FIRETHORN, *Pyracantha crenulata,* with a ½ per cent solution; SHARPLEAF WIL-LOW, *Salix acutifolia,* and common buckthorn, *Rhamnus cathartica,* with a ⅒ per cent solution; and common privet, *Ligustrum vulgare,* with a 1 per cent solution. The common privet required twice as strong a solution as I found necessary for California privet.

Wild garlic, *Allium vineale,* a weed that is spreading with alarming rapidity in the eastern United States, is also easily controlled with MH. When sprayed on young plants, MH moves to the growing point, where it stops growth and prevents formation of the bulb. Results will not be apparent until the season following the treatment because maleic hydrazide does not kill the current season's growth but prevents formation of the bulbs that give rise to the next season's plants.

In the South, MH is sprayed on tobacco plants to prevent the formation of suckers, or side shoots. These formerly were removed by hand, a costly operation.

MH has been found to retard the aging processes in the flowers of *Magnolia grandiflora.* Its ability to slow down maturing of the flowers is related to the amount of starch present at the time it is applied. If abundant starch is present, MH retards its digestion and thus slows down flower development.

Because MH will also retard terminal growth on trees, it is now being tested to compare its effectiveness with hand pruning on street trees that interfere with electric wires.

Two investigators at the University of Missouri found that submersion of unopened rose buds for one minute in an MH solution retards the opening sufficiently to permit storage of roses for twenty-two days at normal refrigeration temperatures. Not only does this treatment increase the storage period, but more consumer satisfaction is assured because treated flowers last three days longer than untreated ones in the home.

The most recently discovered of maleic hydrazide's remarkable properties is its ability to alter the sex of flowers. In an article entitled "Chemical Induction of Male Sterility in Cucurbits" in a recent issue of *Science,* S. H. Wittwer and I. G. Hillyer of Michigan State College reported that maleic hydrazide suppresses the formation of male flowers in certain members of the cucumber family, thus permitting the production of female flowers primarily. A single application of MH at a dosage ranging from 250 to 500 ppm, when 1 or 2 true leaves had developed on TABLE QUEEN SQUASH, resulted in the production of only female flowers. Normally a goodly percentage of the flowers in such plants are males.

Other Growth-Regulating Substances

Two scientists at the University of Wisconsin recently discovered KINETIN, a chemical that works in a way that is just the reverse of that of maleic hydrazide. KINETIN forces plants to grow after they've stopped making normal growth. In other words, it causes dormant cells to divide and grow again just as they did when young, and the cells continue to grow as long as the chemical is applied.

Some very unusual properties are attributed to the chemical alpha methoxyphenylacetic acid by Dr. J. W. Mitchell of the United States Department of Agriculture. He found that after this compound was applied to leaves it was absorbed and moved down the stem into the roots and out into the soil. Then it was readily absorbed by the roots of nearby plants and translocated to their leaves, where it checked growth.

Only nine hours were required for the chemical to make the trip from the leaves of one plant to those of a neighbor in sufficient amounts to check growth.

Although no practical use has yet been found for a material with such unusual properties, gardeners can rest assured that scientists will uncover one soon!

WEED KILLERS

As mentioned earlier in this chapter, the only justification for discussing weed killers in this chapter is that many of our most effective herbicides are true growth regulators or hormone-like substances. Many of them, of course, cannot be classified as hormones or hormone-like substances, but will be discussed in this chapter nevertheless.

Importance of Weeds

Before we go into the problem of how to control weeds, let's see just how important these pests are. Remember a weed is a plant that grows where it is not wanted, or one whose virtues are yet to be discovered.

Estimated losses caused by weeds on farms in the United States have reached the staggering figure of four billion dollars annually. Farmers spend a billion and a half dollars every year fighting weeds. This is equal to more than 7 per cent of the value of their crops. A single railroad may spend a half million dollars a year to keep its rights of way free from unwanted vegetation.

So important are weeds in our economy that a national organization, the Weed Society of America, was founded on December 8, 1954, to further man's knowledge of weeds and their control.

Surprising as it may seem, weeds also occupy an important place in the plant disease picture. They must be kept under control for, besides competing with garden plants for water, food, and sunlight, they serve as breeding places for many insects that attack garden plants. Moreover, certain weeds act as reservoirs for a number of plant viruses. Chickweed, for example, can harbor the virus known as spotted wilt, which can be highly destructive to tomatoes and dahlias.

Controlling weeds by mechanical means, that is, with the hoe or the cultivator, is costly and time-consuming. Hence the American farmer and many home gardeners are turning to chemicals for help on weed control, just as they have come to depend on chemicals to help combat insect pests and plant diseases.

Nonselective Weed Killers

Chemicals that kill all plants, the good as well as the bad, are known as general, or nonselective, weed killers. These are used to keep industrial sites, railroad rights of way, clay tennis courts, and driveways free of all vegetation. Among the older materials used for these purposes are sodium chloride, potassium chlorate, arsenites, and borax. But all have some serious drawback such as fire hazard and toxicity to people and pets, just to mention a few.

Ammonium sulfamate, sold as AMMATE, has long been successfully used as a general weed killer. It is particularly useful on small properties infested with poison ivy. It is nonflammable and there is no danger that its fumes will drift and damage nearby desirable plants, as is the case with some weed killers like 2,4-D, discussed later in this chapter.

AMMATE can, in a sense, be used as a selective killer too. For example, poison ivy growing on apple trees can be killed without hurting the tree if the spray is directed on the poison ivy vines in such a way that very little falls on the bark of the tree and none on the apple leaves. It cannot be used where poison ivy is growing in privet or other hedges because there is no way to avoid hitting the desirable plants.

AMMATE is also effective against the Japanese knotweed, *Polygonum caespitosum* var. *longisetum,* originally introduced for ornamental purposes from Japan and now a most troublesome weed in many parts of the eastern United States. It is overrunning turf areas in cemeteries and golf courses on Long Island, ornamental plantings in the Hudson Valley, and park areas and lawns in and around New York City. An extremely vigorous grower, it produces rapidly spreading below-ground shoots. Some of its roots are known to penetrate as deep as 6 feet in certain soils.

AMMATE sprays, applied when the shoots are less than a foot high, are said to be effective. The soil around the shoots should also be soaked with the solution and the treated area left undisturbed for a month. Repeat the application to destroy shoots missed by the first treatment.

Following are a few new nonselective weed killers on the market:

BARON, developed by the Dow Chemical Company, can be sprayed on the leaves which take it up directly; or it may be sprayed on the soil, from which it is taken up by the roots. When applied to the soil, it prevents regrowth of weeds for approximately an entire season.

CHLOREA, containing sodium chlorate, borate, and a material known by the letters CMU, is recommended for industrial, agricultural, and railroad use. It combines the proved effectiveness of chlorate on deep-rooted weeds with the prolonged soil-surface action of CMU on shallow-rooted grasses and annual seedlings. CHLOREA is nonpoisonous to animal life and, because of its borate content, creates no fire hazard when used as directed.

KARMEX and TELVAR are trade names for two du Pont weed killers. The former is for agricultural use, and the latter for industrial situations such as around factories and rights of way. Both are of low toxicity to livestock and humans, and are noncorrosive to equipment, nonflammable, and nonvolatile.

KURON is the trade name of a weed killer that is highly effective as a foliage spray on post oak, blackjack oak, white oak, and pin oak growing along railroad rights of way.

UREABOR is a new grass and weed killer containing borates and a urea compound. It requires no mixing or spraying but is applied dry, just as it comes from the bag.

Selective Weed Killers

Chemicals that have the unusual property of killing some plants without harming others are known as selective weed killers. It is with this group that the greatest advances have been made in recent years and it is here that many growth regulators are found. As a matter of fact, specificity appears to be the order of the day in weed control investigations. Specific compounds are being developed for specific weeds in specific crops.

By far the best known of the selective weed killers is 2,4-dichlorophenoxyacetic acid, commonly known as 2,4-D. This hormone-like substance has the ability to destroy broad-leaved weeds without harming narrow-leaved plants like the grasses growing near by.

Although it was just a laboratory curiosity when its unusual properties were first discovered, a dozen or so years ago, by Drs. P. W. Zimmerman and A. E. Hitchcock at the world-famous Boyce Thompson Institute, 28 million pounds of 2,4-D compositions were used in 1954. Most of this huge amount was used by American farmers to control broad-leaved weeds among such crops as corn and the small grains. Some was used in lawn preparations for combating broad-leaved weeds like dandelions. (Illustration following page 160)

An important disadvantage of hormone weed killers containing 2,4-D and a close relative, 2,4,5-T, is that they are so highly volatile. Even minute traces of them reaching grapes, tomatoes, beans, and vine crops will cause severe growth reactions and even death to the plant. Hence they must always be handled with due appreciation of this characteristic. Sprayers used to apply them should be set aside for weed control only, because 2,4-D and similar materials cannot easily be washed out of the sprayers.

An ingenious way to spot-treat broad-leaved weeds in lawns with a minimum of drift hazard and little effort is with Bridgeport Brass Company's SPOT WEED KILLER. The 2,4-D comes in a can under pressure and to eliminate bending or stooping, the bottom of the can is attached to a yard-long, reusable applicator handle. An exclusive "Control-Cone," attached to the working end of the can, directs and traps the 2,4-D on the weed.

Other Selective Weed Killers

ALANAP is usually applied after the crops are planted but before they emerge from the soil. Some members of the Cucurbit family like cucumbers, muskmelons, and watermelons are resistant to it and hence weeds around these crops can be controlled even after the plants have been set out in the garden. Squash and pumpkin are susceptible to ALANAP and therefore should not be sprayed with it. It will not harm humans and animals. (Illustration following page 160)

CRAG HERBICIDE 1, a close relative to 2,4-D, is among the more interesting and unsual of the selective weed killers developed in recent years. It is commonly sold as a pre-emergence weed killer, that is, it kills both germinating and very young weeds including chickweed, crab grass, pigweed, and purslane. It does not control weeds after they have grown very large. Nor does it harm cultivated plants with well-established roots. It is unusual in that it is inactive when first applied to the soil but becomes effective as soon as soil microbes act on it, changing it into 2,4-D. At the start of the treatment the soil must be free of any large, established weeds.

Thus far CRAG HERBICIDE 1 has found its greatest use in beds of established vegetables such as corn, lima and snap beans, and asparagus, and small fruits such as strawberries and raspberries. It is also recommended as a pre-emergence weed killer around established shrubs and evergreens and in beds of perennial flowers, bulbs, and roses. A 4-ounce package of the material is enough to treat 3,000 square feet of garden, and one treatment will prevent regrowth of certain weeds for three to six weeks.

On strawberries it should not be applied when the runners are making roots, or during flowering, fruiting, or bud development.

As already mentioned in the chapter on lawns, CRAG HERBICIDE 1 can also be used to control crab grass.

The action of the new selective weed killers may be likened to a gigantic magnet which attracts and kills harmful weeds without harming the cultivated crop.

A new pre-emergence weed killer CDEC (chloroallyl diethyl dithio-carbamate) at the rates of 3 to 6 pounds per acre will control certain grassy weeds. This is a grass-specific pre-emergence herbicide for such crops as sweet corn, onions, carrots, broccoli, spinach, snap beans, lima beans, turnips, radishes, and table beets. Broad-leaved weeds like purslane and pigweed, in addition to annual grass pests such as giant foxtail, wild oats, cheat grass, and crab grass, also have been controlled. CDEC will probably be on the market in 1956.

CHLORO IPC, suggested for preventing fruit formation on ginkgo, is excellent as a pre-emergence herbicide on onions and lettuce. It is most effective when applied to bare soil before the weed seeds germinate. It is relatively ineffective on weed seedlings and on adult weeds. It also gives good control of weeds when sprayed in the fall on dormant apple rootstocks.

DALAPON is an effective herbicide for grassy weeds growing in row crops of fruit trees and vines. At much higher concentrations it becomes nonselective and can be used to destroy all kinds of vegetation around industrial plants or along railroad rights of way. It is especially active against such grasses as JOHNSON, BERMUDA, and QUACK, and shows exceptional promise in the control of the giant plume grass, *Phragmites communis.*

D-LEET is a selective weed killer being marketed by the Monsanto Chemical Company. It contains the material MeCP, a selective chemical which, like 2,4-D, kills broad-leaved weeds in lawns without harming the desirable grasses. Unlike 2,4-D, however, it is also harmless to clover and therefore can be used on lawns containing this plant.

GOODRITE NIX is a weed killer that destroys all the small succulent weeds that it actually wets. It has no growth-regulating effect like 2,4-D and no soil-poisoning effect like many of the general nonselective weed killers.

NATRIN is another weed killer related to 2,4-D and 2,4,5-T which shows promise as a weed preventer rather than a weed killer in tomato plantings. The material is applied as a spray to bare soil before the weeds are visible. A light rain or sprinkling within a day or two after the spraying activates the chemical and assures good contact with sprouting seeds.

SHELL AA-WEED SEED KILLER, containing allyl alcohol, is another newly developed herbicide for use against weed seeds in tobacco beds. Applied as a drench in tobacco seedbeds about two weeks before the seed is sown, the material volatilizes and thus kills weed seeds.

WEEDAZOL, one of the many excellent weed killers marketed by the American Chemical Paint Company, appears to offer great promise as a control for such pestiferous weeds as nut grass, Canada thistle, quack grass, milkweed, Johnson grass, poison ivy, ash, scrub oak, and Bermuda grass.

The commercial grower and the home gardener now have a number of chemicals that will make vegetable growing easier and more profitable. Following is a list of fruits and vegetables together with weed killers that have been used successfully on these crops:

Asparagus. CMU, ¾ ounce per 1,000 square feet in 5 quarts of water or 2 pounds per acre in 50 gallons of water, applied once before and once after the cutting season.

Beans. The dinitros sold as DOW PREMERGE and SINOX P.E., 3 ounces in a gallon of water per 1,000 square feet or 1 gallon in 35 to 60 gallons of water per acre, applied before the bean seedlings emerge, control chickweed, pigweed, red root, lamb's-quarters, and mustard.

Carrots, Parsley, Parsnip, Fennel, and Dill. STODDARD SOLVENT, 1 to 1½ gallons per 100 square feet or 50 to 75 gallons per acre, sprayed when the plants are small and not later than thirty days before harvest. The crowns will be injured if the spray is applied on more mature plants. Weeds in celery can be controlled with the same material but the application must be made before 2 true leaves have developed. I have seen severe injury in celery when this precaution was not observed.

Onion. POTASSIUM CYANATE, the same material suggested for crab grass control in lawns, will control weeds in onions when applied as a spray at intervals starting before the onion seedlings emerge and as the onion plants get taller. When used as directed on the container, it will kill ragweed, red root, mustard, chickweed, and smartweed without harming the onions. It will not control purslane.

Peas. The same materials suggested for potatoes and beans do an excellent job of weed control in peas. The dosage is ¾ of an ounce in a gallon of water per 1,000 square feet or 1 quart in 30 to 50 gallons of water per acre sprayed when the peas are 3 inches tall.

Potatoes. DOW PREMERGE and SINOX P.E., 4 ounces in a gallon of water per 1,000 square feet or 4 to 6 quarts per acre in 30 to 50 gallons of water applied before the potato plants emerge from the soil, will prevent weed development for about four weeks.

Spinach. CHLORO-IPC used as directed by the manufacturer will control pussley in summer plantings of spinach, and chickweed in fall plantings. Best results are obtained when the CHLORO IPC is applied just after the seeds are sown and then is immediately watered in.

Strawberries. CRAG HERBICIDE 1, ¾ ounce in 5 quarts of water per 1,000 square feet or 2 pounds in 50 gallons of water per acre kills germinating weed seeds when applied about seven days after the berries are set. Special precautions noted on the package must be observed when this weed killer is used on strawberries.

Vine Crops—cucumbers, watermelons, and muskmelons. ALANAP ¾ to 1½ ounces in 5 quarts of water per 1,000 square feet or 2 to 4 pounds in 50 gallons of water per acre before the plants emerge from the soil. It is not safe for use on squash and pumpkins.

Other Specific Uses for Weed Killers

Modern weed killers also play an important role in controlling diseases. For example, they are now being used successfully to eradicate the common or European barberry bushes, which carry the alternate stage of the highly destructive wheat rust fungus. The old-fashioned method of controlling this plant was to grub it out, and nearly 450 million bushes have been destroyed in this way on nearly 150,000 rural and urban properties in the wheat-producing areas. In areas where the bushes are numerous, the barberry eradication program has been stepped up 500 per cent by the use of hormone-type weed killers. The chemical ME CP (formerly MCP), applied at the bases of the canes and at the ground line, has been found especially effective, as have mixtures of 2,4-D and 2,4,5-T in pentachlorophenol.

Weeds in gladiolus plantings can also be controlled with certain herbicides. The weed killers do their best job in wet seasons, when cultivation is difficult or impossible. Areas treated with chemicals should not be cultivated until weed growth again becomes a problem. Cultivating immediately after spraying with a weed killer will bring uninjured weed seeds to the surface, where they will germinate.

Among the chemical weed killers found effective for gladiolus plantings are CRAG HERBICIDE 1, CHLORO IPC, CMU, and dinitro compounds such as PREMERGE and SINOX P. E.

In the large bulb-growing areas of the Pacific Northwest, commercial growers of bulbous iris, tulips, and KING ALFRED daffodils control the weeds with one of the four following materials: IPC, diesel oil, dinitro general, and dinitro amine. The amine is sold as SINOX P. E. and PREMERGE.

Some nurserymen are maintaining weed-free premises almost exclusively with chemicals. At first they direct a contact weed killer containing 2,4-D, NIX or CHLORO IPC directly at the weeds. Which material they use depends on the weed species present. After this treatment they further restrict weeds by spraying with materials like CRAG HERBICIDE 1 or ALANAP, which act as pre-emergence weed killers.

The so-called weed trees, with trunks several inches in diameter, are more easily killed by painting Dow's ESTERON BRUSH KILLER on their trunks than by spraying their foliage. In this way there is no risk of injuring nearby plantings because of drifting spray. Moreover, a gallon of spray applied to the bases of the trees will go as far as will 20 gallons on the leaves.

Aquatic Weed Control

Gardeners with ponds, lakes, or streams on their property are frequently faced with the problem of controlling weeds in the form of algae, or pond scum, and of several kinds of higher plants. Some of the latter may grow below the surface of the water, others may be partly submerged, and still others grow mainly on the surface.

Control of Algae. The chemical copper sulfate has long been used to control algae in ponds and lakes. The concentration known to be effective against these tiny green plants is about 1 part in 1 million parts of water by weight. Two disadvantages of the copper sulfate treatment are that it will kill fish if it is too strong and it will not kill the larger weeds. A concentration of about 2 parts per million will kill many different species of fish, including trout, carp, catfish, pickerel, goldfish, perch, and sunfish.

One of the latest materials tested for control of algae in ponds is PHYGON XL. It will kill the so-called bloom-producing blue-green algae, when applied at the rate of 1 to 2 pounds per acre of water surface, and the filamentous green algae, at the rate of 5 to 10 pounds per acre. PHYGON XL is said to be much less toxic to fish than is copper sulfate. It is manufactured by the Naugatuck Chemical Division of United States Rubber Company at Naugatuck, Connecticut.

DELRAD, made by Hercules Powder Company, has also been found to be unusually effective in controlling algae in farm ponds, lakes, irrigation canals, and other bodies of water.

Control of Higher Plants. Though aquatic species of higher plants are not easily controlled with copper sulfate, heavy applications of plant fertilizers to the water sometimes help to control submergent and emergent types. But some of the newer materials do an even better job.

One of the best chemicals developed for the control of aquatic weeds is BENOCLOR, a preparation containing chlorinated benzenes plus emulsifying agents. Actually, two types are available: BENOCLOR and BENOCLOR 3C. BENOCLOR is a heavy liquid that readily disperses in water to form a milky emulsion. In flowing water the highly stable form, BENOCLOR 3C, must be used because the emulsion will not break while moving over distances up to 3 miles. In lakes or ponds the less miscible and less stable form, BENOCLOR, is used because it settles to the bottom, where it continues to act on weeds without tainting the water.

Details on how to use BENOCLOR and BENOCLOR 3C may be obtained from the manufacturer, Cloroben Corporation, Jersey City, New Jersey.

The JMF Chemical Company of Bryan, Texas, markets KINGOCIDE, a chemical that has been used with great success in the South to control water hyacinths, water lilies, lotus, and water primrose, which clog rivers and waterways. KINGOCIDE destroys the roots as well as the tops of the plants, causing the dead mat to sink. According to the manufacturer, it is absolutely harmless to fish.

Gardeners who want to delve deeper into ways to control weeds and algae in ponds should get a copy of Cornell Extension Bulletin 910, by Wilson F. Clark, from the University at Ithaca, New York.

Weed-Free Mulches for Strawberries

Anyone with a strawberry patch soon finds that the only way to keep this highly desirable crop in production for more than a year or two is to control weeds completely and to mulch the beds every fall. Chemical weed killers are available for combating the weeds, but no good substitute for straw mulches has yet been developed.

The trouble with straw mulches, however, is that they contain seeds of grain, ragweed, dock, quack grass, and other weeds which germinate and soon choke out the strawberry plants. As a result of some recent research, it is now possible to treat bales of straw with a fumigant, DOWFUME MC-2, to destroy all seeds in the straw before it is applied. A 1-pound can of DOWFUME MC-2 will treat 4 bales of straw. The bales are enclosed with the fumigant for twenty-four hours in a tubular plastic bag, which is sealed at both ends. After this period the straw may be stored for future use or spread on the strawberry bed immediately as a mulch without danger of introducing weed seeds.

Lest some of my readers get the impression that all new weed control practices involve the use of chemicals, I hasten to assure them that this is not so. Only recently C. L. Hamner and G. S. Rai of Michigan State College reported a nonchemical method for combating weeds which appears to be practical, effective, and economical for gardens. It is a simple method. Merely place around the plants wet newspaper pulp, which dries to form a cardboard-like cover over the soil. Besides preventing weed growth, this cover acts as a mulch to conserve moisture in the soil.

The paper pulp is prepared by soaking old newspapers in water and stirring the material until it forms a pulpy mass. Obviously the more water is added, the thinner will be the consistency. The pulp is then spread over the soil and around the plants, where the excess water either enters the soil or evaporates, leaving a hard, cardboard-like mulch.

The mulch layer must be thick enough to discourage the growth of perennial, biennial, and annual weeds. Three inches is the usual thickness. The thicker the layer, the longer it will take to disintegrate and become incorporated in the soil.

Because this mulch is not highly durable, its greatest use in the vegetable garden will be for quick-maturing crops. But it can be used with almost any type of crop, including annual and perennial flowers and even larger woody ornamentals.

Chapter 13

INSECTS, DISEASES, OTHER PESTS AND HOW TO CONTROL THEM

With more than 2,500 trade-marked insecticides, fungicides, and related items now on the market, the average gardener must certainly be confused when faced with the problem of choosing the right spray for his particular needs.

A few years ago one had to know about only a few standard materials and their capabilities. Most gardeners, for instance, knew that lead and calcium arsenate were the most effective against chewing insects; that nicotine sulfate was to be used for sucking insects; and that bordeaux mixture was the only preventive for blights and leaf spots caused by bacteria and fungi. Alas, no longer is this true! Most of these materials have been replaced by new ones with such strange names as chlordane, lindane, dieldrin, captan, and ferbam, to name a few.

Today we not only have a wider variety of new chemicals, but to make matters more confusing, we have a number of different formulations of a single material. DDT, for example, comes in dust form, at anywhere from 2 to 10 per cent concentration for use on soils and lawns, as a 50 or 75 per cent wettable powder for spraying on foliage, and as a 25 or 30 per cent emulsion for use in pressure sprayers or mist blowers.

Labels Dependable Source of Information. Perhaps the most dependable source of information is the label on the package itself. The information printed thereon represents years of research to determine the most effective way to use the product and at the same time to protect the user, his animals, and his plants. As a matter of fact, the Federal Insecticide, Fungicide and Rodenticide Act requires the manufacturer to produce convincing evidence that his product, when used as recommended, will control the pest as claimed and will not produce serious adverse effects. Such evidence must be supplied even before the product is registered.

Furthermore, the law requires that the manufacturer include on the labels necessary warnings, precautionary measures, and antidotes. Thus if the user of pesticides adheres closely to the manufacturer's directions, no undue hazards should be encountered.

Use Care in Handling. Before listing some of the more important ingredients in present-day pesticides, I believe it might be wise to discuss some of the hazards involved. There has been so much adverse publicity on the dangers associated with the use of insecticides that some folks actually "worry themselves sick" when exposed to them.

It is true that practically every insecticide has properties toxic to warm-blooded animals and man. If it didn't have such properties, it would not be capable of killing insects, which also belong to the animal kingdom. But merely because insecticides are toxic to man and animals does not mean they cannot be used safely!

Only a few deaths have been attributed to the handling and application of pesticides, despite the use of millions of pounds annually for many years. Most, if not all, of these deaths were attributed to accidental or deliberate misuse of these materials. In 1949, for example, fifteen deaths were attributed to accidental use of insecticides. In that same year, however, ninety-nine persons died from accidental use of aspirin and other salicylates, and 112 died from petroleum products.

I do not, for one moment, want to minimize the inherent dangers in all pesticides. I believe these products should be regarded with mixed feelings. On the one hand, they should be welcomed because of their ability to control harmful pests and diseases of plants, animals, and humans. On the other hand, they must be feared because they are capable of harming the user, his pets, and his plants. A thorough appreciation of both properties will lead to their correct use. After all, even fire, one of man's best friends, can be his worst foe.

INSECT CONTROL
Insecticides Used as Sprays or Dusts

The modern, widely available insect killers in common use fall mainly into three groups: the organic phosphates, the chlorinated hydrocarbons, and the botanicals, or those of plant origin.

Modern spraying equipment. Top, a modern orchard sprayer in action. Left, the PISTOL-GRIP *duster can be operated with one hand. Right, the new* HYDRA-GUN *hand-operated sprayer is suitable for the smaller home garden. Bottom, the* SUBURBAN *is a new 10-gallon capacity power sprayer for general garden use.*

Organic Phosphates. One of the newest and most widely available of the organic phosphates is malathion. It is perhaps the best all-purpose insecticide yet developed and the safest of the organic phosphates to handle. It controls most of the hard-to-kill insects, such as scales, mealy bugs, and white flies, as well as mites. It is compatible with most other pesticides, but in combination sprays it may decompose on standing.

Malathion has two drawbacks. One, a disagreeable odor when in concentrated form and when first applied to plants, may soon be eliminated by the manufacturer. The second is that it is far less effective in combating pests like the leaf nematode of hardy chrysanthemums than its more deadly predecessor, parathion.

Chlorthion, a close relative of malathion, with very much the same properties, is not yet widely available.

Parathion, of course, is not available to amateur gardeners but is, to professional growers, who presumably are used to and know how to handle dangerous sprays.

My spray assistant, Martin McLoughlin, at The New York Botanical Garden has been spraying parathion on outdoor chrysanthemums, euonymous, and other plants for more than four years now with no apparent ill effects. But he is an expert with the spray gun and knows how and when to apply such a dangerous material.

TEPP (HEXATOX) is another deadly organic phosphate which is sometimes used by amateur gardeners on outdoor plants to control mites and aphids. Like parathion, it must be handled with great care, particularly in its concentrated form.

The newest highly potent bug killer DDVP or dimethyl dichloro vinyl phosphate, was recently discovered by scientists in the United States Public Health Service. Although DDVP belongs to the organic phosphate group, it appears to be considerably different from other well-known members such as malathion and parathion.

The government scientists first detected DDVP as an impurity in another insecticide. When finally isolated and concentrated, it was found to be ten times more effective against houseflies than the parent material and about equal to parathion in killing power. It was also found to be ten times more toxic to rats than the product from which it was isolated and five to ten times less toxic than parathion.

This does not imply that DDVP will necessarily be a safe material to handle. We must await further toxicological tests before we know just how safe it is for humans, pets, and farm animals.

Early tests with DDVP have dealt mainly with fly control, especially those known to be resistant to DDT, the first and best known of the modern insecticides. Within four hours of its application, 8 grams or slightly more than a ¼ ounce of DDVP killed nearly every fly in a large dairy barn. Because the flies in this barn were resistant to DDT, 10,000 grams or more than 22 pounds of DDT would have been required to do the same job!

DDVP is also expected to be particularly effective against pests such as aphids, mites, and fruit flies.

Research workers of the United States Department of Agriculture recently reported that the residual action of organic phosphates, such as DDVP, could be extended appreciably by the addition of resin-like chemicals known as chlorinated terphenyls.

Chlorinated Hydrocarbons. DDT, the best known of the chlorinated hydrocarbons, is still widely used to control many pests of ornamental and nonfood plants. Because of its long-lasting residual effect, it is not recommended for food crops, except early in the growing season. Near harvest time it is best to use materials that decompose rapidly, like malathion, and that are less toxic, like methoxychlor. Used at the rate of 2 tablespoons of the 50 per cent wettable powder in a gallon of water, DDT gives excellent control of gypsy moth, canker-worms, borers, bark beetles, Japanese beetles, gladiolus thrips, and rose midge.

Certain insects develop a resistance to DDT after it has been used for some time. DIPTEREX is a new insecticide for use against flies which have developed resistance to DDT and for roaches resistant to chlordane.

Another drawback of DDT is that it does not control mites and certain species of aphids. In fact, these pests will actually be more numerous where too much DDT is applied.

Methoxychlor, a close relative of DDT, controls much the same pests as DDT but is less toxic to man and pets and to vegetables like cucumbers, squash, and tomatoes.

Chlordane, another chlorinated hydrocarbon, is extremely effective against soil-inhabiting pests such as ants, Japanese beetle grubs, chinch bugs, and sod webworms.

Heptachlor, a close relative of chlordane, controls pests like the apple maggot, plum curculio, onion thrips, cucumber beetle, and European corn borer, in addition to those pests controlled by chlor-dane. Moreover, it is less expensive and is effective at lower doses.

Endrin, another close relative of chlordane, is one of the most effective materials yet discovered to combat the corn-ear worm.

Lindane, a purified form of benzene hexachloride, is very effective against aphids, lace bugs, and leaf miners in particular. It is not so generally effective as malathion because it does not control mites, scales, and mealy bugs.

Dieldrin is one of the newest insecticides now available in small packages for home garden use. It is effective against most of the pests readily controlled by DDT, such as leaf-chewing caterpillars, grubs, beetles, and weevils, and against leaf miners, borers, and bark beetles.

It controls turf grubs like the Japanese beetle grub as well as any material now available. To do the right kind of a job it must be applied uniformly over the lawn before a rain or before sprinkling, never when the soil or grass is wet. Children and pets should not be allowed on the treated area until the insecticide has been washed off the grass into the soil by drenching or sprinkling and the grass has dried completely. Dieldrin is considerably more toxic to man and pets than is DDT, but is far safer than parathion and TEPP.

Aldrin, a close relative of dieldrin, controls much the same kinds of pests. It is a more volatile chemical, however, and hence its effects are not so long-lasting.

Chlordane, dieldrin, aldrin, and DDT are all now available in granulated form, that is, in a form in which they are adsorbed on granular materials. In this form they can be easily applied to the lawn with a lime or fertilizer spreader for controlling grubs and other insects.

The chlorinated hydrocarbons have a lower order of toxicity to warm-blooded animals than do the phosphates like parathion. They are, however, more persistent on the foliage and in soil, and hence are more hazardous to use where residues or contamination of the treated products is a factor. Insecticide residues on plants will tend to disappear in the following order: lindane, aldrin, chlordane, parathion, dieldrin, and DDT; in other words, lindane disappears most quickly and DDT most slowly.

Insecticides from Botanicals. Rotenone and pyrethrins are the two best known insecticides of plant origin. They are among the safest to use because they are relatively unstable and hence have no prolonged residual effect.

Nicotine sulfate, an old reliable for sucking insects, and also derived from plants, is one of the deadliest of all materials in the concentrated form. When diluted and applied to plants, it quickly loses its deadly properties. It is always more effective in combating sucking insects if used when the air temperature is above 85 degrees, or when diluted and used in lukewarm water.

RYANIA, an extract from the South American shrub *Ryania speciosa,* gives excellent control of the European corn borer and the cranberry fruitworm, with no danger to man and his pets.

A new pyrethrin-type insecticide, CYCLETHRIN, recently developed by Carbide and Carbon Chemical Company, is extremely lethal to houseflies and other insects and relatively nontoxic to man and animals.

Systemic Insecticides

Leonardo da Vinci, most famous as an artist, is credited with being the first to consider pest control by treating plants internally, in his case with arsenic. But several German workers were primarily responsible for the recent rapid progress in treating plants with systemic insecticides. These materials are absorbed either through the roots or through the leaves of actively growing plants and in sufficient amounts to kill insects and related pests feeding on or breeding in them even at considerable distances from the point of application. They also make possible the control of pests such as root aphids and leaf nematodes, which spend some or all of their lives in areas not readily accessible to the standard surface sprays.

The systemics available at this writing are effective primarily against aphids, mealy bugs, and mites, but are not very effective against scales, thrips, leaf miners, and leafhoppers. For the present, surface sprays of malathion are recommended for the latter group.

Organic Phosphates. The two most widely used systemics are the organic phosphates known by the common names demeton (trade name SYSTOX) and schradan (PESTOX 3, OMPA). The latter was named in honor of Gerhard Schrader, who discovered the organic phosphates about 1936.

These are used mostly as soil drenches to control aphids and mites on several important ornamental plants like roses and chrysanthemums grown outdoors and on many ornamental plants grown under glass.

On outdoor roses and chrysanthemums SYSTOX is used at the rate of 1 liquid ounce, properly diluted in water, for each 100 square feet of flower bed.

The systemics are used on greenhouse plants as follows: For chrysanthemums and carnations, 1 pint of 21–23 per cent demeton (SYSTOX), or 2 pints of 90 per cent schradan (OMPA) per 1,000 square feet of bed. For African violets, cyclamen, delphinium, and foliage plants, 2 pints 21-23 per cent demeton (SYSTOX), or 2 pints 90 per cent schradan (OMPA) per 1,000 square feet. Sufficient water must be used to assure good distribution through the soil. The solution must be used as a soil drench, never as a spray.

SYSTOX is also the first systemic to be approved for use on food crops. In this country it may be used early in the growing season on apples, potatoes, and English walnuts. In Europe it is permissible to use it on a far wider range of edibles.

The state of California recently permitted the use of SYSTOX on cabbage, broccoli, brussel sprouts, and cauliflower—plants of the crucifer family—for the control of the cabbage aphid, the green peach aphid, and the turnip aphid. A single pint of SYSTOX per acre will control aphids. A second application is permitted, if needed, but it must be made at least twenty-one days before harvest. Crucifers so treated must be consumed within the state.

One important reason for permitting the use of SYSTOX on certain food crops is that it does not last very long after it gets inside the plant. In fact, it breaks down so rapidly inside the plant that the residues are essentially nontoxic.

SYSTOX has also been found to be relatively harmless to bees and to certain species of wildlife.

Some of the newer systemics are also effective when applied as foliage sprays. One investigator found that 69 per cent of the schradan (OMPA) applied to bean leaves was absorbed in fourteen hours. Another found that 50 per cent of the same material entered citrus leaves within two days of the foliar application.

Obviously the less toxic an insecticide is to humans and pets, the more widely it can be used. Chemists are therefore concentrating their efforts on developing less toxic organic phosphates.

The first such systemic to be developed is META-SYSTOX, which is far less toxic to test animals (rats) than is SYSTOX, but it must be used at twice the strength to achieve the same degree of aphid and mite control.

Selenium Compounds

Sodium selenate, a very deadly poison, can also be used as a systemic insecticide to control pests like aphids, mites, and particularly leaf-infesting nematodes on certain plants.

Its use is recommended only for ornamental, other nonedible

plants, and soils that are never to grow food crops. No one really knows how long this chemical will last in a treated soil.

Sodium selenate comes as a pure powder. It is dissolved in water as directed on the container, then applied to the soil around the plants. A second treatment is necessary three weeks after the first.

It is also available in capsule form, under the names KAPSULATE and SEL-KAPS, for the control of pests of African violets, and in a 2 per cent mixture adsorbed on superphosphate, under the name P-40, for direct application to soil in which chrysanthemums are growing.

Sodium selenate has proved most effective in combating pests of herbaceous ornamentals, where such plants are kept growing vigorously. It is relatively ineffective on woody plants and slow-growing nursery plants and trees.

Newest Approach to Insect Control

The latest and newest concept of insect control is the use of chemicals that prevent insects from "growing up." Rather than killing the insects outright, the "Peter Pan" chemicals merely prevent them from reaching adulthood, thus making them incapable of laying eggs to start the next generation. Piperonyl butoxide is the first of such chemicals. When added to the medium on which housefly larvae are grown, it slows down larval development, in some cases it actually prevents them from changing to adults. Although there are no immediate practical applications, this approach may provide another way to control destructive insects.

Mite Control Now Easy

Because mites have become a major pest of many plants, including arborvitae, birch, boxwood, cedar, cypress, hawthorn, hemlock, oak, peach, phlox, pine, rose, and spruce, I think it wise to discuss these pests in some detail in this chapter.

One reason for the increased numbers of mites is the widespread use of the newer organic insecticides such as DDT, heptachlor, aldrin, and dieldrin. These chemicals give remarkable control of injurious insects, but they also control the natural insect predators of mites and thus indirectly help to increase the mite population.

There are, of course, many other reasons for the increase. Mites can infest plants that have not been sprayed with any of the newer insecticides. Even the nutrition of the plant may influence their prevalence. One investigator noted, for example, that four times as many mites developed on rose leaves low in nitrogen as on leaves high in this element.

Plant-infesting mites fall roughly into four major groups. The largest, and the one I shall discuss in greatest detail, is the spider mite group. In it are included the common red spider, the spruce mite, European red mite, Pacific mite, oak mite, and boxwood mite. Other groups include the cyclamen mite, which is common on cyclamen and delphinium, the bulb-infesting mites, and those that produce galls on leaves and stems.

Mites are not true insects. They belong to that class of animals which includes scorpions, spiders, and ticks, all of which have four pairs of legs. True insects have but three pairs.

Most mites vary from 1/64 to 1/32 inch in length. They may be green, orange, red, brown, or black.

The life cycles of most spider mites are much the same. Winter is passed in the egg stage around leaf scars and the rough and protected places on the smaller twigs. Eggs are 1/64 inch in diameter, oval in shape, and pink or red. During the summer eggs are also deposited on the leaves, chiefly on the lower surface.

Overwintered eggs usually hatch in late April or early May. The young mites feed on the leaves by sucking out the juices. In the cool spring the complete life cycle takes about three weeks; in summer, ten days to two weeks. Each female may lay seventy-five to more than a hundred eggs. As many as five hundred eggs and mites may be found on a single rose leaf in midsummer.

Injury caused by spider mites is rather distinctive, and the gardener soon learns how to distinguish it from that caused by true insects. The green coloring matter, chlorophyll, is destroyed wherever the mites insert their mouth parts to suck out the juices. This gives the leaves a stippled or mottled appearance. At first the leaf color is grayish green, then it turns yellow, and finally brown.

Mite injury is not plainly discernible in May even though mites may be present. It becomes more evident as the season advances, and as the weather becomes warmer and drier for them, the mite population increases by leaps and bounds. This is why it is important to learn how to spot mite infestations early and to apply the proper spray in time to keep injury to a minimum.

Most species of mites are so tiny that a magnifying glass is of great help in detecting their presence. The gardener who does not have such a glass can collect a small branch of the plant suspected of having mites and tap it vigorously on a piece of white paper or cardboard. If mites are present, they will fall on the paper and will be plainly visible as tiny moving specks against the white background.

Pesticide manufacturers have gone all out during the past several years to develop mite-killing chemicals, or acaricides, as they are called. As a result, we now have a number of acaricides that are far more effective than the old-fashioned sulfur dusts and lime-sulfur sprays.

The four best-known mite-killing chemicals are ARAMITE, DIMITE, malathion, and OVOTRAN.

ARAMITE comes as a 15 per cent wettable powder and is used at the rate of 2 level tablespoons in a gallon of water. It destroys the immature and mature mites but not the eggs. Hence it must be used a second time about five to seven days after the first application. It is more effective against the two-spotted mite than against the European red mite. ARAMITE is relatively nontoxic to humans and pets. It is compatible with DDT, lead arsenate, lindane, and ferbam.

Hydrangeas are damaged by sprays made with ARAMITE wettable powder and by sprays from aerosol bombs containing a mixture of ARAMITE and lindane. Malathion would be safer to use on such plants.

DIMITE is a liquid and is usually diluted at the rate of 1 teaspoon for each gallon of water. It controls the delphinium mite better than other acaricides but must be used frequently, starting early in the growing season. It is not toxic to users and has long residual value against mites. It is compatible with lindane, lead arsenate, ferbam, and zineb.

Malathion, mentioned earlier, comes as a 4 per cent dust, a 25 per cent wettable powder, and a 50 per cent emulsion. The 4 per cent dust can be applied directly on plants susceptible to attack by mites. The dilution rate for the 25 per cent wettable powder is 4 level teaspoons in a gallon of water, and for the 50 per cent emulsion, 2 level teaspoons per gallon. Because it controls many other pests, malathion is usually preferred by most gardeners. It is relatively safe to use provided directions on the container are followed carefully. Malathion is compatible with nicotine, oils, sulfur, ferbam, and zineb.

OVOTRAN is perhaps the most effective acaricide of all because it destroys mite eggs in addition to the adult mites. It is especially recommended for the control of the spruce mite on conifers, particularly on arborvitae, cypress, fir, hemlock, juniper, and spruce. It is more toxic to certain plants than the other mite killers discussed. In early spring it will injure the tender foliage and buds of certain plants. It should never be used before June 15 on hollies, dogwood, black raspberries, hawthorns, and flowering fruit trees. OVOTRAN is the preferred treatment after the middle of June where only a single application can be made. It is compatible with DDT, lindane, lead arsenate, lime sulfur, bordeaux mixture, and ferbam.

OVEX and ORTHOTRAN are two products similar to OVOTRAN.

CHLOROBENZOLATE is being tested extensively at this writing as a mite killer by the Geigy Company, originators of DDT.

GENITE EM-923 is one of the newest mite killers to appear on the market. It is outstandingly effective, safe, and economical for use in early-season control of the European red mite and the clover mite on various fruit and nut trees.

DISEASE CONTROLS
New Controls for Diseases

In the field of disease prevention perhaps the newest and most widely publicized material is captan (ORTHOCIDE 406). This is the common name given to the organic fungicide M-trichloromethyl-thiotetrahydrophthalimide—quite a mouthful! I am sure all my readers will agree that when the correct chemical name is difficult to pronounce or where it is inconveniently lengthy, a shorter coined name is highly desirable. That is why we have so many new coined names, like dichlone, ferbam, glyodin, maneb, nabam, thiram, zineb, and ziram for many of the modern fungus killers.

Captan is effective against the following diseases: apple scab, peach brown rot, cherry leaf spot, rose black spot, and brown patch of turf grasses. It is considered one of the better fungicides where rust and mildew diseases are not a problem.

Ferbam (trade names FERMATE, KARBAM BLACK) is the best known of the newer fungicides belonging to the chemical group known as dithiocarbamates. This iron-containing black, soot-like fungicide leaves a residue on blooms which is objectionable to flower show exhibitors, but which is less prominent on foliage. Ferbam provides good protection against such common diseases as scab and rust on apples, black rot of grapes, and black spot of roses. It is compatible with lime sulfur and most insecticides, but its compatibility with calcium arsenate, lime-sulfur, lime, and bordeaux mixture is questionable. Ferbam is not highly toxic, but it may cause skin irritation if inhaled.

The usual dosage of ferbam for foliage sprays is 2 level tablespoons in a gallon of water.

Maneb, the coined name for the manganese-containing relative of ferbam, is excellent for preventing blights of potato, celery, and tomato; leaf spots of hawthorn and certain fruit trees; downy mildew, purple blotch, and blast of onions; black rot of grapes; and in California the shot-hole disease of almonds and peaches. It not only gives good control of black spot of roses, but it also provides some control of red spider, a characteristic rarely found in fungicides, MANZATE is a trade name of maneb, containing 70 per cent of the active ingredient. It is also sold under the trade name DITHANE M22.

The zinc relative of ferbam, ziram, gives excellent control of leaf spots of iris and chrysanthemum as well as those on many vegetables.

Zineb, another dithiocarbamate fungicide, is sold under several trade names, including BLIGHTOX, DITHANE Z-78, DU PONT FUNGICIDE A, and PARZATE. It, too, is excellent for many fungus leaf spot and leaf blight diseases.

Mildew Control. One of the more difficult-to-control diseases, both under glass and outdoors, is the so-called powdery mildew. Several species of fungi cause mildew. These grow mainly on the leaf surfaces, where they produce a white powdery coating.

Sulfur sprays or dusts once were about the only fairly effective control materials. But recently a so-called dinitro material, named dinitro capryl phenyl crotonate, has been found especially effective against this group of fungi. This chemical is sold under the trade names MILDEX and KARATHANE.

Like maneb, mentioned earlier, MILDEX (KARATHANE) also controls mites to some degree, in addition to mildew, particularly on such plants as apple, cantaloupe, cucumber, squash, watermelon, and roses.

As with all other fungus diseases, correct timing of the spray applications is essential. Mildew is more easily controlled if the sprays are applied when the disease first appears. It is far more difficult to control on plants that are already heavily infected.

MILDEX, or KARATHANE, is compatible with other fungicides and insecticides used in combination sprays. It should be omitted from spray mixtures during midsummer, however, because it burns foliage when applied during hot weather (above 85 degrees); and anyway mildew is no problem at that time.

It should not be used stronger than an ounce in 25 gallons of water, especially when temperatures are near the 85 degree mark or on young leaves in spring. Nor should it be combined with sulfur or applied to leaves recently dusted or sprayed with sulfur. It should be applied when the foliage will dry rapidly, never during muggy weather.

The usual dosage for small quantities is ½ to ⅔ teaspoon in a gallon of water.

To get the best control of mildew with MILDEX, or KARATHANE, use just enough spreader, like TRITON X-100, TWEEN 20, DREFT, or DU PONT SPREADER-STICKER, to give good wetting of the surface. Spray the leaves, especially the undersides, thoroughly to ensure complete coverage. Start the applications at the first sign of infection, and repeat at four- to seven-day intervals where mildew infection is heavy. Three-ounce packages of MILDEX are obtainable from Gro-Wel Products, Sanford, North Carolina.

Antibiotics Now Protect Many Plants

An important milestone in the science of plant protection was reached with the recent marketing of antibiotics for the control of plant diseases.

The first of these antibiotics to be made available to the general public was the Upjohn Company's ACTI-DIONE for controlling turf grass diseases known as melting-out, brown patch, dollar spot, and snow mold; for rust on mint; and for leaf spot of cherry. ACTI-DIONE contains the antibiotic cycloheximide as the active ingredient. For use specifically on turf, the new FERRATED ACTI-DIONE is recommended because it contains ferrous sulfate in addition to the antibiotic. The iron is said to make the treated grass greener.

Streptomycin, the antibiotic first isolated from a soil-inhabiting organism by Rutgers University scientists, is the principal active ingredient in the newest antibiotic formulations available for horticultural use.

At this writing three companies are offering either streptomycin or a mixture of streptomycin and TERRAMYCIN for the control of certain bacterial diseases of plants. The names of these products and their manufacturers are: AGRI-MYCIN 100, Charles Pfizer and Company; AGRISTREP, Merck and Company; and PHYTOMYCIN, Olin Mathieson Chemical Corporation.

At present these preparations are being used mainly to control fire blight, the destructive bacterial disease of apples, pears, and other plants in the rose family. The annual losses due to this disease in commercial apple and pear orchards alone exceeds 70 million dollars. This disease, plus an insect pest known as pear psylla, has limited the production of high-quality BARTLETT and CLAPP'S FAVORITE pears in the past.

Prior to the advent of antibiotics, fire blight in pears and apples was controlled only moderately well with copper sprays or dusts and a strict sanitation program which included the removal and burning of all blighted twigs and branches. But copper sprays often affected fruit quality by causing a russeting of the skin.

Tobacco growers in the South will also be important users of the antibiotics because streptomycin will control the bacterial disease of tobacco known as "wildfire." Recent tests indicate that an important fungus disease of tobacco, blue mold, can also be controlled with it.

So much research with antibiotics is being conducted at this time that almost every week a new disease is reported conquered with streptomycin mixtures. Fire blight in a collection of crab apples, consisting of fifty-six trees of twelve varieties, was kept under control in 1954 by spraying with the antibiotic. The bacterial canker disease of tomato was markedly reduced by soaking the seeds in a streptomycin solution. The bacterial spot of pepper plants was almost completely controlled by spraying badly infected plants three times with 500 parts of streptomycin in a million parts of water.

Streptomycin has also been found to exhibit activity against the organisms that cause the following plant diseases: canker of stone fruits, bean blight, wilt of carnation, crown gall, pea blight, cotton wilt, cabbage rot, soft rot of carrots, tobacco wilt, cucumber wilt, tomato leaf spot, Stewart's wilt of sweet corn, chrysanthemum blight, soft rot and black leg of potato, and walnut blight.

One of the newest antifungal agents, FILIPIN, was recently isolated by scientists at the University of Illinois from a species of *streptomyces,* a soil-inhabiting organism related to the one that produces streptomycin. FILIPIN appears to be toxic to a number of species of fungus spores and relatively harmless to higher plants.

Antibiotics are so powerful that only minute quantities are needed to control plant diseases. Dosages are figured in parts per million rather than pounds per gallon, as with the usual spray materials. Dosage units are measured in gamma, and there are more than 28 million gamma in 1 ounce of streptomycin. One and a third ounces in 100 gallons of water gives a dilution of approximately 100 parts in a million parts of water. Although this is one of the most frequently used dilutions, at times the dosage may run as high as 500 parts per million.

How to Use Antibiotics for Fire Blight. For best results in the control of fire blight, antibiotics should be applied at the early-bloom and full-bloom stages. Control is poor if the sprays are delayed until the petal-fall stage. In the eastern United States three applications are needed for good control. In California, where the blossoming period is longer, as many as five properly spaced sprays during the blooming period are necessary.

Sprays must be applied during the blooming period because the bacteria that cause fire blight are carried from flower to flower by insects in their search for nectar and by wind-splashed rain.

Antibiotics sprayed on the leaves and flowers are absorbed through these parts and move through the plant. At high concentrations they actually kill germs inside the plants, but at lower dosages they merely prevent bacterial infections from becoming thoroughly established.

As a supplement to the use of antibiotic sprays, a second precautionary treatment is advised. This involves the eradication of so-called fire blight cankers on the trunks of infected trees. Such cankers, if left untreated, will kill large branches or even entire pear trees and the more susceptible varieties of apple trees of high vigor.

A ready-to-use canker paint containing cadmium sulfate, obtainable in farm supply stores, can be used to kill bacteria in fire blight cankers on the trunk and branches. The paint must be applied exactly as directed on the container.

Antibiotics Are Safe to Use. The newest antibiotics available for plant disease control are safe to use. Thus far no effects toxic to people have been reported except in a few cases where constant handling of the powders has caused a temporary skin irritation.

Carefully conducted tests have shown also that pears and apples harvested from trees sprayed up to seven times during and after the blossoming period contained no detectable antibiotic activity.

There are two reasons why little or no antibiotic remains in mature fruits that have been treated with these drugs. First, the antibiotics are usually applied to apple and pear trees before the fruits form. Second, the antibiotics disappear rapidly, usually within ten days of application, from any fruits sprayed with them. Even in tomatoes and peppers harvested from plants treated throughout their growing period, including some sprayed a day before harvest, no antibiotic activity could be detected.

Less streptomycin is absorbed into the plant if rain falls within a few hours after application. A rain one or more days after the application has little effect on the amount absorbed.

As a rule, streptomycin rarely damages plants. A few varieties of apples and pears show yellowing along the leaf margins. The condition appears to be temporary and will cause no permanent damage. In my own greenhouse tests on more than twenty different kinds of ornamental plants in 1953, I noted this leaf yellowing only on one variety of Japanese holly, *Ilex crenata convexa*. After I discontinued the antibiotic spray, the green color returned.

The currently available brands of antibiotics are said to be compatible with most of the commonly used fungicides and insecticides. Despite this fact, however, it is wise for the present, at least, to apply the antibiotic by itself, before using the regular sprays. In this way there will be no possibility of interference in absorption of the antibiotic.

Dry forms of the antibiotics may be stored indefinitely. Once in solution, however, they begin to lose their potency after a few days. They are not stable in soil and at present are not recommended for soil applications. Action by soil microbes and adsorption on soil colloids are two causes of the loss in potency when antibiotics are added to soils.

Virus Diseases Can Be Prevented. Virus diseases of plants also may soon be combated with antibiotics. Scientists recently reported that an antibiotic MK 61, produced by an Actinomycete provisionally identified as *Nocardia formica,* markedly inhibited the production of local lesions, as well as systemic infections, caused by the bean mosaic and the tobacco mosaic viruses in healthy plants.

It appears that the antibiotic interfered with the reproduction of the virus in the host plant rather than with the virus itself. The virus infections were inhibited when the sprays of the antibiotic were applied to the leaves, beginning one hour to one day after the inoculations, as well as when sprays were applied for several days before inoculation.

Plant virus inhibitors are apparently more common than most of us realize. In addition to being present in many species of fungi and bacteria, they also occur in higher plants. Pokeweed, carnations, cucumbers, and peppers, for example, are a few of the plants known to inhibit plant virus development.

Antidotal materials have been discovered for the virus disease of tomato known as mosaic, and for viruses affecting plums, peaches, and cherries. Among these are thiouracil; chloramphenicol, which is the Parke-Davis Company's CHLOROMYCIN; and guanazola, which is Lederle Laboratory's ATRIAZOLOPYRIMIDINE.

The United States Patent Office recently awarded a patent to a Finn on a method of combating virus diseases and of preventing them by treating plants with a protein-free ethyl alcohol containing 3 to 6 per cent of croton aldehyde.

Systemic Fungicides. The success achieved in combating insects with systemic insecticides has stimulated interest in the possibility of combating plant diseases with systemic fungicides. Although I am unaware of any successful systemic fungicides on the market, the hunt for them is being vigorously pursued at a number of experiment stations and private laboratories. Several American research workers have reported controlling fungus and virus diseases by injecting chemicals into the plants or by adding them to the soil to be absorbed by the roots. Either their results have been unverified, or the materials are not commercially available. A European worker has reported that GRISEOFULVIN, an antibiotic, is effective as a systemic fungicide, but this, too, is as yet unverified by American research workers.

Some Connecticut growers are reported to be using systemic fungicides for control of fusarium wilt of carnations and red stele of strawberries. The practice, however, has not achieved widespread use.

COMBINATION SPRAYS

No chapter on insect and disease control would be complete without some mention of combination, or all-purpose, sprays. These are mixtures containing compatible materials to control all the major insect pests, fungus diseases, and mites. There are a goodly number of ready-mixed combinations on the market, most of them in powdered form, which may be applied dry with a dusting machine or diluted in water, as directed, and applied as a spray.

Combination sprays are also available in aerosols. The du Pont Company, for example, has incorporated methoxychlor, lindane, and rotenone in an aerosol can called GARDEN INSECT SPRAYER, which is effective against aphids, Japanese beetles, red spider, leaf hoppers, lace bugs, thrips, and other bad actors of the flower garden. The Bostwick Laboratories of Bridgeport 5, Connecticut, were the first to offer an aerosol containing both insecticides and a fungicide in its product BOSTWICK ROSE and FLOWER SPRAY.

For those who wish to buy the separate ingredients and mix their own, the following formula, which makes a highly effective combination spray, is suggested:

In each gallon of water mix the following: 2 teaspoons of 50 per cent emulsifiable malathion, 2 tablespoons of 50 per cent wettable DDT powder (or 50 per cent wettable methoxychlor powder), 1 tablespoon of 65 per cent wettable zineb powder (or 1 tablespoon wettable captan powder), and ½ teaspoon of MILDEX (or 2 tablespoons of wettable sulfur).

An important advantage of a homemade spray mix is its flexibility. When aphids and mites are absent, malathion can be omitted. In very hot weather, when there is little likelihood of fungus infections, the zineb or captan can be left out, as should be the MILDEX (KARATHANE) or sulfur, because these may burn plants when temperatures are very high.

As a final word of advice, I would warn gardeners that the mere selection of the right spray material is not enough to assure successful insect and disease control. Even the best pesticides will fail if not used strictly according to the directions and at the right time.

PEST CONTROL

Besides bugs and blights, gardeners occasionally must cope with large and small animal pests. Some merely damage plants, others are a hazard to people and pets, and some are just plain nuisances. Some of these pests are peculiar to rural areas, others are commoner in cities and towns.

Nematodes or eelworms are microscopic worms that attack plants both below and aboveground. Soil-inhabiting kinds are controlled by placing or injecting special fumigants into the soil where their volatile gases kill the pests. These fumigants usually contain either dichloropropene or ethylene dibromide as the active ingredient. The former is sold under trade names like D-D and NEMAFUME; the latter as GARDEN DOWFUME, SOILFUME 60-40, BROMEX, and BROMOFUME.

A new phosphorous compound, V-C 13 NEMACIDE, is reported to successfully control nematodes without destroying plant life near the infested area. The nematode killer is sprayed or sprinkled on the infested area and then soaked into the soil with additional water.

Two of the newest nematode killers are NEMAGON, made by the Shell Chemical Corporation, and VAPAM 45, manufactured by the

Stauffer Chemical Company. The latter also controls certain fungi, bacteria, soil insects, and weeds, in addition to the nematodes. In all probability neither product will be generally available to home gardeners for some time.

Birds. Even the most ardent bird lover will admit that some birds can be a nuisance. Take starlings for example. They have become real pests in the sixty-five years since they were introduced from Europe. They roost in trees by the thousands, and their noise in the morning and evening is almost unbearable to people living near by. During the day the starlings fly to more rural areas, where they feed on fruits and berries and gorge themselves on insects, including the grubs of that widespread pest, the Japanese beetle.

Many means of dispensing hordes of starlings have been tried in the past, but the most recent and what looks like the most effective method involves an entirely new approach—the use of recordings of the distress call of starlings. Professor Hubert Frings of Pennsylvania State University told about this method at the National Shade Tree Conference in 1954.

The distress call was recorded by trapping a starling and holding it tightly. This recording is played back on a machine just as the starlings arrive in the trees or other spots to roost in early evening after a day of foraging. The sound is turned on intermittently every evening for three to five nights. By this time the starlings become tired of hearing the distress call and move to quieter lodgings.

The Starner-Ray Company of Scarsdale, New York, has BIRD EVICTION MACHINES which faithfully reproduce the starling's distress call and rid communities of this pesky bird.

I wonder where the poor starlings would go if every community used a BIRD EVICTION MACHINE?

For birds, including starlings, that eat cherries, sweet corn, and other crops, the United States Fish and Wildlife Service has developed another unusual control. Firecrackers strung like beads on long fuses are suspended in trees or near the crop to be protected. One end of the string is lighted and explodes one firecracker at a time at periodic intervals when crop protection is desired. Commercial growers find this method economical and effective. The method, obviously, can be used only in those farming areas where it is legal to set off firecrackers.

To discourage pheasants from digging up newly planted grain seeds, California scientists recently reported that a coating of lindane

Installing an underground sprinkler system.

1. Lay out system aboveground to test coverage and tightness of connections.

2. Slit ground to 5-inch depth with flat spade. Rock spade back and forth to open slit width of the hose.

3. Slip hose into cut. Set sprinkler heads flush with ground level. Tamp sod back into place gently with foot.

…. A five-headed sprinkling system can be …aid out completely installed in two hours.

The Orlyt Greenhouse was designed especially for home gardeners.

Heating cables are easy to install in hotbeds, coldframes, or greenhouses.

The *Trim Master* is an excellent tool for edging lawns.

The *Start-A-Plant,* excellent for rooting cuttings, almost completely automatic.

E. F. BRITTEN & CO., INC.

─A-PLANT DIVISION, CARSTENITE SALES COMPANY,
GO, ILL.

Here are power tools for every garden job. The Farm-Ette *"Trigger-Tach"* is a fine example of a single power unit which can be attached to any one of several tools within a minute.

FARM-ETTE, TOM MOORE TRACTOR, INC.

Roto-Therm is a compact machine for sterilizing soil.

TARRANT MANUFACTURING CO.,
SARATOGA SPRINGS, N.Y.

Close-up of the *Irrometer,*
a small compact moisture recorder.

Dr. Luther Baumgartner, Director of
the Baumlanda Horticultural Research
Laboratory, recording the moisture
content of the soil with an *Irrometer.*

T. W. PROSSE
RIVERSIDE,

T. W. PROSSER CO.,
RIVERSIDE, CAL.

insecticide on the seed prior to planting is effective. Such a treatment also controls insect pests that attack grain seeds below ground. Of course, the old stand-by, STANLEY'S CROW REPELLENT, has long been used to treat corn seeds so that crows and other birds will not bother them.

Pigeons are more of a problem on buildings and other structures in the larger cities than they are in gardens. They, like the starlings, can be quite messy. The latest pigeon repellent to appear on the market is ROOST NO MORE, made by the National Bird Control Laboratories of Skokie, Illinois. This gelatin-like compound comes in an aerosol can and is applied to the birds' usual landing places such as cornices, ledges, window sills, and gutter edges. The birds find it very disagreeable underfoot and go elsewhere to roost. It does not harm them in any way, nor is it harmful to humans. The manufacturer claims that when ROOST NO MORE is applied properly, it remains effective for a year or more, and since birds are creatures of habit, they will seldom return to treated buildings.

ROOST NO MORE is nonflammable, odorless, and will cling to any metal, hard stone, wood, or other building material without staining.

Deer. As soon as heavy snows fall, deer no longer have access to their regular forage and hence turn to trees and shrubs for food.

To protect valuable trees, shrubs, and berry bushes from foraging by deer, the repellent GOODRITE Z.I.P., distributed nationally by Larvacide Products of New York, should be applied as a spray in late fall. A pound of Z.I.P. in 25 gallons of water is the standard dosage for deciduous trees and shrubs after the leaves have fallen but before the first snow.

The coating of Z.I.P. makes the leaves so unpalatable to deer that a few bites are enough for them. The animals, therefore, will not establish themselves in the vicinity of sprayed plants but will move to unsprayed areas before bad weather restricts their travel.

In addition to deer, Z.I.P. will repel other animals. Horses will not nibble on trees and shrubs sprayed with it. And when painted or sprayed on fences, posts, and buildings, it controls cribbing. Some users report that goats, cattle, and raccoons also stay away from treated plants. The repellent does not harm any animal which tastes treated plants. Nor is it harmful to the plants themselves. Because Z.I.P. contains a special adhesive, its effectiveness is not impaired by rain, snow, or wind.

Another type of deer-repelling spray is bone tar oil. Apple trees, nursery plantings, and other crops can be successfully protected for a month with one spraying.

Bone tar oil also appears to be effective in repelling beavers and woodchucks, which also cause considerable damage to crops under certain conditions. It does not repel rabbits, however.

Gardeners who feel squeamish about applying chemicals for repelling deer might want to investigate a scientifically designed electrical device known as the DEER FLY. This device emits short bursts of sound, which have proved particularly unpleasant to deer, at irregular intervals from dusk until morning. DEER FLY is operated on a 6-volt battery, is easy to install, and is completely automatic. Additional information on this electronic deer repellent may be obtained from its manufacturer, Wildlife Associates, Inc., Pittsfield, New Hampshire.

Rabbits. Timid, soft-eyed, cottontail rabbits may be things of beauty to children but they are serious pests in flower borders, in vegetable gardens, and on many kinds of trees and shrubs. They not only chew the leaves of ornamentals like pansies, tulips, and iris, and of many kinds of vegetables, but they severely damage and may even kill trees like dogwood and apple by chewing the bark at the base of the tree.

A 1-inch mesh galvanized wire fence about 2 feet high placed around susceptible flower and vegetable plants will keep rabbits out. The fence should be embedded lightly in the ground or staked down at intervals to prevent the rabbits from crawling under it.

The material NO-NIBL, sold by the same company which handles the deer repellent Z.I.P., is effective in repelling rabbits. NO-NIBL comes in a shaker-top can, from which it may be dusted directly on the rabbit-susceptible plants, or it can be made into a spray and applied in that form, which is slightly more effective.

To prevent bark chewing, a mechanical barrier such as aluminum foil, ½ inch mesh hardware cloth, or even ordinary window screening wrapped around the tree is effective. The barrier should be wide enough to go slightly below ground and high enough to protect the bark even if the rabbit stands on a blanket of snow.

Certain harmless repellents can also be painted around the base of the tree to repel rabbits. GOODRITE Z.I.P., mentioned under deer control, and CRYSTAL'S RABBIT REPELLENT, made by Crystal Soap and Chemical Company of Philadelphia, are two good ones.

A new material, soon to be made available, which contains trinitrobenzene-analine complex with acetone as a diluent, is particularly distasteful to rabbits.

In areas where it is permitted, shooting will help to reduce the rabbit population. Where this is not permitted or where a person hesitates to kill the rabbits, live-trapping with special box traps furnished by the state conservation department offers a way out. The live rabbits are then moved from garden areas to understocked rural areas.

Squirrels sometimes cause considerable damage to trees by feeding on seeds, nuts, and fruit, by cutting twigs and eating the buds, and by gnawing the bark. I know of no effective repellent for them.

Live-trapping in special box traps, as suggested for rabbits, and releasing them in more rural areas is one way for the suburban gardener to combat squirrels.

Dogs. Among the many effective dog repellents on the market are DOG CHECK, made by the Nott Manufacturing Company of Mount Vernon, New York; LIQUID CHAPERONE, Sudbury Laboratory, South Sudbury, Massachusetts; and RIDZ DOG REPELLENT, Boyle-Midway, Cranford, New Jersey.

Mice and moles do a great deal of damage to plants, particularly in fall. They are discussed together because the types of injury they cause are closely associated.

Moles are blamed more frequently than mice for plant damage because the tunnels and mounds they make are very prominent. Actually, moles are not vegetarians, but feed on grubs and worms in the soil. The damage they cause results from loosening of the soil around roots, which causes the plants to wilt and die. The tunnels made by moles do provide easy access for mice, which feed on bulbs, tubers, and tender roots.

The use of chlordane or dieldrin, as suggested in *Chapter 9,* will destroy soil-inhabiting insects and thus remove the principal source of mole food. These pests will then move elsewhere and will no longer be a problem.

Immediate control measures for moles include the use of a harpoon-type mole trap. Before setting the trap, flatten down all mole ridges in the lawn early in the morning and vacate the area for a few hours to give the moles a chance to raise the soil. This will indicate which mole runs are being used and the traps can be placed accordingly.

Moles and woodchucks can be killed by blowing into their burrows CYANOGAS A-DUST, made by American Cyanamid Company, New York. This dust works especially well if all exits are sealed immediately after the chemical is blown in. A CYANOGAS FOOT PUMP is available for pumping the CYANOGAS into the pests' runways or nests.

TAT MO-GO, an extremely toxic poison bait consisting of thallium sulfate on Spanish peanuts, recently has been found unusually effective in controlling moles. Using a teaspoon, place two poisonous peanuts into the mole run at 4-foot intervals through a small hole made by poking a lead pencil through the soil. The small openings can be closed by pinching the soil, if the soil is moist, or covering with sticks, stones, or leaves, if the soil is dry. *Thallium sulfate is a violent poison for humans and pets, and hence must be handled with extreme care!*

Mice in mole runs can be easily controlled by using ready-prepared mouse bait available in hardware and seed stores.

A bait containing 2 per cent zinc phosphide in cracked corn mix has found favor with orchardists and nurserymen in rural areas to control meadow mice in the fall. The phosphide is very poisonous and hence must be handled with great care. The danger to wildlife, other than mice, from this bait is said to be very low.

Slugs and snails chew ragged holes in the leaves of vegetables and flowering plants. They are usually most troublesome in heavily shaded gardens, and in spring and fall during periods of cool, damp weather.

Baits in meal or pellet form containing metaldehyde as the attractant and lead arsenate as the poison are usually effective in combating these pests. These are spread over the ground late in the day and will attract and destroy the snails or slugs during the night.

Where proprietary baits are ineffective, 5 or 10 per cent metaldehyde dusts applied to susceptible plants at the rate of 2 pounds per 1,000 square feet give excellent control of slugs. A 15 per cent dust at one pound per 1,000 square feet is just as effective. The dusts should be applied at night for three or four times at seven- to ten-day intervals. Thorough coverage of the foliage, soil, pots, and bench surface is essential for control in greenhouses.

In some parts of the country where the European brown snail occurs, metaldehyde dusts do not work as well as the baits.

Wasps, including hornets, yellow jackets, *Polistes,* and mud daubers, frequently build nests in and around homes. Some of the commonest places are beneath eaves, on porches, behind blinds, in trees, in shrubbery, and in the ground. These insects cause painful stings, occasionally even fatal ones, if their nests are disturbed or if they are molested in any way.

Wasps can be controlled by applying chlordane or DDT to their nests. These insecticides are best applied at night, when the wasps are least active and when most of them are in their nests.

The concentrations to spray on the nest are: 3 ounces of 50 per cent wettable DDT powder or 1½ ounces of 40 per cent wettable chlordane powder in a quart of water. If the emulsifiable concentrates are used, then dilute 9 tablespoons of 50 per cent DDT or 4½ tablespoons of 45 per cent chlordane in a quart of water. Additional details on the life history of wasps and how to control them are given in the United States Department of Agriculture leaflet 365, obtainable for five cents from the Superintendent of Documents, Washington, D. C.

Clover Mites in Homes. Clover mites, *Bryobia praetiosa,* have become important household pests in some parts of the country. Only 3/100 inch long, these tiny reddish-brown members of the spider family migrate into dwellings in large numbers in late summer and early fall. Although they cause no damage in homes and are generally supposed not to feed on man or pets, I know of several cases of skin rash on children and adults attributable to them.

David H. Brannon, Extension entomologist at Washington State College, recommends spraying odorless white kerosene directly on the mites as well as in cracks and other areas in which they hide. Also effective are sprays containing chlordane or pyrethrum in kerosene. Kerosene-based sprays obviously should not be used near open flames.

To prevent re-entry of the mites into homes, outside window sills and doorsills as well as the lawn and fruit trees near the house may be sprayed with ARAMITE as directed by the manufacturer.

Ticks. The wood tick, *Dermacentor variabilis,* is a serious pest in some parts of our country because it may carry a virus disease, Rocky Mountain spotted fever, to man. The tick is picked up by dogs that roam over uncultivated fields and brushland. It also comes from other vegetation, where it is waiting to drop on people or animals that move through such places. Persons unacquainted with ticks may not realize the pests are on them until the mouth parts are well embedded in some part of the human skin. Persons having chills, fever, and headache anywhere from two to twelve days after being bitten by ticks should be placed under a doctor's care immediately and the doctor told of the pest's bites.

Though in many parts of the country the tick population is heavy, 95 per cent control can be achieved by spraying the vegetation with about 2 pounds of actual DDT per acre (4 pounds of 50 per cent wettable DDT). A 10 per cent DDT dust at the rate of 20 pounds per acre can also be used but is somewhat less effective. Dieldrin sprays also do a good job of controlling ticks.

Ticks gather in largest numbers along roads and paths. Treating a 4-foot band along each side is a good plan. A single treatment will control the pests for about two weeks and sometimes for an entire season.

Black Widow Spider. Lindane insecticide is very effective in killing black widow and other spiders, according to W. M. Cory, University of California farm adviser. It kills spiders on contact and, when applied as a spray, leaves a residue that will kill spiders coming in contact with it for a month or two.

It can be used as either an emulsion or in the water suspension form. The latter is more economical to use but must be kept agitated. It also leaves a visible deposit on the surface. Make the spray solution by mixing ½ pound lindane in 5 gallons of water. The solution should be agitated to keep the lindane from settling to the bottom of the sprayer.

Chapter 14

GARDENING GADGETS AND EQUIPMENT

Because manufacturers of gardening equipment have kept pace with the plant hybridizer, the weed control specialist, and the pest control scientist, gardening today is no longer the back-breaking job it once was. Tools and gadgets are available that eliminate the tough part of gardening and give the gardener more time to enjoy the fruits of his labor.

It is the wise gardener, therefore, who takes time to select the right kind of garden equipment and lets the equipment do most of the work.

Sprinklers and Sprinkling Systems

An important part of every gardener's time is spent on the lawn. Because of this, manufacturers have developed many time- and labor-saving devices to help make lawn maintenance easier.

To do well, lawns must be watered, mowed, and fed properly. Equipment is available to do all three jobs most efficiently and with the least expenditure of time and labor.

Of course, old-fashioned gardeners still water their lawns by standing, hose in hand, hour after hour. This practice not only takes up the gardener's time but it is generally ineffective. Automatic sprinklers certainly do a better job and free the gardener for other chores. Such sprinklers are available in rotary types, which spray the water in a circular pattern, and in oscillating types, which deliver water in a rectangular pattern. The latter eliminate overlapping of watered areas, and hence prevent excessive watering in some spots.

One drawback of on-the-ground automatic sprinklers is that their position must be changed from time to time. Gardeners who dislike having to do this will like the SUNBEAM RAIN KING because it will move under its own power. This sprinkler can be adjusted so that it will move slowly, anywhere from 5 to 50 feet, along the lawn and even around corners. Moreover, the spread of its spray is adjustable.

The nonautomatic tube-type flexible sprinklers have also become extremely popular in the last two years because they are relatively inexpensive, easy to store, and have no moving parts to wear out. They can be used on lawns, along narrow grass strips, and even between rows in the garden. SUPPLEX is a triple-tube flexible sprinkler with holes on one side only, compared with some kinds of flexible sprinkler hoses that have holes on two sides. It lies flat and can be turned upside down for use as a soil soaker.

The latest in lawn-watering equipment is the underground sprinkling system. Heretofore such systems were expensive and required specialists to install them. Now, instead of metal pipes, inexpensive plastic or rubber pipe and hose connections are available, which can be installed by the home gardener himself.

These underground sprinkler systems are available in units for any size lawn. A knife, spade, hammer, and wooden stakes are the only things needed to install the basic unit, which will water anywhere from 900 to 1,600 square feet of lawn and which costs less than fifty dollars. The stakes are driven into the lawn where the sprinkler heads are to go, each sprinkler to deliver water in a pattern about 15 feet in diameter. The flexible pipe is then laid out within this pattern. The whole unit is buried in a 6-inch-deep slit in the lawn. Finally the sprinkler system is connected to an outside faucet on the house. (Illustration following page 224)

Sprinkler systems made of plastic pipe will not rust, rot, crack, or corrode, and will withstand ten times the average city water pressure. Some of them have sprinkler heads that are set flush with the ground and hence are out of the way of the lawn mower and of children playing on the lawn. Others have spray heads that pop up when the water is turned on and retract below the surface when not in use.

Among the buried sprinkler units presently on the market and their manufacturers are: EASY DEW, Permaproducts Corporation, New York; EVERSPRAY, Everhot Products Company, Chicago; NOMA SPRAY, Noma Lites, Miami, Florida; RAINRITE, Sprinkler Company, Burbank, California; and TUFF-LITE, Better Lawns Company, Metuchen, New Jersey.

The Goodyear Tire and Rubber Company makes an all-rubber underground sprinkler system with much the same desirable properties as those of plastic hose systems.

Gardeners should be warned that some communities require a permit for installation of buried sprinkler systems. A special check valve and a syphon breaker must be installed to prevent water in

the sprinkler system from backing up into the water supply lines.
It would be well, therefore, for gardeners planning to install such
a system to check with their local water supply authorities and to
comply with the regulations of their local sanitary codes. Compliance
is especially important where the water source is situated well below
the level of the buried sprinkler system, for it is under such conditions
that water in the sprinklers is apt to back up into the water supply
system.

Mowers

Until plant scientists develop a grass that requires no mowing, or
until they develop a foolproof grass-growth inhibitor, we will have
to depend on lawn mowers to keep grass looking neat and trim.

Nearly a quarter century ago my good wife Loretta purchased an
old reel-type lawn mower at an auction sale for twenty-five cents. I
used this mower for many years because it was solidly built and did
a good job of mowing the lawn. But it did take lots of elbow grease
to push it along. That was all right in the days when I had plenty of
energy, but today electric- and gasoline-powered mowers do the same
job much more easily.

There are three types of power mowers—reel, rotary, and sickle
bar. The reel-type mower cuts grass with the scissors action of a reel
of five or more curved blades which revolve against a straight-edged
bed knife. This type mower is preferred for level terrain and where
the home owner wants to have a particularly trim lawn. In the rotary
mowers the grass is cut by a fanlike blade that revolves at high speed.
This is better suited for rough areas. The sickle bar mower operates
much like a barber's clippers or a harvesting machine, that is, the
grass is lifted by the metal teeth and a sharp cutting edge moves back
and forth near the teeth to shear the grass. It is most efficient for
cutting tall grass.

With so many types to choose from, the average home owner finds
it difficult to decide what kind to buy. For a gardener with lots of pep
and a relatively small area, a manually operated mower may do well
enough. To save energy, an electric or gasoline model is suggested.
Electrically driven mowers are relatively noiseless compared to gasoline driven ones, but the area they can cover is limited by the length
of the electric cord, or anywhere from 50 to 100 feet. For very large
lawns, a self-propelled power mower, or even one that can be ridden,
is most satisfactory.

In recent years variations from the standard type power mowers have appeared on the market. The HENDERSON CONTOUR MOWER, although resembling a reel-type mower, works on a so-called "Cyclo-Safe" cutter which looks somewhat like the tines on a rotary tiller. Small cutter blades, mounted on a high-speed revolving shaft, cut and chop the grass. The blades are not exposed and are adjustable to cut the grass to a height of 1 to 2½ inches.

Another departure from the ordinary types of power mowers is the MC CULLOCH TWIN ACTION SAFETY MOWER, which has two cup-shaped cutters revolving toward the center at high speed. Two-inch cutter blades mounted on pivots are set on the rim of each of the cup-shaped cutters. The double-support wheels inside the cup-shaped cutters are so placed that no wheels go over the grass until after it is cut. Mowing height can be adjusted from the top of the machine merely by turning two knobs. A gauge on the side indicates the height to which the cutters are adjusted.

Gardeners really interested in conserving their energy will welcome a power mower that can be ridden. Even if the gardener already owns an ordinary self-propelled power mower, he can convert it to a riding mower with a MOWER-CYCLE. This attachment goes in front of the mower, and the whole unit resembles somewhat a child's tricycle with the mower trailing behind.

The HUFFY rotary mower has four small cutting blades on one disk instead of the standard single blade. An advantage of this type mower is that when one of the small cutters hits a stone or other hard object, the blade flips back. This not only avoids damage to the blade but reduces the jars and jolts. The HUFFY is quieter because its engine operates the four cutters at a much slower speed.

To make the job of operating power mowers even more pleasant, some manufacturers are now equipping their machines with electric starters that work like self-starters on automobiles. The starting motor, which does away with the customary rope-pulling starter, is powered by a 6-volt battery. It automatically disengages as soon as the mower engine starts.

Manufacturers have even remembered those unfortunate commuters who arrive home so late at night that little or no daylight is left for lawn mowing. Battery-powered headlights are available for attaching on power mowers so these gardeners can mow their lawns even on dark nights!

No matter what kind of reel-type mower one purchases, some thought should be given to the width of its cut. Sometimes by buying a machine with a few inches wider cut, the gardener can save a great deal of time and labor at only a slight extra cost. For example, on every swath the average practice is to allow a 2-inch overlap. Hence an 18-inch cutting blade actually gives only 16 inches of neat mowing. For a 22-inch cutter, the effective cut is 20 inches, or a 25 per cent increase in cutting area.

Grass Trimmers

One of the most time-consuming jobs associated with lawn maintenance is that of trimming grass along walks, fences, and other areas that are inaccessible to mowers.

In three minutes a man with a POWER TRIMMER, made by the Porter-Cable Machine Company of Syracuse, can trim the same amount of grass he could with hand shears and an hour's labor on hands and knees.

The TRIM MASTER, made by E. P. Britten and Company of Cranford, New Jersey, not only clips grass along walks and around trees and bushes, but it can be tilted upward to edge lawns, drives, walks, and flower beds. (Illustration following page 224)

Lawn Sweepers

Hand-operated and power-driven lawn sweepers for gathering leaves in the fall eliminate the slow, back-breaking job of leaf raking. A hand-operated model costing less than sixty dollars has an 8-bushel capacity, with an adjustable sweeping height for lawns, sidewalks, and driveways. A power-driven model that sells for just over a hundred dollars has a ⅓ horsepower engine, a 28-inch sweeping width, a 5½ bushel capacity, and a height adjustment from 0 to 2 inches.

Feeding Lawns

Feeding lawns was discussed in detail in *Chapter 9*. Little more need be said on the subject here.

Dry fertilizers, like 5-10-5, are applied by hand or with a fertilizer spreader. All-soluble, high-analysis fertilizers can be applied in solution with a sprinkling can, or with some special feeding gun such as the HAYES 6 SPRAY GUN.

Monsanto Chemical Company sells the FOLIATOR, an attachment that enables the gardener to feed the lawn while watering. It can be attached either at the faucet or between lengths of hose. A small plastic tube inserted into a pail containing the concentrated, dissolved plant food sucks in the nutrient solution, which in turn enters the

Modern fertilizing equipment. Left, Breck's QUICK-LIFE MIX-MIZER. *Right, the Doggett-Pfeil Company's* HYDROMIX. *The latter not only dispenses fertilizers but insecticides as well. Bottom, the Monsanto Chemical Company's* FOLIATOR.

main volume of water and is finally released through the sprinklers on the end of the hose.

Brecks of Boston sells a QUICK-LIFE MIX-MIZER which adds the correct proportion of water-soluble plant food to the water supply right at the faucet.

HYDROMIX, discussed later in this chapter under spraying apparatus, can be used to apply soluble liquid plant foods as well as insecticides.

Spraying Equipment

Because insect and disease control is a necessary, though unpleasant, phase of all gardening activities, many kinds of application devices are constantly being developed.

Good spraying equipment is an absolute must for properly applying insecticides and fungicides. Ordinarily, equipment for spraying ranges from a hand atomizer for house plants up to 50-gallon sprayers, electric- or gasoline-powered, for large gardens and estates. Even larger spraying machines are available for tall trees, but these are used mainly by professional arborists and foresters.

Widely used by home gardeners is the so-called knapsack compressed-air sprayer of 1½- to 5-gallon capacity. This type retails for about ten dollars and will last many years with reasonable care. To supply the necessary pressure, it must be pumped up before use. The operator usually wears it strapped on his back, but special carts are also available to carry it.

Another type of knapsack sprayer is similar to the portable fire pumps used in the Forestry Service. Pressure is maintained at a constant level by pushing a lever up and down while spraying.

The trombone, or slide-type, sprayers can be regulated to deliver a fine mist for low-growing shrubs and flowers or a solid stream capable of reaching the tops of 40-foot trees.

The H. D. Hudson Manufacturing Company of Chicago, Illinois, long known for its fine line of sprayers and dusters, has a new 10-gallon power sprayer, the SUBURBAN. It will do all the spraying required around the average garden. It is compact, easy to wheel about the yard and along garden paths, and takes only 3 square feet of storage space. It is one of the outstanding small-capacity power sprayers. This company also makes larger power sprayers. (Illustration page 207)

Hudson recently introduced its new HYDRA-GUN, designed as an all-purpose sprayer for the small home garden with only a few trees, shrubs, and flowers. It is a corrosion-proof, all-brass sprayer attached to a standard mason jar cover so that it can be screwed on any standard fruit jar. It operates on the same principal as the well-known Hudson trombone pump. (Illustration on page 207)

ECLIPSE is the name of a new hand sprayer made of stainless steel also recently introduced by the Hudson Company. I have used all kinds of sprays in this sprayer for more than a year now, and it still looks like new. A light twist of the spray nozzle changes the spray from a fine mist to a coarse one, depending on the job to be done.

A fully automatic sprayer equipped with a cylinder of carbon dioxide to eliminate all hand pumping is available for the really lazy gardener. A regulator valve on the cylinder maintains a constant spraying pressure. Because no air space is required above the liquid, the sprayer can be filled to capacity. The carbon dioxide cylinder contains enough gas to apply as much as 15 gallons of spray. It is refillable at low cost.

Some of the newer spray gadgets are designed for attachment to the garden hose or house faucet, so that the flow of water dissolves or dilutes the pesticide or plant food in an attached jar or cartridge and then applies the diluted solution to the plants.

After years of research and testing, the Doggett-Pfeil Company of Springfield, New Jersey, has developed a highly efficient and extremely accurate device of this sort, HYDROMIX, for applying insecticides and soluble plant foods. When attached to the water faucet or to a jar set upright between lengths of garden hose, HYDROMIX turns the working end of the garden hose into the equivalent of a garden sprayer. The water, under pressure, moving through the noncorrosive plastic device sucks in some of the insecticide, which changes to a fine emulsion by the time it leaves the hose nozzle. (Illustration on page 236)

I was privileged to witness a preview of the HYDROMIX several years ago and was highly impressed with its efficiency and with the ease of operation. I have since used the sprayer with two of the insecticides sold with it in my experimental garden at The New York Botanical Garden and around my home and have obtained excellent results. One, HYDROMIX GARDEN INSECTICIDE, is a green-colored malathion-methoxychlor concentrate for general garden use; and the other, HYDROMIX LAWN AND TERMITE SPRAY, is a yellowish brown-colored chlordane-dieldrin concentrate for use against lawn-infesting insects and termites. Because the colored insecticide does not mix with the water in the bottle as the water replaces the insecticide, it is very easy to see how much insecticide is left. The plant food concentrate is also colored, green, hence one can readily see when it is used up.

A new and convenient way to apply small quantities of insecticides is with pressurized aerosol bombs or dispensers, mentioned in *Chapter 6*, on HOUSE PLANTS. These are made by adding a gas propellent, reduced to liquid form, to an insecticide concentrate in a can strong enough to withstand high pressure. The nozzle of the bomb must be held 12 to 18 inches from the plant before the release button is pressed. This allows the propellent to evaporate before it reaches the plant but still permits deposition of the insecticide. Holding the nozzle too close may result in some plant damage. Gardeners are admonished to follow carefully the manufacturer's directions for use.

Dusting Equipment

For applying insecticides and some fungicides in dry form, many highly efficient applicators are available. These come in a number of general types, including sifter-top cans, plunger dusters, bellows blowers, knapsack-bellows, rotary hand dusters, and compressed-air dusters. Perhaps the most popular and inexpensive type is the small plunger-type duster of 1 pint capacity, which retails for less than two dollars.

Jackson and Perkins, world-famous rose growers, recently introduced the MIDGET rotary duster made of rustproof metal and weighing only 1¼ pounds. This handy duster throws an 8-foot dust cloud with one turn of the crank, and one filling will treat two hundred or more rose bushes. The same company sells a combination rose dust that will control virtually every pest and disease of roses.

Vaughan's Seed Company of Chicago and New York also sells a small hand duster, called PISTOL-GRIP duster, made of aluminum alloy and with precision-engineered gears. It can be operated with one hand. (Illustration on page 207)

The Champion Sprayer Company of Detroit, Michigan, makes the CHAMPION, a bellows-type hand duster that is light in weight and easy to operate. It will work with as little as a teaspoonful or as much as 8 pounds of dust.

A New Mulching Material

The newest mulching material to appear on the market is ground black walnut shells sold under the trade name O-G-M, which is the abbreviation for organic granule mulch. Dr. Luther Baumgartner, Director of the Baumlanda Horticultural Research Laboratory at Croton Falls, New York, found it superior to several of the older, commonly used types of mulches. O-G-M does not rot readily and exhibits no evidence of reducing soil nitrogen. Water passes through the ground walnut shell mulch without washing it away. The mulch does not swell when wetted and it keeps pots or soil on which it is placed neat-looking for long periods of time. A coarser grade of ground walnut shells makes an excellent surface for garden paths, according to Dr. Baumgartner. O-G-M is made by Composition Materials Company of New York City.

Soil Pasteurizer

Florists, nurserymen, and gardeners who have need for large amounts of weed-, insect-, and fungus-free soil will welcome the appearance on the market of ROTO THERM, an automatic soil pasteurizer. This compact machine not only pasteurizes soil quickly and efficiently, but it can also be used to sterilize pots, to screen soil, and, in an emergency, to provide heat for a small greenhouse. Three models are available from the Tarrant Manufacturing Company, Saratoga Springs, New York. (Illustration following page 224)

Power Saws

Although chain-type power saws are used mostly by professional arborists and shade tree maintenance men, some home gardeners may be interested in trying one of the smaller, easier-to-handle kinds. One which operates at the rate of 160 strokes a second and which is capable of felling a tree 18 inches in diameter with a single cut is made by the Wright Power Saw and Tool Corporation of Stratford, Connecticut. Because it weighs only 25 pounds, it can also be used to remove limbs high in the tree.

Garden Tractors

Garden tractors, great time and labor savers, are available in all shapes and sizes. Among the lighter models made by S. L. Allen and Company of Philadelphia are PLANET, JR. TUFFY and SUPER-TUFFY. The former has a 1-horsepower engine and weighs 80 pounds; the latter has a 1½-horsepower engine and weighs 90 pounds. Accessory equipment available for both models include a rotary tiller and mower, cultivator, reel-type mower, trailer cart, snow plow, lime and fertilizer spreader, and seed planter. The Allen Company also makes other Planet models ranging up to 5 horsepower.

Two- or 3-horsepower tractors are powerful enough for use in most large vegetable gardens and on large estates. Some can be ridden by the operator. Among the manufacturers of these kinds of tractors are: Bolen Products, Port Washington, Wisconsin; Farm-ette, Mantua, Ohio; Garden-All Tractor, Inc., Liberty, Indiana; Midland Garden Tractors, Columbus, Ohio; Simplicity Manufacturing Company, Port Washington, Wisconsin; and Springfield Tractors, Quick Manufacturing Company, Springfield, Ohio. All sorts of accessories are available from these manufacturers to do all kinds of jobs. (Illustration following page 224)

The rotary tiller and cultivator has become popular because it enables the most inexperienced gardener to prepare his soil in a single operation. Nearly all kinds of rotary cultivators work on the same principle—a revolving set of digging knives, hoelike blades, or tines cut into the soil, break it up, and leave it in a homogeneous, fluffy mass. This type of garden machinery works best in soils relatively free of stones.

REDHEAD, made by Wiscon Products Company of Racine, Wisconsin, is one of the lightest rotary cultivators on the market. Weighing only 65 pounds, it is ideally suited for back yards and is adjustable to till soil in widths of 14 to 21 inches.

For very small plots, a 15-pound, electrically operated tiller is available from Rototiller Company of Troy, New York. With the several attachments available, this versatile machine can perform many outdoor chores, including digging, hoeing, mowing, and sawing.

New Greenhouse Developments

The gardener who can afford a greenhouse, however small it may be, will be interested in the newest developments in this field.

Aluminum is the backbone of the newest kinds of greenhouses just made available. The very first of a whole series of aluminum greenhouses to be introduced by the world-famous Lord and Burnham Company is the ORLYT. Designed especially for home gardeners, the ORLYT is 14 feet wide and of any desired length. Its aluminum frame never needs to be painted, an expense that is ever present with standard greenhouses. All screws, bolts, hinges, and other fittings are of stainless steel, hot-galvinized steel, or aluminum, thus making all parts of the greenhouse completely rustproof. Glass panels are set in place in a special rubber channel, making them watertight and relatively shockproof. (Illustration following page 224)

Plastic sheets, discussed under plant propagation *(Chapter 8),* also enter the greenhouse field. A greenhouse which previously cost four thousand dollars for materials can now be built for two hundred and fifty, exclusive of labor. This tremendous reduction is possible through the substitution of a polyethylene film, VISQUEEN, for the standard glass and glass sash.

Following are some of the details as reported by specialists at the Kentucky Agricultural Experiment Station:

"A house 18 by 84 feet can be covered for $26.00 for the outside layer of .002 in plastic film and about $16.00 for the inside layer of .0015 inch film (at wholesale prices), not counting labor. The framework, doors and lath used to hold the plastic costs about $150.00 if cheap, unplaned lumber is used. If a better lumber is used the cost will be approximately $200.00. Thus materials for the plastic house cost only $200.00 to $250.00, while the material for a glass house of the same size would cost about $4,000.00."

The double layer of VISQUEEN makes possible a considerable saving on heating costs because the air between the layers acts as an insulator. Less watering is required in a VISQUEEN greenhouse because it retains moisture more effectively than do the standard houses. Details on construction and operation of the VISQUEEN greenhouses may be obtained from the Plastics Division of the Visking Corporation, Terre Haute, Indiana.

Even in existing glass greenhouses, a single sheet of polyethylene film can be used as an inner insulating barrier. Sheets of the plastic are clamped together to cover the interior wall and ceiling space, and 4 to 6 inches of dead air space is left between the plastic and the glass to act as an insulating barrier. Heating costs are thus cut from 25 to 30 per cent and the need for watering is reduced by nearly 50 per cent.

The newest type of greenhouse construction material to appear on the market is FIBERGLAS—a plastic made by pouring a syrupy resin on a blanket of glass fibers. FIBERGLAS admits enough light to permit the growing of many kinds of plants. It can be cut, sawed, bolted, or nailed. It is light and tough, and is sunproof, hailproof, and warpproof. "Do-it-yourself" FIBERGLAS greenhouse kits will soon be available for both amateur and professional gardeners.

Miscellaneous Garden Gadgets

Garden Carts. One of the handiest gadgets a gardener can own is a garden cart. These carts are designed to do more than just a carting job. The GENERAL LAWN TENDER, for example, when not used for carting materials, can be adjusted for seeding and feeding the lawn. The HANDYMAN has rollers instead of conventional wheels so that it can be used as a lawn roller after its bucket is filled with sand or stones. When the bucket is removed, HANDYMAN is converted into a flat cart or a hand truck.

Wood Chippers. Professional arborists now use so-called wood chippers to aid in brush disposal. Pruned branches no longer are loaded on trucks and carted to the city dump. Instead, they are run through the wood chipper, which quickly reduces the branches to small chips that take up relatively little space.

Wood chippers are also available for grinding the wood into even finer particles than is possible with the brush-grinding outfits of arborists. Such materials can be used for mulching plants and for bedding and litter for livestock.

Leaf Mulchers. These gadgets gather fallen leaves, grind them in small pieces, and spread the chopped pieces back on the lawn.

They must be used wisely, however. For example, if a heavy accumulation of leaves is run through a mulcher and the ground material is left on the lawn, the grass is likely to rot. The wise procedure is to rake off most of the leaves and use the leaf mulcher on those that are left. Or use a leaf mulcher model that catches the chopped leaves in a vacuum-cleaner-type bag, which then can be emptied on the compost pile.

Heating Cables. The General Electric Company makes cables for use in hotbeds, cold frames, and greenhouses to supply bottom heat for speeding seed germination and root development on cuttings. These cables are easy to install and are inexpensive. Details on installation may be obtained from the Construction Materials Division of General Electric Company, Bridgeport, Connecticut. (Illustration following page 224)

Root Fence. Keeping roots of many trees and shrubs within bounds so that they do not interfere with smaller plants growing near by need no longer be a problem. In many situations the problem can be solved by using a so-called root fence made of corrugated steel sheets 12 inches high. These sheets come in sections which interlock to form any desired length. To use them, the required number of pieces are first interlocked. Then the roots of the offending trees or shrubs are severed with a spade at the point where the fence is to be inserted and also at a point 6 inches outward to make a trench 6 inches across. The soil is removed from this trench to spade depth, and the bottom of the trench is grooved 4 inches deeper. The assembled fence is then set into the ground and the soil replaced to ground level. Keelor Steel, Inc., of Minneapolis, and Handy Manufacturing Company of Newark, New Jersey, are two firms that make 12-inch root fences.

An Unusual Garden Tool. The SOAK-O-HO, manufactured by the Hoke Tool Works of Raeford, North Carolina, is an unusual combination tool that can do about everything required of a garden tool. It can be used as a long-handled scuffle hoe and weed puller, and when attached to the garden hose, it becomes a lawn sprinkler or a deep root soaker. SOAK-O-HO can also be used as a broom, a rake, or a self-watering brush for cleaning porches, walls, or terraces.

Soil Moisture Recorders. An important decision frequently faced by gardeners is when to water. For anyone who wants to take the guesswork out of this question, I suggest the use of an automatic moisture recorder. Reasonably accurate moisture-recording meters are now available which quickly reveal the moisture content of the soil. One model measures the moisture content in the root zone of plants 6, 12, or 24 inches deep—without disturbing the plants.

A small, more compact, more efficient moisture recorder is known as the IRROMETER. Manufactured by the T. W. Prosser Company of Riverside, California, it is available in the eastern United States from the Nursery Specialty Products Company, Croton Falls, New York, the same company that makes the anti-desiccant WILT-PRUF. (Illustration following page 224)

These new gadgets, tools, and devices help the gardener to do a better job with far less effort. More and more of them will appear on the market as research progresses.

Like varieties of ornamental and crop plants, chemicals to feed plants, condition soils, regulate plant growth, kill weeds, and control pests, gardening equipment changes with the times. What's new today may be obsolete tomorrow. Those who love plants and enjoy working with them are always on the lookout for new varieties of plants, new materials, new equipment, and new methods to add to the pleasures of gardening. Research, then, is certain to keep pace with the 30 million Americans ever alert to what's new in gardening.

Index